e-Résumés

Third Edition

WITHDRAWN

A guide to successful online job hunting

Pat Criscito, CPRW
President and Founder
ProType, Ltd., Colorado Springs
and author of Barron's
How to Write Better Résumés and
Cover Letters, Designing the Perfect Résumé,
and *Guide to Distance Learning*

D1278089

BARRON'S

The screen shots in this book are reprinted courtesy of America Online, Microsoft, Corel, Brandego, Google, Yahoo! Resumix, NationJob, Monster.com, and CareerBuilder.

All inquiries should be addressed to:
Barron's Educational Series, Inc.
250 Wireless Boulevard
Hauppauge, New York 11788
http://www.barronseduc.com

Library of Congress Catalog Card No. 2004052971

International Standard Book No. 0-7641-2896-5

Library of Congress Cataloging-in-Publication Data

Criscito, Pat, 1953–
    E-résumés : a guide to successful online job hunting / by Pat Criscito.
        p. cm.
    Rev. ed. of: Résumés in cyberspace. 2nd ed. c2000.
    Includes index.
    ISBN 0-7641-2896-5
    1. Résumés (Employment)—Data processing. 2. Job hunting—Data processing. 3.
Internet I. Criscito, Pat, 1953- Résumés in cyberspace. II. Title

    HF5383.C744 2004
    650.14'2'0285—dc22

                                                                2004052971

PRINTED IN THE UNITED STATES OF AMERICA
9 8 7 6 5 4 3 2 1

Dedicated

To Anthony and Christian
who bring a special joy to my life.

Thank you

To Jefferson Daniel Wood for his talented drawings.
A graduate of the Savannah College of Art and Design,
Jeff found a way to make a complicated,
cold subject like computer technology warm and friendly.

Contents

Preface

This book is the latest edition of Barron's *Résumés in Cyberspace,* but just like its new name, *e-Résumés,* the content is also new. Job seekers no longer need to know how to turn on their computers and log onto the Internet like they did in 1997 when this book was first published. Instead, they need to know how to sift through the extraordinary wealth of career information on the Internet to get to the real treasures, the accurate facts, and the hidden job market. They need to know how to maximize their time online and how to avoid getting bogged down in minutia.

Job seekers still need easy-to-understand instructions on how to write and design the perfect résumé for use on paper, in e-mail, and on the Internet. If your résumé isn't designed right, it won't scan properly. If the right keywords aren't there, your résumé won't be selected in a keyword search of an applicant database. If the wording isn't dynamic and easy to read, hiring managers won't read it, no matter how many keywords it contains.

In this third edition, you will learn how to do all of this and more. You will learn how to write, design, and use an e-résumé that will exploit the Internet. At the book's companion Web site *(www.patcriscito.com),* you will find thousands of up-to-date links to Internet addresses where employers post job openings and accept résumés online. You will learn how to use the Internet to make networking contacts and to research potential employers before an interview.

You will also learn how to design a paper résumé that will make it through the scanning process without becoming a jumble of incomprehensible words, increasing your chances of popping to the top in a keyword search. The book will give you insights into how companies use these applicant tracking systems, which will forever change the way you search for a job.

When you are finished with this book, you will have an advantage over your competition in today's tight job market.

■ *Overview*

E-Résumés is logically organized to take you step by step through the process of writing, designing, and then using the perfect electronic résumé. The first four chapters help you write and design your paper résumé, which can then be turned into an electronic version for e-mail or posting on the Internet.

Once you have written and designed both your paper résumé and e-résumé, the book walks you through the process of understanding the technology of the Internet and e-mail. At the book's companion Web site there are thousands of online resources where you can place your résumé, search for job openings, set up job agents, and tap into the hidden job market. These resources are categorized by industry and type so you don't waste time wading through hundreds of addresses that would be useless in your own personal job search. All of the online addresses or URLs (Universal Resource Locators) have been researched to ensure that they are relevant, and they are kept current on the Web site.

Chapter 8 contains a comprehensive guide to career resources. Everything you always wanted to know about job searching—and a lot you didn't even know you wanted to know—can be found on the Web. Nearly every job site has an archive of career information and sometimes an expert guru just waiting to answer your questions. The thousands of resources listed in this book and on its companion Web site will help you avoid the bad advice and target the really useful, accurate information.

But don't stop there. Use Chapter 9 to build an online network through newsgroups, company Web sites, colleges, professional associations, and other resources so you can tap into the hidden job market. Chapter 9 will help you discover the treasures you need to ace your interviews. Gather information on your target company, its products, and competition so you can ask intelligent questions during the interview. Research the company and its competition before an interview, and don't limit yourself to the company's own Web site, either. Be prepared with recommendations for improving a potential employer's market position.

In Chapters 10 and 11, you will discover whether a Web portfolio is right for you. Then you will learn how to create a home page résumé, how to make it multimedia, where to place it on the Internet, and how to get the word out to potential employers that you are there.

Finally, in Chapter 12, you will learn how to keep up with the times by using search engines to find the latest online resources and potential employers.

Appendix A provides you with convenient forms that are keyed to Chapter 2's twelve-step résumé writing process. They can be used to gather the information you need to write your résumé, or you can take the completed forms to a professional résumé writer and possibly save some money since you've done a lot of the legwork.

The Glossary makes the technical terms discussed in the book easier to understand, and the Index will help you locate all the key concepts discussed and every job title covered in the sample résumés.

This comprehensive resource is the most user-friendly guide to e-résumés and online networking you can find today. All you need is a computer, an Internet connection, and this essential guide to:

- Use the power of the Internet to find your next job.
- Search the most current job banks and tap into thousands of job openings around the world.
- Access listings of thousands of current Internet career resources.
- Design an attention-getting electronic résumé, e-mail it to recruiters, and then post it on the Internet.
- Create your own Web portfolio on the Internet.
- Use online resources to network and find job leads in the hidden job market.
- Research potential employers before the interview.
- Effectively utilize strategies for keeping up with the times.

About the Author

Pat Criscito is a Certified Professional Résumé Writer (CPRW) with more than 25 years of experience and résumé clients in 42 countries. As the president and founder of ProType, Ltd., in Colorado Springs, she has written more than 15,000 résumés in her career and speaks nationally on the subject, appearing regularly on television and radio shows, as well as at Harvard, Yale, Tulane, SMU, Thunderbird, and other major universities.

Pat is also the author of Barron's *How to Write Better Résumés and Cover Letters, Designing the Perfect Résumé*, and *Guide to Distance Learning.* She is a contributing writer to *The Wall Street Journal's careerjournal.com, The Boston Globe, Colorado Springs Business Journal,* and other publications. In fact, her twelve-step résumé writing process, which you will find in Chapter 2 of this book, was excerpted in *The Wall Street Journal's National Employment Business Weekly* and selected as one of the ten best articles of 1997.

Pat is a member of the National Résumé Writers' Association *(www.nrwa.com)* and sits on their Board of Directors. For more information and the handy online hyperlinks from this book, check her Web site at *www.patcriscito.com.*

1 What Is an e-Résumé?

When I was researching the first edition of this book in 1996, using the Internet in a job search was a relatively new concept. There were a limited number of Web sites that listed jobs and/or accepted résumés, and the majority of e-résumés ended up in a company's applicant database by being scanned from a paper résumé. In 1998, Forrester Research estimated that only 15,000 businesses and 17 percent of Fortune 500 companies recruited online.

Not now! In 2003, that estimate was more than 120,000 businesses and 50 percent of Fortune 500 companies. According to a recent Forrester study, expenditures on Internet-based recruiting will be $7 billion by the end of this year. It is estimated by experts that, by 2008, 99 percent of all companies will use the Internet for their recruitment needs.

Today, job seekers turn to the Internet even before they open the local newspaper. They use job banks (such as Monster.com) like they once used classified advertisements. They set up job agents at sites like CareerBuilder.com that send them e-mails every day notifying them of jobs that match their profiles. They post their résumés directly to company Web sites and add them to online résumé databases. And many employers now accept more electronic résumés by e-mail than they do paper résumés by snail-mail.

According to Charlene Li, a Forrester Research analyst who studies online recruiting, "The Internet is transitioning people from print." This change is being driven by a growing consumer reliance on the Internet for job information and low rates for online advertising. E-recruiting is faster, reaches a larger audience, and is much more cost effective than print advertising.

A Society for Human Resource Management (SHRM) study in 2003 reported that the average cost per hire for an Internet recruiting strategy was $377 compared to the average cost per hire of $3,295 for a major metropolitan newspaper. Employment classified advertising in U.S. newspapers was worth $8.7 billion in 2000. That revenue plummeted to about $4.3 billion in 2002 and less than $4 billion in 2003.

Even though these changes in the marketplace are significant, a résumé is still a résumé. It still has just one purpose—to entice potential employers to open their doors for an interview. Résumés are marketing tools designed to give job seekers an opportunity to sell themselves in person.

Electronic résumés serve the same purpose as printed résumés but use a different medium—computers. It wasn't all that long ago that finding your dream job depended on who you knew, how good your résumé was, and how many newspapers you were willing to thumb through. Today, however, the rules are different.

Dick Knowdell, president of Career Research and Testing, draws some interesting word pictures of how job hunting has changed in the last 50 years. In the 1950s, your career was like a train. You got on the, let's say, "Accounting Train" right out of school and stayed on it until you reached your destination. Someone else was driving and there was little opportunity to change trains. At the end of the track, you simply stepped off the train with your gold watch and retired.

In the 1960s and 1970s, your career became more like a bus. It was now acceptable to get on the "Accounting Bus" and then transfer to the "Sales Bus" somewhere down the road. However, someone else was still driving.

Today, your career is more like an ATV (all-terrain vehicle). You are definitely the driver, but you often don't know your destination at the beginning. Your career path can change rapidly as you careen from one obstacle to another—downsizing, subcontracting, re-engineering, and so on.

According to the U.S. Department of Labor, the average worker today will change jobs 15 times in his or her career and hold 9.2 jobs between the ages of 18 and 34. Your career choice is now up to you, and it is an ongoing process of change and adaptation.

Just before the turn of the century, David Lynch and Del Jones, in an article in *USA Today*, stated, "If the job markets of the 21st century are going to be in constant flux, employers and employees are going to need better ways to find each other than the local help-wanted ads. As good jobs become more technical and more specialized, companies increasingly will recruit nationally—or even globally—not locally."

What a great projection! Not only are employers looking nationally for workers, they are also outsourcing work globally. We've all read about the offshoring of jobs. *Forbes* magazine reports that technology giants Hewlett-Packard and Microsoft are shifting more technology, software development, and customer service functions to China and India. However, many companies that have sent customer service and call center jobs offshore are beginning to return them to lower-cost centers in the United States because of customer dissatisfaction and complaints about communication difficulties. Technology jobs, on the other hand, will continue to leak offshore.

Anne Fisher, career columnist for *Fortune* magazine, says, "So far, according to the best industry estimates, only about 5 percent of U.S. technical jobs have been shipped to India, New Zealand, and Eastern Europe. But by 2007, at least 23 percent will have gone." A typical software engineer in Bangalore, India, earns $20,000 a year, about one-third what U.S. starting engineers make. Call center employees start at only $250 a month.

With those kinds of savings, no wonder the Bureau of Labor Statistics and Forrester Research project that more than 3,400,000 jobs will be moved offshore by 2015. That projection can be divided between the following industries:

- Office Jobs: 1,600,000
- Computer Jobs: 542,000
- Business Jobs: 356,000
- Management Jobs: 259,000
- Sales Jobs: 218,000
- Architecture Jobs: 191,000
- Legal Jobs: 79,000
- Life Sciences Jobs: 39,000
- Art and Design Jobs: 30,000

Some of this job loss is offset by foreign companies that are coming to the U.S. and creating high-skilled, high-paying jobs that can be filled by those workers willing to adapt (meaning retooling, re-education, or specialization). And Fortune 500 companies like Intel, Microsoft, and General Motors are recruiting in the U.S. for management jobs overseas. What does this mean to you? To survive in today's dynamic, evolving workplace, you must be willing to "adapt or die."

The evolution of the Internet and the job market has created an international job network that requires a unique set of job-hunting skills to which you must adapt. Instead of just a simple paper résumé, you must now have several kinds of electronic résumés.

1. The first is an MS Word document that you can print and take with you to an interview or to hand to networking contacts. It is also the file you will attach to e-mail messages. When printed, this résumé will become an electronic version without your knowing it when you send your paper résumé by mail and it is scanned into a computerized applicant tracking system.

2. The second is an ASCII text, e-mailable version that you create especially to send through cyberspace without ever printing it onto paper. This is the file you will use to cut and paste into e-mail messages or into e-forms on the Internet.

3. And the third is a multimedia résumé (or portfolio—e-folio) that is given a home page at a fixed location on the Internet for anyone to visit at will. Let's look at each kind in turn.

■ *The Scannable Résumé*

With this first kind of e-résumé, you innocently create a handsome paper résumé and mail it to a potential employer. Without your knowing it, that employer has implemented a computerized system for scanning résumés as they arrive in the human resource department. Instead of a human being reading your résumé and deciding how best to forward it along or file it, a clerk sets your résumé on the glass of a scanner bed and the black dots of ink are turned into words in a computer. The paper is then either filed or thrown away.

Also falling into this class is your paper résumé when it is faxed to a potential employer. Instead of receiving a printout of your résumé, a potential employer allows your fax to sit in a computer's queue until such time as a clerk can verify and summarize the information into the same computerized database where the scanned paper résumés have been stored.

According to *U.S. News & World Report*, more than 10,000 unsolicited résumés arrive every week at most Fortune 500 companies, and before the days of computerized applicant tracking systems, 80 percent were thrown out after a quick review. In a recent conversation with a Chicago recruiter with access to Coca-Cola's résumé database, I learned that Coke receives as many as 100,000 résumés a month!

It was simply impossible to keep track of that much paper until now. Instead of opening and reading thousands of paper résumés, companies can scan them or receive them by e-mail or via their online application forms and sort them by keywords. The resulting applicant database becomes an HR department's most valuable asset that contains the credentials of hundreds of thousands of potential employees.

Recent sources indicate that nearly all large companies with 1,000 employees or more are using computerized applicant tracking systems that scan résumés. Even if they don't do it themselves, companies turn to service bureaus to manage their résumé scanning or to recruiters to find potential employees for them, who in turn scan résumés into their proprietary databases. Even though these numbers sound large, in actuality they represent only 24 percent of companies nationwide. According to a survey conducted by the Society of Human Resource Managers, 76 percent of companies do not scan résumés.

As more and more companies have established a presence on the Internet and opened up their computer databases to e-mailed résumés, the scannability of your résumé has become less of an issue. The majority of résumés are sent as attachments to e-mails or in the body of e-mail messages.

When you e-mail your résumé directly to a company, you have total control over whether or not your information is correct. You are not at the whim of a scanner's ability to read your font or formatting. However, Fortune 1000 companies that scan résumés will continue to use their investment in this technology as long as they receive enough paper résumés to make the process worthwhile.

The U.S. government has invested a great deal of money over the past five years creating their Resumix applicant tracking system, so making your paper résumé scanner-friendly will continue to be important when sending your résumé to government agencies.

■ *The e-Mailable Résumé*

When you type words onto a computer screen in a word processing program, you are creating what is called a *file* or *document*. When you save that file, it is saved with special formatting codes like fonts, margins, tab settings, and so on, even if you didn't add these codes. Each word processing software (WordPerfect, Microsoft Word, etc.) saves its files in its own native format, making the file readable by anyone else with the same software version or with some other software that can convert that file to its own native format.

Only by choosing to save the document as a generic ASCII text file can your document be read by anyone, regardless of which word processing software he or she is using. This is the type of file you should create in order to send your résumé via e-mail, whether or not you attach a Microsoft Word file to the message. You will find complete instructions for creating and using this file in Chapter 7.

An ASCII text file is simply words—no pictures, no fonts, no graphics—just plain words. If you print this text, it looks very boring, but all the words are there that describe your life history, just like in the handsome paper résumé you created to mail to a potential employer or take to an interview. This computer file can be sent to a potential employer in one of two ways.

First, you can send the file directly to a company's recruiters via an e-mail address, if you have that address. Second, you can use this file to post your résumé onto the Internet (to the home page of a company, to a job bank in answer to an online job posting, or to a newsgroup). In any case, the file ends up in the same type of computerized database in which the scanned paper résumés have been stored.

A recent survey conducted by the Society of Human Resource Managers found that more than one-third of human resource professionals would prefer to receive résumés by e-mail—your job is to make them happy!

There are many advantages to e-mailed résumés. First, they save you money over conventional mailing of a paper copy of your résumé with a cover letter, envelope, and postage. Second, they are faster, getting to a potential employer in only seconds instead of days. You also make a powerful first impression when you understand the technology enough to e-mail your résumé correctly. And, lastly, your résumé will be accessible every time the hiring manager searches the résumé database using keywords. Your résumé will never again be relegated to languishing in a dusty filing cabinet.

■ *The Web Portfolio*

If you are a computer programmer, home page developer, graphics designer, artist, sculptor, actor, model, animator, cartoonist, poet, writer, or anyone who would benefit by the photographs, graphics, animation, sound, color, or movement inherent in a multimedia résumé, then this résumé is definitely for you.

If you have more information about your career than you can practically include in a résumé, then a Web portfolio (or e-folio) is a great option for making this additional information available to a potential employer. It might just set you apart from the other candidates competing for the same job. Chapters 10 and 11 will give you everything you need to know to take full advantage of this medium to sell your special abilities and manage your career.

Don't make the mistake, however, of thinking that a home page or e-folio can take the place of your paper and other e-résumés. In today's harried world, most recruiters and hiring managers have so little time to read résumés that they are turning to e-mailed and scanned résumés and applicant tracking systems to lighten their load. Unless they are highly motivated, they won't take the time to search for and then spend 15 minutes clicking their way through a multimedia presentation of someone's qualifications, either online at your home page or on a disk you might mail to them.

Having said that, however, I have spoken with private recruiting firms that use search engines to find Web résumés of potential candidates, so it doesn't hurt to have one. You might just be the lucky person who's e-folio or Web résumé is discovered.

The real purpose of an e-folio is to provide extra information for when a potential employer is trying to narrow down his or her applicant pool. In an e-folio, you can display examples of your work, college transcripts, letters of recommendation, charts of revenue or other growth achievements, writing samples, scanned product images, or other information that expands on or supports the information in your résumé.

Your e-folio may just tip the scales when a hiring manager is trying to choose between you and someone else. It never hurts to add this networking tool to your job search. You can always direct your reader to your e-folio by listing the URL (Universal Resource Locator—pronounced "earl") on your résumé and letterhead. That way, your reader has the option of going there for more information. Or you can direct the hiring manager to your Web site during the interview.

Most Internet service providers and online services provide some space on their servers for subscribers' own home pages at no extra charge. For instance, AOL allows its subscribers 12 megabytes of space per screen name to establish a personal home page in *AOL Hometown*. Your URL is your home page address and would look something like this: *http://hometown.aol.com/criscito*. Granted, you don't have your own domain name *(http://www.patcriscito.com)*, but it's FREE!

The other alternative is to pay a professional Web developer or online portfolio development service to create a slick presentation of your qualifications. The higher your annual salary, the more I recommend this kind of service. You need to make a very professional impression, and that can't be done with a do-it-yourself, first-generation Web site. For detailed information on these services, see Chapter 10.

A word of caution about using photographs and video in your e-folio. You don't want to set yourself up for discrimination based on sex, race, age, or even something as silly as the color of your hair or the length of your nose. If there is something about your appearance that would make it hard for an HR professional not to discriminate, then don't include your photograph on your Web site. If your appearance is a bona fide occupational qualification for a job (modeling, television, acting, etc.), then you should use your photograph on all of your résumés, including your e-folio.

■ *The Paper Résumé Is NOT Dead!*

This world of computers and the Internet will coexist with the more traditional world of paper and human networking contacts forever. Face it—computers generate more paper than they save! Therefore, you should think about having several résumés:

1. A pretty paper one for human eyes—for use in networking, interviews, and Postal Service mailings.

2. An ASCII text file—for pasting into e-forms and e-mail messages.

3. An MS Word file (or Rich Text File, RTF)—for attaching to e-mails.

4. An e-folio or home page résumé—for expanding on your résumé and managing your career.

Your paper résumé for human eyes should be one page (no more than two, unless you are an executive or are in a medical or academic field and need a curriculum vita) and designed in such a way that it is appealing to a human reader, both in words and in appearance (see the samples on pages 9, 10, 11). This is the résumé you will carry to an interview or mail to a small- or medium-sized company, since only large companies have the need and budget (the software and hardware can be a major investment) to process large volumes of résumés. *How to Write Better Résumés and Cover Letters* and *Designing the Perfect Résumé*, both from Barron's, can help you create the perfect paper résumé, so I won't go into a lot of detail here.

If you are in a more creative industry where the chances of your résumé being scanned are extremely low, then you have some license to design your paper résumé with imagination. You are not limited in font selection, margins, graphics, or style. For instance, if you are a cartoonist, you can scan cartoons onto your résumé. If you are an artist, use one of your paintings as a watermark in the background of your text (see the sample on page 10). Get creative. The chances that an art gallery will scan your résumé are nonexistent and it is your individuality that is your strongest selling point. This visual selling component of your résumé is really the determinant for choosing to create a e-folio at your home page on the Internet instead of worrying about whether your paper résumé will scan (see Chapters 10 and 11).

On the other hand, if you are a computer programmer and will be sending your résumé to both small companies and to Fortune 1000 companies, then you had better be certain your paper résumé will not only look good but also scan perfectly. Chapter 5 will cover all the basics of how to design a paper résumé that does just that. The résumé on page 11 is a good example of a handsome, yet scannable, résumé.

Everyone should have both MS Word and ASCII text files of his or her résumé for use in e-mails and electronic application forms (e-forms) on the Internet. For creative résumés, you should also create a PDF file using Adobe Acrobat to ensure that the receiver sees all of the graphics and special features of your artistic résumé. See Chapters 6 and 7 for complete instructions on creating and saving these files.

1234 Westminster Boulevard #123
Arvada, Colorado 80003
Phone: (303) 555-1234

OBJECTIVE

A challenging opportunity in corporate or industrial training.

> This résumé is not scannable because of the font and reverse box for the name.

SUMMARY OF QUALIFICATIONS

- Five years of experience as an instructor in both the corporate and public sectors.
- Strong background in developing company training programs and computer-based instruction.
- Skilled in organization, leadership, management, and problem solving.
- Effective team player with proven interpersonal, communication, and presentation skills.
- Comfortable with IBM PCs, Windows, MS Word, Excel, PowerPoint, and telecommunications software.
- Certifications: Indiana Teaching Certificate.

PROFESSIONAL EXPERIENCE

CONFERTECH INTERNATIONAL, Westminster, Colorado   1997 – Present
Corporate Instructor (1998 – Present)
- Administer professional development, supervisory, and software training programs in three locations.
- Conduct on-site visits to monitor operations and compliance with policies and procedures.
- Act as liaison between managers, instructors, supervisors, and trainees.
- Develop learning objectives for in-house computer training programs and devise instructional materials.
- Make presentations, including lectures, seminars, and orientations for groups of six to ten employees.
- Devise evaluation instruments to analyze performance; institute program changes to meet training goals.
- Wrote and designed computer-based training manuals, user materials, and training publications.

Operations Manager (1997 – 1998)
- Managed the operations of a 300-employee department.
- Administered all policy and procedure documentation and ensured consistency with corporate objectives and training efforts.
- Created, implemented, and monitored personnel training programs.
- Developed new guidelines for the call center.

DICKINSON MIDDLE SCHOOL, South Bend, Indiana   1996
Teacher
- Instructed 25 junior high school students in after-school programs.

PROJECT HEAD START, Bloomington, Indiana   1995
Teacher
- Taught basic skills to preschool children.

EDUCATION

BACHELOR OF SCIENCE, Indiana University, Bloomington, Indiana   1996
- Major in Education

CONTINUING EDUCATION, University of Colorado, Denver, Colorado   2000 – Present
- Studies toward a Master of Arts in Instructional Technology

AFFILIATIONS

- International Society of Performance Improvement
- American Society of Training and Development

Not Scannable

12345 Northface Court
Colorado Springs, Colorado 80919
Phone: (719) 555-1234

Education

BACHELOR OF ARTS (1998–2000)
Whittier College, Whittier, California
- Studio arts major
- Emphasis in oil painting

DENMARK INTERNATIONAL STUDIES (1999)
Copenhagen, Denmark
- Studied abroad for a semester

UNIVERSITY OF NORTHERN COLORADO (1996–1998)
Greeley, Colorado

SAVANNAH COLLEGE OF ART AND DESIGN (1994–1995)
Savannah, Georgia

Exhibitions

- Two paintings chosen for the Whittier College "Literary Review" (2000)
- Two works selected for display at the Whittier College "Senior Art Exhibit" (2000)
- Abstract oil painting exhibited for two months at Whittier College Library (2000)
- Hired to paint a mural for a Whittier College dormitory (1998)
- Designed a t-shirt print for a fraternity fund raiser (1999)
- Selected to paint a homecoming parade float for the University of Northern Colorado radio station (1996)

Other Experience

RECEPTIONIST (2000), Whittier College Computer Center, Whittier, California
- Provided customer service and answered telephones.

COOK (Summers 1997–1999), Old Chicago's Pizza, Colorado Springs, Colorado
- Prepared food (pizza, pasta, dough).
- Opened and closed the pizza line and pasta bar.

CUSTOMER SERVICE (1997), Pudge Brothers', Greeley, Colorado
- Managed the cash register and assisted customers in a newly opened pizza delivery restaurant.

Portfolio

Available upon request

SCANS PERFECTLY

QUALIFICATIONS	• Demonstrated success in management positions for more than 22 years. • Definitive abilities in leadership, planning, organization, and decision making. • Well organized, efficient administrator capable of shouldering responsibility and using initiative to successfully bring a project to conclusion within budget. • Skilled in discovering resourceful and enterprising solutions to problems. • Steady, focused team player committed to professionalism and integrity.
EXPERIENCE **Management**	• Managed the daily operations of a land development company and its 1600-acre master planned community, including contract negotiation and administration, transaction closings, architectural review of plans, and construction management. • Created a management and financial partnership with the city for infrastructure development. • Coordinated with legal counsel, co-brokers, builder sales teams, title insurance firms, and appraisers. • Served as liaison with lenders, city government, and engineering and land planning firms.
Marketing	• Conceptualized land use and marketed major land assets to builders, developers, and individuals. • Organized and marketed two of the most successful parades of homes ever conducted in the region.
Supervision	• Supervised both office and field personnel and administered insurance and employee benefit programs. • Provided direction to subcontractors for planning, engineering, and infrastucture construction.
Financial	• Generated budgets and forecasts for partners and other senior management. • Developed market data files and statistical tracking strategies that supported the internal financing requirements of the development together with the marketing strategies of the firm. • Ensured compliance with governmental regulations and property tax obligations.
Consulting	• Provided management guidance and support for a bankrupt wholesale floral enterprise; directed the filing of Chapter 11 petition for the company. • Initiated administrative cost reduction measures, inventory control, and product purchasing disciplines. • Sold unprofitable operations and property; instituted effective management and accounting systems. • Reduced accounts receivable, restaffed key positions, restructured the financial obligations, and provided the basis for a reorganization plan acceptable to the bankruptcy court.
WORK HISTORY	**Business Manager**, Hausman Management Corporation, Colorado Springs, Colorado, 1996 – present **Real Estate Consultant**, Independent Broker, Colorado Springs, Colorado, 1995 – 1996 **Management Consultant**, RF Wholesale, Las Vegas, Nevada, 1994 – 1995 **Business Manager**, Hausman Management Corporation, Colorado Springs, Colorado, 1987 – 1994
EDUCATION	**BACHELOR OF SCIENCE**, 1979 **California State Polytechnic College**, San Luis Obispo, California **Colorado State University**, Fort Collins, Colorado
LICENSES	Colorado Real Estate Broker, 1979 – present
AFFILIATIONS	• Land Developer Representative on Joint City / County Drainage Board (appointed by City Council of Colorado Springs and El Paso County Board of Commissioners), 1990 – 1994 • Colorado Springs Board of Realtors and Home Builders Association, 1987 • Director, Pueblo Association of Home Builders, 1985 • Advisory Board Member, University of Southern Colorado College for Community Services, 1980 • Officer and Director, Pueblo Board of Realtors, 1979 • Instructor, University of Colorado Real Estate Certificate Program, 1979
ADDRESS	1234 Del Oro Circle, Colorado Springs, Colorado 80919 (719) 555-1234

11

SCANS PERFECTLY
1234 Del Oro Circle
Colorado Springs, Colorado 80919
Phone: (719) 555-1234
E-mail: johndoe@thespringsmall.com

QUALIFICATIONS
~~~~~~
Demonstrated success in management positions for more than 22 years. Definitive abilities in leadership, planning, organization, and decision making. Well organized, efficient administrator capable of shouldering responsibility and using initiative to successfully bring a project to conclusion within budget. Skilled in discovering resourceful and enterprising solutions to problems. Steady, focused team player committed to professionalism and integrity.

EXPERIENCE
~~~~~~
MANAGEMENT: Managed the daily operations of a land development company and its 1600-acre master planned community, including contract negotiation and administration, transaction closings, architectural review of plans, and construction management. Created a management and financial partnership with the city for infrastructure development. Coordinated with legal counsel, co-brokers, builder sales teams, title insurance firms, and appraisers. Served as liaison with lenders, city government, and engineering and land planning firms.

MARKETING: Conceptualized land use and marketed major land assets to builders, developers, and individuals. Organized and marketed two of the most successful parade of homes ever conducted in the region.

SUPERVISION: Supervised both office and field personnel and administered insurance and employee benefit programs. Provided direction to subcontractors for planning, zoning, engineering, and infrastucture construction.

FINANCIAL: Generated budgets and forecasts for partners and other senior management. Developed market data files and statistical tracking strategies that supported the internal financing requirements of the development together with the marketing strategies of the firm. Ensured compliance with governmental regulations and property tax obligations.

CONSULTING: Provided management guidance and support for a bankrupt wholesale floral enterprise; directed the filing of Chapter 11 petition for the company. Initiated administrative cost reduction measures, inventory control, and product purchasing disciplines. Sold unprofitable operations and property; instituted effective management and accounting systems. Reduced accounts receivable, restaffed key positions, restructured the financial obligations, and provided the basis for a reorganization plan acceptable to the bankruptcy court.

WORK HISTORY
~~~~~~
Business Manager, Hausman Management Corporation, Colorado Springs, CO, 1987 - 1994 and 1996 - present
Real Estate Consultant, Independent Broker, Colorado Springs, CO, 1995 - 1996
Management Consultant, RF Wholesale, Las Vegas, NV, 1994 - 1995
Office Manager, Jones-Healy, Inc., Pueblo, CO, 1979 - 1987

EDUCATION
~~~~~~
Bachelor of Science, 1979
California State Polytechnic College, San Luis Obispo, California
Colorado State University, Fort Collins, Colorado

12

■ *Some Options*

What if you are uncertain whether your résumé will scan well and you have learned from Chapter 3 of this book that the company to which you are sending your résumé does, in fact, scan every paper résumé it receives? What do you do?

Well, you can always take the computer file of your paper résumé, strip it of all its fancy formatting codes, add some white space to help define the sections, print it on a nice white bond paper (see the sample on page 12), and send it along with your handsome résumé. That way the company can decide which résumé will suit its purposes best and you haven't lost anything. This version of your résumé is now ready to save as an ASCII text file from your word processor (see Chapter 6 for the details of creating this ASCII file) for transmission via e-mail or for use on the Internet while filling in those little boxes on e-forms.

Once your résumé has entered the electronic world, you immediately have an advantage over the paper résumé that is stored in a wall of filing cabinets waiting for a recruiter or clerk to remember it is there. Recruiters or hiring managers can now search through an entire database of e-résumés in a matter of seconds, using keywords to narrow the search to those potential candidates who are the most qualified.

Let's talk now about writing the perfect résumé and how to use those keywords to your advantage. The next chapter will walk you through a step-by-step process for getting those keywords down on paper. When you are finished, you will have the perfect résumé for both the Internet and paper worlds.

2 How to Write the Perfect e-Résumé

Writing your résumé is one of the most difficult things you will ever do! Think about it . . . you must turn your life history into a one- or two-page advertisement that highlights a lifetime of experience, accomplishments, and education. Since we have been taught all of our lives not to brag, most people find this ultimate brag piece difficult to write.

This chapter will develop a résumé for an experienced electrical engineer with a background in the support of complex computer networks. The finished résumé can be found on page 33.

Before we get down to the business of writing your new résumé, let's look at the expectations of today's discerning hiring manager. The National Résumé Writers' Association *(www.nrwaweb.com)* publishes a test to help job seekers decide whether their résumés are ready for a job search. With their permission, let's evaluate your old résumé's effectiveness. Put a checkmark by every box that applies to you.

❑ My résumé uses the same marketing techniques used by companies to sell my unique "brand" to employers.

❑ My résumé is packed with industry-specific language and crucial keywords.

❑ My résumé emphasizes and quantifies my achievements to show not only what I have done, but also *how well* I have done it.

❑ My résumé uses varied action verbs and powerful marketing phrases.

❑ My résumé contains superior grammar, spelling, sentence structure, and punctuation.

❑ My résumé emphasizes how I will benefit employers and meet their precise needs.

❑ My résumé engages the reader from the outset and maintains interest throughout.

❑ My résumé clearly communicates my job target and the key strengths I bring to the table within the first few lines of text.

- ❏ My résumé utilizes accomplishment statements in a compelling way.
- ❏ My résumé communicates and targets my key transferable skills.
- ❏ My résumé minimizes my potential weaknesses and turns negative "red flags" into positive assets.
- ❏ My résumé uses an eye-catching, inviting, and original design (not a template).
- ❏ My résumé includes ASCII (plain-text) and scannable versions to enable e-mail, Internet, and electronic distribution/storage.
- ❏ My résumé uses the most effective format, style, and strategy for my particular situation.

How did you do? If you checked 13–14 boxes, your résumé writing abilities appear to be sound. You can still benefit from some of the strategies and tips in this chapter, or you might want to avail yourself of a critique from a professional résumé writer to be sure you didn't miss anything important.

If you checked 10–12 boxes, you have some distinct abilities that will help you write a résumé more solidly than most. Without the help of this chapter, however, you may leave out some critical components that can cost you interviews. Optimize your results by following all 12 steps in this chapter.

If you checked less than 10 boxes, you need this chapter! You will miss opportunities that may be perfect for you unless you apply all the suggestions listed.

■ Step-by-Step Writing Process

Using this twelve-step process to write your résumé will help you clarify your experience, accomplishments, skills, education, and other background information and make the job of condensing your life onto paper a little easier. I expanded this twelve-step process into an entire book for Barron's in 2003—*How to Write Better Résumés and Cover Letters*—which you can find at your local bookstore or online. If you want to download the questionnaires developed for that book, you can find them free at my Web site—*www.patcriscito.com*—by clicking on *bookstore*. You can also copy the forms from the Appendix in the back of this book.

❏ Step One—Focus

The first step in writing the perfect résumé is to know what kind of job you will be applying for. A résumé without a focus is never as effective as one that relates to a specific job description.

Now, decide what type of job you will be applying for and then write it at the top of a piece of paper. This can become your objective statement, should you decide to use one, or it can become the first line of the profile section of your résumé to give your reader a general idea of your area(s) of expertise.

An objective is not required on a résumé, and often the cover letter is the best place to personalize your objective for each job opening. There is nothing wrong with using an objective statement on a résumé, however, provided it does not limit your job choices. As an alternative, you can alter individual résumés with personalized objectives that reflect the actual job title for which you are applying. Just make sure that the rest of your information is still relevant to the new objective.

Never write an objective statement that is not precise. You want to name the position so specifically that, if a janitor came by and knocked over the stacks of sorted résumés on a hiring manager's desk, he could put yours back in its right stack without even thinking about it. That means saying, "A marketing management position with an aggressive international consumer goods manufacturer" instead of "A position that utilizes my education and experience to mutual benefit."

❑ Step Two—Education

The second step in writing your résumé is to think about your education. That means all of your training and not just formal education (college, university, or trade school).

The education section of your résumé will include degrees, continuing education, professional development, seminars, workshops, and sometimes even self-study.

Under your objective statement, list any education or training that might relate. If you are a recent college graduate and have little

Objective: An electrical engineering position utilizing an extensive background in the design and support of complex, large computer networks.

Objective: An electrical engineering position utilizing an extensive background in the design and support of complex, large computer networks.

Education:

1. Master of Science, Electrical Engineering (1989-90)
Air Force Institute of Technology,
Wright-Patterson AFB, Ohio
Concentration in Electro-Optics
2. Bachelor of Science, Electrical Engineering (1981-85)
United States Air Force Academy, Colorado
Concentration in Communications
3. Continuing Professional Education (1985-89)
Air Force Institute of Technology
Wright-Patterson AFB, Ohio
Digital Signal Processing, Fiber Optic Communications,
Local Area Networks, Electrical Power Distribution,
Spread Spectrum Communications, Optimizing . . . .

relevant experience, then your education section will be placed at the top of your résumé. As you gain more experience, your education almost always gravitates to the bottom.

There is an exception to every rule in the résumé business, however, so use your common sense. If you are changing careers and recently returned to college to obtain new credentials, your education section will appear at the top of the résumé even if you have years of experience. Think about your strongest qualifications and make certain they appear in the top half of page one of your résumé.

If you participated in college activities or received any honors or completed any notable projects that relate directly to your target job, this is the place to list them.

Computerized applicant tracking systems are programmed to show that you have college study but not a degree if they see from–to dates. For instance, writing 1999–2001 implies that you did not graduate. If you graduated with a degree, list only the year you graduated (2001).

When you attend a trade school, you receive either a diploma or certificate. This type of schooling can be listed under the "Education" heading or under a separate heading called "Training" or "Technical Training."

Listing high school education and activities on a résumé is only appropriate when you are under 20 and have no education or training beyond high school. Once you have completed either college courses or specialized technical training, drop your high school information altogether.

Continuing education shows that you care about lifelong learning and self-development, so think about any relevant training since your formal education was completed. *Relevant* is the key word here. Always look at your résumé from the perspective of a potential employer. Don't waste space by listing training that is not directly or indirectly related to your target job. This section can include in-services, workshops, seminars, corporate training programs, conferences, conventions, and other types of training.

❏ Step Three—Job Descriptions

Get your hands on a written description of the job you wish to obtain and for any jobs you have held in the past, as well as for your current job. If you are presently employed, your human resource department is the first place to look. If not, then go to your local library and ask for a copy of *The Dictionary of Occupational Titles* or the *Occupational Outlook Handbook* (which can also be found on the Internet—see next page). These industry standard reference guides offer volumes of occupational titles and job descriptions for everything from Abalone Divers to Zoo Veterinarians (and thousands in between).

Another resource available at your local library or college career center is *Job Scribe*, a computer software program with more than 3,000 job descriptions.

Other places to look for job descriptions include:

- Your local government job service agencies
- Professional and technical organizations
- Recruiters
- Associates who work in the same field
- Newspaper advertisements for similar job
- Online job postings, which tend to have longer job descriptions than print ads.

Here are some other sources for job descriptions on the Internet:

- America's Career InfoNet: *www.acinet.org*
- Career Guide to Industries: *www.bls.gov/oco/cg/*
- Careers Online Virtual Careers Show: *http://www.careersonline.com.au/show/menu.html*
- Dictionary of Occupational Titles: *www.oalj.dol.gov/libdot.htm*
- JobProfiles.com: *www.jobprofiles.org*
- Occupational Outlook Handbook: *www.bls.gov/oco/home.htm*
- Occupational Outlook Quarterly: *www.bls.gov/opub/ooq/ooqhome.htm*

Performance evaluations, depending on how well they are written, generally list a description of your major responsibilities, a breakdown of individual tasks, and highlights of your accomplishments. You should *always* keep a folder at home of performance evaluations from every job you have ever held. If you haven't kept them up until now, please start.

Now, make copies of these performance evaluations so you can highlight them as you write your résumé. Use a different colored pen to highlight accomplishments—the things you did above and beyond the call of duty.

Also make copies of the job descriptions you discovered and mark the sentences that describe anything you have done in your past or present jobs. These job descriptions are important sources of keywords, so pay particular attention to nouns and phrases that you can incorporate into your own résumé.

❏ *Step Four—Keywords*

In today's world of computerized applicant tracking systems, make sure you know the buzzwords of your industry and incorporate them into the sentences you are about to write. Keywords are the nouns, adjectives, and sometimes verbs and short phrases that describe your experience and education that might be used to find your résumé in a keyword search of a résumé database. They are the essential knowledge, abilities, and skills required to do your job.

Keywords are generally concrete descriptions like: C++, UNIX, fiber optic cable, network, project management, among others. Even well-known company names (Intel, IBM, Hewlett-Packard) and universities (Harvard, Yale, Princeton, SMU, Stanford, Tulane, Columbia, etc.) are sometimes used as keywords, especially when it is necessary to narrow down an initial search that calls up hundreds of résumés from a résumé database.

Acronyms and abbreviations here can either hurt you or help you, depending on how you use them. One example given to me by an engineer at Yahoo! Resumix was the abbreviation "IN." Think about it. "IN" could stand for *intelligent networks, Indiana,* or the word *in.* It is better to spell out the abbreviation if there could be any possible confusion. However, if a series of initials is so well known that it would be recognized by nearly everyone in your industry and would not likely be confused with a real word, then the keyword search will probably use those initials (i.e., IBM, CPA, UNIX). When in doubt, always spell it out at least one time on your résumé. A computer only needs to see the combination one time for it to be considered a "hit" in a keyword search.

Soft skills are often not included in search criteria, especially for very technical positions, although I have interviewed some companies that use them extensively for the initial selection of résumés for management positions. For instance, "communicate effectively," "self-motivated," "team player," and so on, are great for describing your abilities and are fine to include in your profile, but concentrate more on your hard skills, especially if you are in a high-tech field.

In the next chapter, you will find a more in-depth description of keywords and some examples of keywords for specific industries, although there is no such thing as a comprehensive listing of keywords for any single job. The computerized candidate management programs used by most companies and online résumé databases allow the recruiter or hiring manager to personalize his or her list of keywords for each job opening, so it is an evolving process. You will never know whether you have listed absolutely every keyword possible, so focus instead on getting on paper as many related skills as possible, remembering to be absolutely honest and accurate.

The job descriptions and performance evaluations you found in step three are some of the most important sources for keywords. You can also be certain that nearly every noun and some adjectives in a job posting or advertisement will be keywords, so make sure you use those words somewhere in your résumé, using synonyms wherever you can. Just make sure you can justify every word on your résumé—don't exaggerate. If you don't have the experience or skill, don't use the keyword.

Make a list of the keywords you have determined are important for your particular job search and then list synonyms for those words. I have provided a form for this purpose in the appendix. As you incorporate these words into the sentences of your résumé, check them off.

One caution. Always tell the truth. The minute a hiring manager speaks with you on the telephone or begins an interview, any exaggeration of the truth will become immediately apparent. It is a bad idea to say, "I don't have experience with Excel computer software" just to get the words *Excel* or *computer software* on paper so your résumé will pop up in a keyword search. In a cover letter, it might be appropriate to say that you "don't have five years of experience in marketing but can add two years of university training in the subject to three years of in-depth experience as a marketing assistant with Hewlett-Packard." That is legitimate reasoning, but anything more manipulative can be hazardous to your job search.

❑ *Step Five—Your Jobs*

Now that you have the basic information for your résumé, you need to create a list of jobs and write basic sentences to describe your duties. Start by using a separate "Experience" form (you will find them in the appendix) for each job you have held for the past 10 to 15 years. You can generally stop there unless there is something in your previous work history that is particularly relevant to the new job you are seeking.

> *United States Air Force (1985-Present)*
>
> *Chief, Network Control Center, USAF Academy, CO*
>
> *Managed an eight-person help desk to assist more than 9,000 customers with trouble shooting their own software problems or to assign technicians to correct the problems on site. Programmed hubs and routers; ran unshielded twisted pair and fiber optic cabling. Diagnosed client software and hardware problems. Used HP OpenView, Cabletron's LanView, for SNMP management of local area networks. Selected, trained, and supervised 27 civilian and military personnel with a wide range of responsibilities, including client configuration, network connectivity, and file server availability. Developed infrastructures for Banyan networks, VINES, TCP-IP to include remote, dial-in access via LanExpress. Maintained microcomputers, printers, and more than 90 file servers. Limited project costs to $250,000, while an alternative proposal was provided for $2,500,000.*

Starting with your present position, list the title of every job you have held, along with the name of the company, the city and state, and the years you worked there. You don't need to list full addresses and zip codes, although you will need to know that information when it comes time to fill out an application. You should use a separate page for each job title even if you worked for the same company in more than one capacity.

You can list years only (1996–present) or months and years (May 1996–present), depending on your personality. People who are more detail oriented are usually more comfortable with a full accounting of their time. Listing years alone covers some gaps if you have worked in a position for less than a full year while the time period spans more than one calendar year. For instance, if you worked from December 2000 through January 2001, saying 2000–2001 certainly looks better. If you are concerned about gaps in your work history, then listing years only is to your advantage.

From the perspective of recruiters and hiring managers, most don't care whether you list the months and years or list the years only. However, if you are writing a Resumix résumé for a U.S. government job, you will be required in almost every case to list the beginning and ending month and year for each job. Regardless of which method you choose, be consistent throughout your résumé, especially within each section. Don't use months sometimes and years alone other times within the same section. Consistency of style is important on a résumé, since it is that consistency that makes your résumé neat, clean, and easy to read.

❑ *Step Six—Duties*

Under each job on its separate page, make a list of your duties, incorporating phrases from the job description wherever they apply. You don't have to worry about making great sentences yet or narrowing down your list. Just get the information on paper.

This is the most time-consuming part of the résumé writing process. Depending on how quickly you write/type, it could take an entire day just for this step. Anything worth doing, however, is worth doing right, so you will want to take the time to do this step right.

Under experience, don't forget internships, practicums, and unpaid volunteer work in your experience section. Experience is experience, whether you are paid for it or not. If the position or the knowledge you gained is relevant to your current job search, then list it on your résumé. You can either include unpaid experience along with your paid experience, or you can create a separate section just for your volunteer history.

❑ *Step Seven—Accomplishments*

When you are finished with your work history, go back to each job and think about what you might have done above and beyond the call of duty. What did you contribute to each of your jobs? How did you measure your success? Did you:

- Exceed sales quotas by 150 percent each month?
- Save the company more than $100,000 by developing a new procedure?
- Generate new product publicity in trade press?
- Control expenses or cut overhead?
- Expand the business or attract/retain customers?
- Improve the company's image or build new relationships?
- Improve the quality of a product?
- Solve a problem?
- Do something that made the company more competitive?
- Make money?
- Save money or time?
- Improve quality or service?
- Increase productivity?
- Improve workplace safety?
- Increase efficiency or make work easier?

Go back to the experience forms in the last step and write down any accomplishments that show potential employers what you have done in the past, which translates into what you might be able to do for them in the future.

Quantify and diversify whenever possible. Numbers are always impressive. But don't duplicate wording throughout the résumé. If you use dollars in one case, use percentages in another. Overused words lose their effectiveness, like a song played on the radio again and again.

Remember, you are trying to motivate the potential employer to buy . . . you! Convince your reader that you will be able to generate a significant return on their investment in you. Try to focus on "before" and "after" examples. Identify a problem and explain how you corrected it.

❏ Step Eight—Delete

Now that you have the words on paper, make a copy of each sheet. It pays to be a packrat if you decide to change careers in the future. Store the original worksheets in the same file you created for your performance evaluations and job descriptions. Use the copies for this step.

Decide which jobs are relevant to today's job search. Set aside the jobs that are too old or irrelevant (like flipping hamburgers back in high school if you are now an electrical engineer with ten years of experience). Try to limit your list of final jobs to no more than six, although you can list more if they are truly relevant or contain valuable experience.

Remember, your résumé is just an enticer, a way to get your foot in the door. It isn't intended to be all-inclusive. You can choose to go back only as far as your jobs relate to your present objective.

Then focus on the sentences and do the same. Which ones are the most powerful? Which ones summarize your experience best? Which ones highlight your accomplishments the best? Be careful not to delete sentences that contain the keywords you identified in Step Four.

Next, do the same for your education and training worksheets. Copy them, file away the originals, and cross out anything that doesn't relate to your current job goal.

This does not apply to your formal education, however. Even if you have a graduate degree in your career field and your undergraduate degree is unrelated, leave them both on your résumé. Your reader will need to see the progression of your formal education.

If you have a bachelor's degree and an associate degree, you don't need to list them both unless there is something about the major of your associate degree that you don't have in your bachelor's degree and it is relevant to your current search. Remember, it is okay to list almost anything on your résumé as long as it is relevant to your job search.

One last thing, if you have lied (or exaggerated) anything on your résumé up to this point, delete it now! Did you know that you can go to jail for lying on a résumé? You could be committing a felony. If you are caught and convicted, you could land in jail! And that's not all. If you claim to have a college degree you didn't earn and it leads to higher pay, you could be accused of criminal fraud by your employer, even if this is discovered years later.

According to a survey conducted by the Society for Human Resource Management, among the 87 percent of hiring managers who check all references, 90 percent say they've caught job applicants making false claims and, of those liars, 35 percent fabricated a previous employer. Reuters reports that ADP Screening and Selection Services found that more than 50 percent of the people on whom it conducted employment and education checks in 2003 had submitted false information, compared with about 40 percent a year earlier.

Anne Fisher of *Fortune* magazine says, "The vast majority of companies view lying on a résumé as grounds for firing or for putting a candidate right out of the running, so forget it." Companies are fighting back. They are conducting more thorough background checks of candidates and even long-time employees. This includes not only references but also criminal checks. If you are job hunting, you will likely have to prove you really did earn your degree. Expect to be asked for an official transcript of your college work.

❏ *Step Nine—Sentences*

It's time to do some serious writing now. You must make dynamic, attention-getting sentences of the duties and accomplishments you have listed under each job, combining related items to avoid short choppy phrases. Here are the secrets to great résumé sentences:

- In résumés, you never use personal pronouns (I, my, me). Instead of saying: *"I planned, organized, and directed the timely and accurate production of code products with estimated annual revenues of $1 million"* you should say: *"Planned, organized, and directed. . . ."* Writing in the first person makes your sentences more powerful and attention grabbing, but using personal pronouns throughout a résumé is awkward. Your reader will assume that you are referring to yourself, so the personal pronouns can be avoided.

- Make your sentences positive, brief, and accurate. Since your ultimate goal is to get a human being to read your résumé, remember to structure the sentences so they are interesting to read.

- Use verbs at the beginning of each sentence (designed, supervised, managed, developed, formulated, and so on) to make them more powerful (see the list at the end of this chapter).

- Incorporate keywords from the list you made in Step Four.

- Make certain each word means something and contributes to the quality of the sentence.

If you find it difficult to write clear, concise sentences, take the information you have just written to a professional writer who can help you turn it into a winning résumé. Choose someone who is a Nationally Certified Résumé Writer (NCRW) or

Certified Professional Résumé Writer (CPRW). That way you can be assured that the person has passed the strictest tests of résumé writing and design in the country, including peer review, administered by the National Résumé Writers' Association (NRWA) and Professional Association of Résumé Writers (PARW).

To find certified résumé writers, check these Web sites:

- National Résumé Writers' Association: *www.nrwaweb.com*
- Professional Association of Résumé Writers: *www.parw.com*
- Career Masters Institute: *www.cmi.com*
- Professional Résumé Writing and Research Association: *www.prwra.com*
- Certified Résumé Writers Guild: *www.certifiedresumewritersguild.com*
- Certified Résumé Writers: *www.certifiedresumewriters.net*

What are the benefits of partnering with a professional résumé writer? According to the NRWA, you will gain access to:

- Expert résumé writing, editing, and design skills.
- Needed objectivity and expertise to play up your strengths, downplay your weaknesses, and position yourself for interview success.
- The precise know-how to target your career and industry correctly.
- Winning résumé, job search, interviewing, and salary negotiation strategies from recognized experts.
- Experienced professionals who have passed rigorous résumé industry exams and demonstrated their commitment to the profession by obtaining ongoing training.

Résumé writers work in one of two ways: 1) they gather all of the information they need from you in a personal interview, 2) they require that you complete a long questionnaire before they begin working on your résumé, or 3) they use a combination of both methods. In any case, you have already done most of the data collection if you have followed the steps in this chapter. This preparation sometimes makes the résumé easier to write and many professional résumé writers will pass on that savings to you in the form of lower fees.

❏ *Step Ten—Rearrange*

You are almost done! Now, go back to the sentences you have written and think about their order of presentation. Put a number 1 by the most important description of what you did for each job. Then place a number 2 by the next most important duty or accomplishment, and so on until you have numbered each sentence.

Again, think logically and from the perspective of a potential employer. Keep related items together so the reader does not jump from one concept to another. Make the thoughts flow smoothly.

The first sentence in a job description is usually an overall statement of the position's major responsibilities. The rest of the sentences should begin with your most important duties and accomplishments and proceed to lesser ones.

Let me give you an example of a job description in rough draft format and one that has been rearranged, and I'm sure you will see what I mean.

United States Air Force (1985-Present)

Chief, Network Control Center, USAF Academy, CO

2) Managed an 8-person help desk to assist more than 9,000 customers with trouble shooting their own software problems or to assign technicians to correct the problems on site. 3) Programmed hubs and routers; ran unshielded twisted pair and fiber optic cabling. 7) Diagnosed client software and hardware problems. 6) Used HP OpenView, Cabletron's LanView, for SNMP management of local area networks. 1) Selected, trained, and supervised 27 civilian and military personnel with a wide range of responsibilities, including client configuration, network connectivity, and file server availability. 4) Developed infrastructures for Banyan networks, VINES, TCP-IP to include remote, dial-in access via LanExpress. 8) Maintained microcomputers, printers, and 90+ file servers. 5) Limited project costs to $250,000, while an alternative proposal was provided for $2,500,000.

JOHNSON UNIVERSITY HOSPITAL, New Brunswick, New Jersey (2000 – 2003)
Director, Pediatric Emergency Department
- Recently developed and implemented an expansion of the department into a new children's hospital.
- Hired and managed a staff of 40 employees, directed performance improvement initiatives, and implemented departmental standards of care.
- Analyzed trends for key indicators to improve subsequent code responses.
- Member of the Performance Improvement Committee.
- Analyzed 72-hour readmission trends to find problems with practice patterns.
- Selected for the Code Response Team: Developed a new performance improvement form.
- Redesigned resuscitation guidelines for residents and nursing staff.
- Directed clinical and administrative operations of a 12,000-visit-per-year pediatric emergency department.
- Developed and managed an operating budget of $1.3 million.
- Developed staffing standards and evaluated the qualifications/competence of department personnel to provide appropriate levels of patient care.
- Member of the Health Policy and Strategic Planning Committee responsible for preparing the hospital and staff for JCAHO accreditation reviews.
- Implemented a pain initiative.

After numbering and rearranging the sentences, the section reads much stronger and has a better flow.

JOHNSON UNIVERSITY HOSPITAL, New Brunswick, New Jersey (2000 – 2003)
Director, Pediatric Emergency Department

- Directed clinical and administrative operations of a 12,000-visit-per-year pediatric emergency department.
- Developed and managed an operating budget of $1.3 million.
- Hired and managed a staff of 40 employees, directed performance improvement initiatives, and implemented departmental standards of care.
- Developed staffing standards and evaluated the qualifications/competence of department personnel to provide appropriate levels of patient care.
- Member of the Health Policy and Strategic Planning Committee responsible for preparing the hospital and staff for JCAHO accreditation reviews.

Key Accomplishments:

- Recently developed and implemented an expansion of the department into a new children's hospital.
- Member of the Performance Improvement Committee: Analyzed 72-hour readmission trends to find problems with practice patterns. Implemented a pain initiative. Redesigned resuscitation guidelines for residents and nursing staff.
- Selected for the Code Response Team: Developed a new performance improvement form. Analyzed trends for key indicators to improve subsequent code responses.

Here is my reasoning for rearranging the sentences:

1. The first sentence was selected because it was a good overall statement of the job's major responsibility.

2. The second sentence added a further sense of scope by describing the size of the director's budget.

3. As did the third sentence by discussing the number of employees managed and other supervisory responsibilities.

4. The next two sentences are secondary job duties and special assignments.

5. In order to emphasize achievements, key accomplishments were pulled out into a separate section.

6. The first bullet was the most important accomplishment and the most recent.

7. All of the bullets that applied to the Performance Improvement Committee were listed together in a separate paragraph.

8. The last accomplishment was the least important.

❑ *Step Eleven—Related Qualifications*

At the bottom of your résumé (or sometimes toward the top), you can add anything else that might qualify you for your job objective. This includes licenses, certifications, special skills, languages, credentials, publications, speeches, presentations, exhibits, grants, special projects, research, affiliations, volunteer activities, civic contributions, honors, awards, distinctions, professional recognitions, computer skills, international experience, and sometimes even interests if they truly relate.

For instance, if you want a job in sports marketing, stating on your résumé that you play tennis or are a triathlete would be an asset. In the case of the certified Banyan engineer on page 34, it is relevant that he has served as president of the board of directors of the Association of Banyan Users International and as vice president of the local Banyan Users group.

❏ *Step Twelve—Profile*

Last but not least, write four or five sentences that give an overview of your qualifications.

This profile or qualifications summary should be placed at the beginning of your résumé. You can include some of your personal traits or special skills that might have been difficult to get across in your job descriptions.

> *Qualifications:*
>
> *Experienced electrical engineer with an extensive background in the design and support of complex, large computer networks with primary responsibility for an 8,000-user network.*
>
> *Strong communication, leadership, management, and problem solving skills.*
>
> *Dedicated professional who enjoys the challenge of solving computer problems.*
>
> *Able to work with minimal supervision and as a cooperative team member.*
>
> *Knowledge of Windows 98/NT, MS Word, Excel, Access,, FormFlow, C/C++ languages, among others.*

Some HR professionals might disagree with me. They say that they skip over descriptions of unverifiable claims about personal strengths, but there are just as many HR managers who read every word. Besides, you want to make sure you cover your soft skills for e-résumés where keywords defined in job requisitions often request such strengths.

On the next page is a sample profile section for the electrical engineering résumé we have been developing to this point. It is also acceptable to use a keyword summary that gives a "quick and dirty" look at your qualifications (like the sample on page 34). Although this type of "laundry list" isn't very interesting for a human being to read, some recruiters in high-tech industries like this list of terms because it gives them a quick overview of an applicant's skills. An experienced trial attorney with fewer technical skills might use something like the profile section on page 36.

Busy recruiters spend as little as ten seconds deciding whether to read a résumé from top to bottom. You will be lucky if the first third of your résumé gets read, whether it is an electronic résumé or a paper one, so make sure the information at the top entices the reader to read it all.

This profile section must be relevant to the type of job for which you are applying. It might be true that you are "compassionate," but will it help you get a job as a high-pressure salesperson? Write this profile from the perspective of a potential employer. What will convince this person to call you instead of someone else?

Another important reason for adding this profile section to your résumé is to ensure that the clerk who classifies your résumé into a category and summarizes your information into the applicant tracking software doesn't have to read your entire résumé and guess what words are important. Even large companies that don't scan résumés or receive them through e-mail or Web-based e-forms (which includes the majority of companies) still have computerized systems for tracking résumés or they outsource the scanning of paper résumés, so these words of advice apply to all résumés, not just the electronic kind.

❑ *You're Done—Well, Almost*

Now it's time to put all of this information together into the perfect résumé that will serve as the foundation for your e-résumés. You have a qualifications summary, your education, experience, and other relevant information. The only thing you lack is your contact information.

For the contact information, you can use your full name, first and last name only, or shortened names (Pat Criscito instead of Patricia K. Criscito).

Do not use work telephone numbers or a work e-mail address on your résumé. Potential employers tend to consider that an abuse of company resources, which implies you might do the same if you are working for them. Listing a cellular telephone number on your résumé gives a hiring manager a way to reach you during working hours.

Avoid the use of "cutesy" e-mail addresses on a résumé. If you use *babycakes@ aol.com* for your personal e-mail, create a second e-mail address under your account that will be more professional. If your only access to the Internet is at work, then create a free-mail account at *hotmail.com, juno.com, usa.net, yahoo.com, mail.com, excite.com, e-mail.com,* or *altavista.com.* Check *www.refdesk.com/freemail.html* for a list of even more free e-mail services.

Now it's time to typeset your information in a style that reflects your personality for your paper résumé, which is an entirely different subject. Even though content is extremely important, many times well-qualified people aren't considered for positions because a poorly designed résumé didn't grab the reader's attention long enough to make sure the words were read. Just the opposite can be true as well. Even if your qualifications aren't the greatest, a well-designed résumé improves your chances of getting an interview because it stands out in a crowd of poorly designed one.

There is a science behind laying out a paper résumé just like there is a science behind designing advertisements, and you need to feel comfortable with your word processing software before you even start. If you are not, then you should call in a professional typesetter, designer, or résumé writer for this part. You have just finished the hardest part of a résumé—the writing of it—so you may be able to save some money by shopping around when getting it typeset. Make sure the designer knows you need a résumé that will scan perfectly and that you need a copy of the file on a computer disk so you can create your e-mailable version.

An experienced résumé writer and designer can take the work you have done and enhance it with a wealth of seasoned knowledge, turning it into a finely tuned marketing instrument that truly reflects who you are. The finished résumé will attract a reader to learn more about you in an interview, which is the whole purpose of your résumé anyway.

Whether you typeset your résumé yourself or hire someone else to do it for you, the ultimate responsibility for the accuracy of your résumé is *yours*. Make sure every word is spelled correctly and that your grammar is perfect. Double proofread your dates, address, phone number, and any other numbers that might appear in your résumé. Make sure punctuation is consistent and that you haven't used the ampersand (&) in place of the word *and* (except in the case of a company name when the company uses it that way). When you are absolutely certain it is perfect, then have someone else read it again just to make sure!

Résumé writing and design services that advertise on the Internet are probably comfortable with writing and designing electronic résumés. Use a good search engine to locate them and then contact several to request samples or references. You might also check your local Yellow Pages for companies that mention the Internet or electronic résumés in their advertising. Remember to look for the NCRW or CPRW after someone's name in an advertisement. Go directly to the Web sites of the National Résumé Writers' Association and the Professional Association of Résumé Writers for lists of their members. With today's technology, you aren't limited to writers in your immediate geographic area. Don't hesitate to use a long-distance service if you feel confident with the quality of its work.

- National Résumé Writers' Association
  http://www.nrwaweb.com

- Professional Association of Résumé Writers
  http://www.parw.com

- ProType, Ltd.
  http://www.protypeltd.com

■ Creating an ASCII Text File

After you have saved your résumé to a computer disk, the next step is to take the computer file you have just created for your paper résumé and strip it of all the formatting codes in order to save the file again (under a new name) as an ASCII text file ready for e-mailing or posting online. Chapter 5 will walk you through the process in complete detail, but the following screens will give you a general idea of how it works.

Every word processing software accomplishes this in a different way, but most of them have an option to convert a file to ASCII, MS-DOS text, or some other type of generic text file. For instance, in Corel WordPerfect (see the sample below), you choose the "Save As" option from the "File" menu and select the option "ASCII (DOS) Generic Word Processor." There are other ASCII options, but the text will wrap better when cut and pasted into an e-mail message or onto those little electronic forms on the Internet if you choose this option. After saving the file in the new format, you close it and open it again. If WordPerfect asks you for the file type, choose "ASCII (DOS)

Text CR/LF to Srt." This tells WordPerfect to maintain the wrap at the end of the lines instead of replacing a Soft Return (Srt) with a Hard Return (Hrt). I know this sounds complicated, but it isn't as difficult as it might seem. Try it a couple of times and you'll get the hang of it. For a more in-depth discussion of creating and using ASCII text files, see Chapter 5.

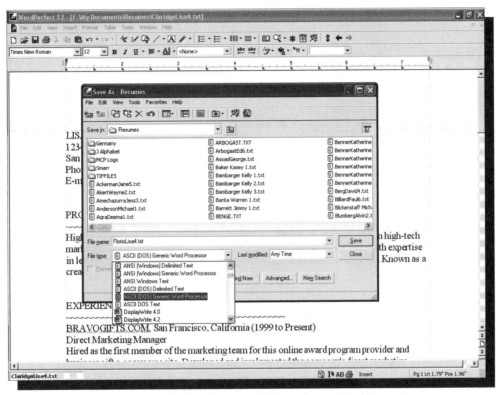

Screen shot of WordPerfect 12 reprinted with permission of Corel Corporation

In Microsoft Word (see sample on next page), you also choose the "Save As" option from the "File" menu, but you will select "MS-DOS Text." If you choose "MS-DOS Text with Line Breaks," then the software will force a carriage return at the end of each line of text, which will cause you problems with pasting the text into an e-form or e-mail where the lines will be shorter than they are on your screen.

■ *Some Don'ts*

There is no need to list references on any résumé, since references are rarely checked until after an interview. However, it is even more important not to list references on an electronic résumé since so many people have access to it. This will avoid the possibility of invading the privacy of friends, associates, or former employers. The only exception might be if you are responding to an advertisement that requests references.

By the way, avoid that needless line at the bottom of a résumé that says, "References available upon request." It takes up valuable white space that you need to help

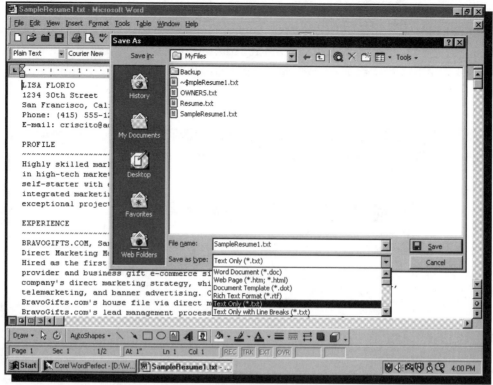

Screen shot of Microsoft Word reprinted with permission from Microsoft Corporation.

define sections on your résumé, which helps to draw the reader's eyes logically down the page. It is assumed that you will provide references when requested, which is usually at the time you complete an application or are interviewed.

Don't send multiple copies of your résumé to the same company within any six-month period if they are *significantly different* in their content, unless they are simply updates. Computerized applicant tracking systems will pick up all versions of your résumé in a keyword search, and you could be blacklisted if multiple versions of your résumé that are very different from each other pop up in the search.

According to Martita Mestey with iHispano.com, if you reply to an online classified advertisement from, say, the Marketing Department of a company one day and then turn around and apply to their Finance Department for a completely different type of job the next day, you won't be taken seriously. Even if you want to work for a specific company very badly, remember that you are applying for a "job" and not a "company."

Martita has been a recruiter in the Chicago area for many years, and according to her, "Applicants often forget that there is a human being at the other end of their computer." Even though you are applying online, you should pretend that you are personally handing your résumé to a recruiter. If you wouldn't walk into a company's HR department and turn in a totally different cover letter and résumé to the same recruiter every other day, then don't do it online. Human resource departments aren't that big, and there is a very good chance that you will develop a "reputation."

On the following pages, you will find some résumés that were discussed in this chapter. On page 33 is the finished version of the résumé we used as a working sample throughout the twelve-step résumé writing process.

Mark A. Phillips

PROFILE

- Experienced electrical engineer with an extensive background in the design and support of complex, large computer networks with primary responsibility for an 8,000-user network.
- Strong communication, leadership, management, and problem solving skills.
- Dedicated professional who enjoys the challenge of solving computer problems.
- Able to work with minimal supervision and as a cooperative team member.
- Knowledge of Windows 98/NT, MS Word, Excel, Access, FormFlow, and C/C++ languages.

EXPERIENCE

UNITED STATES AIR FORCE   1990 – Present

CHIEF, NETWORK CONTROL CENTER
United States Air Force Academy, Colorado (1999 – Present)
- Selected, trained, and supervised 27 civilian and military personnel with a wide range of responsibilities, including client configuration, network connectivity, and file server availability for an 8,000-user local area network valued at over $35 million.
- Managed an 8-person help desk to assist more than 9,000 customers with trouble shooting their own software problems or to assign technicians to correct the problems on site.
- Programmed hubs and routers, and ran unshielded twisted pair and fiber optic cabling.
- Developed infrastructures for Banyan networks, VINES, TCP-IP to include remote, dial-in access via LanExpress.
- Limited project costs to $250,000, while an alternate proposal was provided for $2,500,000.
- Used HP OpenView, Cabletron's LanView, for SNMP management of local area networks.
- Maintained microcomputers, printers, and more than 90 file servers; monitored more than $1 million in annual computer maintenance contracts.

ATMOSPHERIC PROPAGATION ENGINEER
USAF/Phillips Laboratory, Hanscom AFB, Massachusetts (1996 – 1999)
- Developed computer models and conducted field experiments to quantify the atmospheric propagation of light for infrared sensors.
- Defined the parameters for an airborne laser program intended to shoot down missiles.
- Managed a $1.4 million analysis contract supporting electro-optical sensing projects.
- Designed a unique interface software to improve wind sensing accuracy by 50 percent.
- Gained extensive experience with UNIX workstations and PCs.

CHIEF ENGINEER, ELECTRICAL POWER AND COMMUNICATIONS SYSTEM
Utah Test and Training Range, Layton, Utah (1990 – 1994)
- Responsible for the daily operation and maintenance of $70 million of power distribution and microwave communication systems for a 20,000 square mile land/airspace test and training range.
- Installed and maintained power protection equipment, uninterruptible power systems, and automatic transfer switches to protect data processing equipment.
- Wrote specifications for contractor engineering projects to improve system performance.

EDUCATION

MASTER OF SCIENCE, ELECTRICAL ENGINEERING (1994 – 1995)
Air Force Institute of Technology, Wright-Patterson AFB, Ohio
- Concentration in electro-optics

BACHELOR OF SCIENCE, ELECTRICAL ENGINEERING (1986 – 1990)
United States Air Force Academy, Colorado
- Concentration in communications

CONTINUING PROFESSIONAL EDUCATION (1990 – 1994)
Air Force Institute of Technology, Wright-Patterson AFB, Ohio
- Digital Signal Processing, Fiber Optic Communications, Local Area Networks, Electrical Power Distribution, Spread Spectrum Communications, Optimizing Network Server Performance, Acquisition Professional Development Series (4 courses)

ADDRESS   123 East Antelope Drive, USAF Academy, Colorado 80840   (719) 555-1234

Michael L. Patterson, CBI, CBE

12 Parkview, Suite 123
Fort Worth, Texas 76102

Telephone: (817) 555-1234
Voice Mail: (214) 555-1234

Objective   A position as a computer network engineer and instructor for a network and integration company.

Keywords   Banyan VINES network, UNIX, DOS, VAX cluster, gateways, servers, clients, SMTP, DNS, firewall, Internet, dual broadband system, VAX cluster, WAN connections, DMSP ground system, 10base2 wiring, 10baseT wiring, virus scanning, Lotus Notes, ground radar systems, Certified Banyan Engineer, Instructor, and Specialist

---

Experience

Independent Systems Consultant, Fort Worth, Texas .... 1996 to Present
- Develop training and update courses for VINES administrators and conduct classes.
- Provide client support in resolving network problems either directly on-site or via the telephone.

Meridian Oil, Incorporated, Fort Worth, Texas .... 1994 to 1996
SENIOR STAFF INFORMATION SYSTEMS AND TECHNOLOGY ANALYST
- Set up and managed the Internet connection using SMTP, DNS, and a firewall.
- Supported outlying offices with either direct on-site or phone support for resolving network problems.
- Set up and maintained a company-wide virus scanning software on both servers and clients.
- Assisted in a Coopers & Lybrand audit to ensure security on the Internet connection.
- Developed and conducted training and update classes for VINES administrators company-wide.

United States Air Force .... 1973 to 1994
Twenty-one years of progressively more responsible service and training positions that included contact with manufacturers, service contractors, and major computer suppliers. Extensive specialized training at both Department of the Air Force and manufacturers' schools.

CHIEF, HARDWARE SERVICES DIVISION, ACADEMIC COMPUTING SERVICES
Department of the Air Force, Dean of Faculty, USAF Academy, Colorado (1993 to 1994)
- Supervised an office of 10 technicians, with a wide range of responsibilities including the installation of a 65-server Banyan VINES network with 6,000+ clients.
- Prepared and conducted training for group and building VINES administrators for the USAF Academy.
- Worked with the dual broadband system for distribution of VAX cluster output and connections.
- Engineered design and trade-off studies; assembled and distributed systems to operational users.
- Supported base-level contracting with technical information needed to complete purchase requests.
- Improved process methods, reducing expenditures and minimizing total man-hours for all projects.

PROGRAM MANAGER FOR COMPUTER INFORMATION SYSTEMS
Training System Program Office, Wright-Patterson AFB, Ohio (1990 to 1993)
- Managed and provided engineering support for a 12-server Banyan VINES network with 400+ clients.
- Completed an upgrade of the network from 10base2 client wiring to 10baseT wiring, which included WAN connections to an off-site work location during the upgrade with no loss of work time.
- Designed and deployed an extension of the network to a division located in Utah, using Internet for connectivity.
- Engineered design and trade-off studies; supported base-level contracting with technical information.

ASSISTANT TO THE PROGRAM MANAGER
Training Systems Program Office (SPO), Wright-Patterson AFB, Ohio (1987 to 1990)
- Assisted in leading a team of 13 functional experts in defining, acquiring, and fielding maintenance training devices.
- Managed the Support Equipment Requirement Development list for the C-17 Maintenance Training Devices program in coordination with HQ Air Mobility Command, HQ Air Training Command, C-17 Airlifter SPO, and the contractor.

34

Experience (continued)

FIELD ENGINEER, DEFENSE METEOROLOGICAL SATELLITE PROGRAM (DMSP) GROUND SYSTEM
1000 Satellite Operations Group, Offutt AFB, Nebraska (1983 to 1986)
- ◆ Evaluated proposals for any changes to the Satellite Ground Control Facility.
- ◆ Lead Engineer on embedded microcomputer applications for controlling the DMSP Ground System links and equipment.
- ◆ Test Engineer for installation of new electronic systems.
- ◆ Controlled equipment failures and coordinated with DMSP SPO, three contractors, and two detachments when failure trend analysis indicated needed action.

Education

College Degrees
- ◆ Master of Science, Systems Management, Air Force Institute of Technology
- ◆ Bachelor of Science, Electrical Engineering, Texas A&M University
- ◆ Applied Associate of Science, Instructor of Technology, CCAF
- ◆ Applied Associate of Science, Electronics Engineering Technology, CCAF
- ◆ Applied Associate of Science, Ground Radar Systems Technology, CCAF

Certifications
- ◆ Certified Banyan Instructor, 1994 (Advanced VINES Administration and 6.0 Update Courses)
- ◆ Certified Banyan Engineer, 1993 (Recertified 1994, 1995, 1996)
- ◆ Certified Banyan Specialist, 1993 (Recertified 1994, 1995, 1996)

Banyan Courses
- ◆ Train-the-Trainer Update for VINES Administration (VINES 6.0), Banyan, 1996
- ◆ VINES 6.00 Engineering Update, ABUI Training Institute, 1995
- ◆ Train-the-Trainer for VINES Administration (VINES 5.5), Banyan, 1994
- ◆ Advanced VINES Administration and Planning (VINES 5.5), Banyan, 1994
- ◆ Basic VINES Administration (VINES 5.5), Banyan, 1994
- ◆ VINES 5.5 Engineering Update (VINES 5.5), Banyan, 1993
- ◆ Technical Tools II (VINES 5.0), Banyan, 1993
- ◆ Technical Tools I (VINES 5.0), Banyan, 1992
- ◆ VINES Gateways, Banyan, 1992

Other Courses
- ◆ Systems Engineering Course, Systems Management and Development Corp, DSMC, 1992
- ◆ Computer Resources Acquisition Course, AFMC SAS, 1992
- ◆ Advanced Systems Acquisition Management Course, AFSC SAS, 1989

Activities

Association of Banyan Users International (ABUI) . . . . 1990 to Present
President, Board of Directors, with responsibility for overseeing corporate operations as CEO (1995 to Present). Secretary, Board of Directors, with responsibility for overseeing minutes and corporate records (1994 to 1995). Chairman for Asynchronous Technical Wizards Interface Group (TWIG) with the responsibilities of overseeing session content at the semiannual conferences, conducting sessions, and coordinating the tracking of member requirements with a Banyan representative as related to asynchronous and WAN issues (1990 to 1994).

Banyan Users In Colorado (BUIC) . . . . 1993 to 1994
Vice President of the Regional Banyan user group; assisted in the development of the BUIC.

David H. Parker

| ADDRESS | 12 Parkview Boulevard, Colorado Springs, Colorado 80906 | (719) 555-1234 |

PROFILE

- Licensed attorney in private practice since 1969 (Colorado and New Mexico).
- Board Certified Civil Trial Specialist with extensive litigation experience.
- Recognized specialist in workers' compensation law by the New Mexico Legal Specialization Board.
- Admitted to practice before the U.S. Court of Appeals, 10th Circuit; U.S. District Court for the District of New Mexico; U.S. District Court for the Western District of Texas; District Courts of the State Colorado; and all courts in the State of New Mexico.
- Extensive experience in the preparation and trial of injury claims resulting from both workers' compensation and off-the-job injuries.
- Exceptional knowledge of administrative procedures, rules of evidence, and trial practices.

EXPERIENCE

- Member of a three-attorney panel appointed by the New Mexico Court of Appeals to issue advisory decisions in pending civil appeals.
- Wrote the advisory decision in the appeal of *Miller v. NM Dept. of Transportation,* the essence of which was adopted by the New Mexico Supreme Court.
- Selected twice in fifteen months as an arbitrator for the New Mexico trial-level court to arbitrate cases with damage claims less than $15,000, using procedures similar to those governing American Arbitration Association proceedings.

Personal Injury

- Lead counsel or sole counsel for the injured plaintiff/worker in at least 30 jury trials with a minimum trial length of three days, plus another 50 non-jury trials of at least two days.
- Since 1983, have prepared and prosecuted to conclusion, either by trial or settlement, over 650 workers' compensation cases involving both physical and economic injuries.
- Interviewed witnesses, propounded and responded to interrogatories, requested productions and admissions, took and defended depositions, briefed interlocutory motions, filed requested findings and conclusions in non-jury cases, and prepared and argued requested instructions in jury trials.
- Developed considerable experience in determining when the record should be closed or supplemented.

Expert Witnesses

- Defined case issues and facts, then determined what type of expert witnesses would be needed.
- Located highly competent and persuasive experts in the required field.
- Consulted with and prepared the experts based on the definition of the issues and facts.
- Examined and cross-examined all types of fact witnesses and expert witnesses from nearly all areas of medicine and many scientific fields.

Management

- Managed a private law practice for more than 20 years, including all aspects of administration, accountability for profit and loss, controlling costs, and achieving revenue objectives.
- Recruited, supervised, motivated, and evaluated employees, including clerical staff and paralegals.
- Met deadlines for pretrial procedures, trials, and appellate briefings by effectively utilizing attorney associates and support staff.
- Designed a complete set of recurring forms to manage a typical workers' compensation claim from initial client interview through requested findings and conclusions.
- Competent in IBM, Windows, and WordPerfect computer software.

EDUCATION

JURIS DOCTOR — 1969
University of New Mexico School of Law, Albuquerque, New Mexico

GRADUATE SCHOOL — 1966 – 1967
University of New Mexico, Albuquerque, New Mexico
- 18 hours of Modern European History

BACHELOR OF ARTS — 1965
University of Minnesota, St. Paul, Minnesota
- Major in English

SIGNIFICANT CASES

- *Nick Andler v. City of Gallup and NM Self-Insurer's Fund,* NM Dept. of Labor, Workers' Compensation Administration No. WCA 92-03246
- *Greene v. Proto/Stanley-Proto,* San Juan County, N.M. District Court No. CV-88-540-3, 1993 (jury verdict, products liability case, eight-day trial, $282,000 plus costs)
- *Vickaryous v. City of Albuquerque,* Bernalillo County, N.M. District Court No. CV-91-02098, 1992 (alleged police negligence in failing to take keys from DWI driver resulting in paralysis)
- *Chevron Resources ex rel. Blatnik v. New Mexico Superintendent of Ins.,* 838 P.2d 988, 114 N.M. 371 (Ct. App. 1992)
- *Johnson v. Sears, Roebuck & Co.,* 832 P.2d 797, 113 N.M. 736 (Ct. App. 1992)
- *Richardson v. Farmers Ins. Co.,* 811 P.2d 571, 112 N.M. 73 (S. Ct. 1991)
- *Roybal v. Mutual of Omaha,* USDC, DCNM No. CIV 88-01195 SC, 1991 ($300,000 settlement on appeal, breach of insurance contract claims for nonpayment of benefits health/major medical policy)
- *Cano v. Smith's Food King,* 781 P.2d 322, 109 N.M. 50 (Ct. App. 1989)
- *Strong v. Sysco Corp./Nobel Sysco,* 776 P.2d 1258, 108 N.M. 639 (Ct. App. 1989)
- *Rodriguez v. X-Pert Well Serv., Inc.,* 759 P.2d 1010, 107 N.M. 428 (Ct. App. 1988)
- *Jimmy Davis, et al. v. Aztec Drilling, et al.,* San Juan County, N.M. District Court, 1988 (seven-day jury trial, natural gas field explosion, bifurcated liability and damages trials; settled for $500,000 for Jimmy Davis following jury verdict on liability)
- *Thompson v. Ruidoso-Sunland, Inc.,* 734 P.2d 267, 105 N.M. 487 (Ct. App. 1987)
- *Robert Shattuck v. Lovelace Medical Center,* Bernalillo County, N.M. District Court No. CIV 85-03953, (medical/hospital malpractice case settled after two days of trial for $800,000, Nov. 1987)
- *John Sauters v. Jack B. Kelley: American Western Securities, Inc., et al.,* USDC, DCNM No. CV 84-0826 HB, 1986 (bench decision for $180,000 minority shareholders dilution action against broker-dealer and principal broker)
- *Bledsoe v. Garcia,* 742 F.2d 1237 (10th Cir. 1984)
- *Garrison v. Safeway Stores,* 692 P.2d 1328, 102 N.M. 179 (Ct. App. 1984)
- *Moreno v. Marrs Mud Co.,* 695 P.2d 1322, 102 N.M. 373 (Ct. App. 1984) (exception to "firemen's rule" absolute assumption of risk defense to tort claim by policeman/fireman recognized)
- *Kathy Penley v. Buena Suerta Ranch, Inc., et al.,* USDC, DCNM No. CIV 82-0878, JB, 1984 ($60,000 jury verdict in breach of bailment contract by horse owner v. horse ranch and trainer)
- *Patterson v. City of Albuquerque,* 661 P.2d 1331, 99 N.M. 632 (Ct. App. 1983)

AFFILIATIONS

- American Bar Association
- Colorado Bar Association
- New Mexico Bar Association
- Association of Trial Lawyers of America
- New Mexico Trial Lawyers Association (Board of Directors, 1987 – 1988)
- Colorado Trial Lawyers Association
- Albuquerque Lawyers Society

PRESENTATIONS

- "Workers' Compensation: Calculation of Disability Benefits Under the New Grid Systems," New Mexico Trial Lawyers Association, 1994.
- "Direct Examination of a Cardiologist in Heart Attack Cases" and "Establishing Disability with the Dictionary of Occupational Titles," New Mexico Trial Lawyers Association, 1993.

WORK HISTORY

STAFF ATTORNEY, McDivitt Law Firm, Colorado Springs, Colorado	1995 – Present
PRESIDENT, David H. Parker, P.A., Albuquerque, New Mexico	1980 – 1995
PARTNER, Parker & Diamond, Albuquerque, New Mexico	1979 – 1980
PRESIDENT, David H. Parker, P.A., Albuquerque, New Mexico	1976 – 1979
PARTNER, Parker & Shoobridge, Albuquerque, New Mexico	1975 – 1976
PARTNER, Aldridge, Baron, Parker & Campbell, Albuquerque, New Mexico	1973 – 1975
PARTNER, Aldridge & Parker, Albuquerque, New Mexico	1971 – 1973
PRESIDENT, David H. Parker, P.A., Albuquerque, New Mexico	1969 – 1971

■ *Power Verbs*

Just because a computer will screen your résumé in the beginning and look for keywords is no excuse for poor writing. Your ultimate goal is to entice a human being to read your résumé, so keep the sentences interesting by using positive power verbs. Try to use a variety of these words. It's easy to choose the same one to begin every sentence, but there are synonyms buried within this list that will make your writing better.

A

abated
abbreviated
abolished
abridged
absolved
absorbed
accelerated
accentuated
accommodated
accompanied
accomplished
accounted for
accrued
accumulated
achieved
acquired
acted
activated
actuated
adapted
added
addressed
adhered to
adjusted
administered
adopted
advanced
advertised
advised
advocated
affirmed
aided
alerted
aligned
allayed
alleviated

allocated
allotted
altered
amassed
amended
amplified
analyzed
answered
anticipated
appeased
applied
appointed
appraised
approached
appropriated
approved
arbitrated
aroused
arranged
articulated
ascertained
aspired
assembled
assessed
assigned
assimilated
assisted
assumed
assured
attained
attended
attracted
audited
augmented
authored
authorized
automated
averted

avoided
awarded

B

balanced
bargained
began
benchmarked
benefitted
bid
billed
blended
blocked
bolstered
boosted
bought
branded
bridged
broadened
brought
budgeted
built

C

calculated
calibrated
canvassed
capitalized
captured
cared for
carried
carried out
carved
catalogued
categorized

caught
cautioned
cemented
centralized
certified
chaired
challenged
championed
changed
channeled
charged
charted
checked
chose
chronicled
circulated
circumvented
cited
clarified
classified
cleaned
cleared
closed
coached
co-authored
coded
cold called
collaborated
collated
collected
combined
commanded
commenced
commended
commissioned
communicated
compared
competed

compiled
complemented
completed
complied
composed
compounded
computed
conceived
concentrated
conceptualized
concluded
condensed
conducted
conferred
configured
confirmed
confronted
connected
conserved
considered
consolidated
constructed
consulted
consummated
contacted
continued
contracted
contributed
controlled
converted
conveyed
convinced
cooperated
coordinated
copied
corrected
correlated
corresponded
counseled
counted
created
credited with
critiqued
cultivated
customized
cut

dealt
debated
debugged
decentralized
decided
decoded
decreased
dedicated
deferred
defined
delegated
deleted
delineated
delivered
demonstrated
deployed
depreciated
derived
described
designated
designed
detailed
detected
determined
developed
devised
devoted
diagnosed
diagramed
differentiated
diffused
directed
disbursed
disclosed
discounted
discovered
discussed
dispatched
dispensed
dispersed
displayed
disposed
disproved
dissected

disseminated
dissolved
distinguished
distributed
diversified
diverted
divested
divided
documented
doubled
drafted
dramatized
drew up
drove

earned
eased
economized
edited
educated
effected
elaborated
elected
elevated
elicited
eliminated
embraced
emphasized
employed
empowered
enabled
encountered
encouraged
ended
endorsed
enforced
engaged
engineered
enhanced
enlarged
enlisted
enriched
enrolled
ensured

entered
entertained
enticed
equipped
established
estimated
evaluated
examined
exceeded
exchanged
executed
exercised
exhibited
expanded
expedited
experienced
experimented
explained
explored
exposed
expressed
extended
extracted
extrapolated

fabricated
facilitated
factored
familiarized
fashioned
fielded
filed
filled
finalized
financed
fine-tuned
finished
fixed
focused
followed
forecasted
forged
formalized
formatted

formed
formulated
fortified
forwarded
fostered
fought
found
founded
framed
fulfilled
functioned as
funded
furnished
furthered

G

gained
garnered
gathered
gauged
gave
generated
governed
graded
graduated
granted
graphed
grasped
greeted
grew
grouped
guaranteed
guided

H

halted
halved
handled
headed
heightened
held
helped
hired
honed
hosted

hypnotized
hypothesized

I

identified
ignited
illuminated
illustrated
implemented
imported
improved
improvised
inaugurated
incited
included
incorporated
increased
incurred
indicated
individualized
indoctrinated
induced
influenced
informed
infused
initialized
initiated
innovated
inspected
inspired
installed
instigated
instilled
instituted
instructed
insured
integrated
intensified
interacted
interceded
interfaced
interpreted
intervened
interviewed
introduced
invented
inventoried

invested
investigated
invigorated
invited
involved
isolated
issued
itemized

J

joined
judged
justified

L

launched
learned
leased
lectured
led
lessened
leveraged
licensed
lifted
lightened
limited
linked
liquidated
listened
litigated
loaded
lobbied
localized
located
logged

M

made
maintained
managed
mandated
maneuvered
manipulated
manufactured

mapped
marked
marketed
mastered
maximized
measured
mediated
memorized
mentored
merchandised
merged
merited
met
minimized
mobilized
modeled
moderated
modernized
modified
molded
monitored
monopolized
motivated
mounted
moved
multiplied

N

named
narrated
navigated
negotiated
netted
networked
neutralized
nominated
normalized
noticed
notified
nurtured

O

observed
obtained
offered

officiated
offset
opened
operated
optimized
orchestrated
ordered
organized
oriented
originated
outdistanced
outlined
outperformed
overcame
overhauled
oversaw
owned

paced
packaged
packed
paid
pared
participated
partnered
passed
patterned
penalized
penetrated
perceived
perfected
performed
permitted
persuaded
phased out
photographed
piloted
pinpointed
pioneered
placed
planned
played
polled
posted

praised
predicted
prepared
prescribed
presented
preserved
presided
prevailed
prevented
priced
printed
prioritized
probed
processed
procured
produced
profiled
programmed
progressed
projected
promoted
prompted
proofread
proposed
protected
proved
provided
pruned
publicized
published
purchased
pursued

quadrupled
qualified
quantified
queried
questioned
quoted

raised
rallied

ranked
rated
reached
reacted
read
realigned
realized
rearranged
reasoned
rebuilt
received
reclaimed
recognized
recommended
reconciled
reconstructed
recorded
recovered
recruited
rectified
redesigned
redirected
reduced
re-engineered
referred
refined
refocused
regained
registered
regulated
rehabilitated
reinforced
reinstated
reiterated
rejected
related
released
relied
relieved
remained
remediated
remodeled
rendered
renegotiated
renewed
reorganized

repaired
replaced
replicated
replied
reported
represented
reproduced
requested
required
requisitioned
researched
reserved
reshaped
resolved
responded
restored
restructured
retained
retooled
retrieved
returned
revamped
revealed
reversed
reviewed
revised
revitalized
revolutionized
rewarded
risked
rotated
routed

safeguarded
salvaged
saved
scanned
scheduled
screened
sculptured
searched
secured
segmented
seized
selected
sent

separated
sequenced
served as
serviced
settled
set up
shaped
shared
sharpened
shipped
shortened
showed
shrank
signed
simplified
simulated
sketched
skilled
slashed
smoothed
sold
solicited
solidified
solved
sorted
sourced
sparked
spearheaded
specialized
specified
speculated
spent
spoke
sponsored
spread
spurred
stabilized
staffed
staged
standardized

started
steered
stimulated
strategized
streamlined
strengthened
stressed
stretched
structured
studied
subcontracted
submitted
substantiated
substituted
succeeded
suggested
summarized
superceded
supervised
supplied
supported
surpassed
surveyed
swayed
swept
symbolized
synchronized
synthesized
systemized

tabulated
tackled
tailored
talked
tallied
targeted
tasted
taught

teamed
tempered
tended
terminated
tested
testified
tied
tightened
took
topped
totaled
traced
tracked
traded
trained
transacted
transcribed
transferred
transformed
transitioned
translated
transmitted
transported
traveled
treated
trimmed
tripled
troubleshot
turned
tutored
typed

uncovered
underlined
underscored
undertook
underwrote
unearthed

unified
united
updated
upgraded
upheld
urged
used
utilized

validated
valued
vaulted
verbalized
verified
viewed
visited
visualized
voiced
volunteered

W

weathered
weighed
welcomed
widened
withstood
witnessed
won
worked
wove
wrote

Y

yielded

3 | Keywords Are Key!

Using the right keywords for your particular experience and education is critical to the success of your e-résumé. Without the right keywords, your résumé will float in cyberspace forever waiting for a hiring manager to find it. If your résumé contains all the right keywords, then you will be among the first candidates whose résumés are reviewed. If you lack only one of the keywords, then your résumé will be next in line after résumés that have them all, and so on.

Remember, your keywords are the specific terminology used in your job that reflect your experience and skills. For instance, *operating room* and *ICU* immediately classify the experience of a nurse, but *pediatric ICU* narrows it down even further.

■ How to Use Keywords

Don't try to limit your résumé by using fewer words. If your information is longer than one page, a reader looking at a computer screen won't be able to tell, but the computer doing a keyword search will know if a word is not there. Recall, however, that you only need to use a word one time for it to be considered a "hit" in a keyword search. Try to use synonyms wherever possible to broaden your chances of being selected.

You should also understand the difference between a simple keyword search and a concept search. When a recruiter brings up an e-mailed résumé onto the screen and sends the computer on a search for a single word like *marketing*—which one can do in any word processing program with a few clicks of a mouse or function key—he or she is performing a keyword search.

You are also performing a keyword search when you type a word or combination of words into the command line of a search engine like Yahoo! or Google (see example that follows). In that case, sometimes the computer searches entire documents for matches and other times it looks only at headers or extracts from the files.

Screen shot used with permission of Google.

A concept search, on the other hand, can bridge the gap between words by reading entire phrases and then using sophisticated artificial intelligence to interpret what is being said, translating the phrase into a single word, like *network*, or a combination of words, like *project management*.

For example, in a simple keyword search on "Manager of Product Sales," ordinary software would return a match on a candidate's résumé that reads "worked for a Manager of Product Sales." Using a concept search, Yahoo! Resumix can distinguish between this résumé and another candidate's résumé that indicated "served as a Manager of Product Sales."

The software that extracts data from scanned and e-mailed résumés and Web sources is incredibly sophisticated. Yahoo! Resumix, one such programs used by recruiters in large companies and government agencies, reads the grammar of noun, verb, and adjective combinations and extracts the information for placement on the form that will become your entry in a résumé database. Its expert system extraction engine uses a complex knowledge base of more than 197,000 rules and over ten million résumé terms. It recognizes grammatical structure variations, including synonyms and context within natural language text.

It even knows the difference between *Harvard Graphics* (a computer software program) and *Harvard* (the university) by its placement on the page and its relationship to the header that precedes it *(Computer Skills* or *Education).*

Because of this complicated logic, and because each company and each hiring manager has the ability to personalize the search criteria for each job opening, it is

44

impossible to give you a concrete list of the thousands of possible keywords that could be used to search for any one job.

For instance, StorageTek, a high-tech company in Louisville, Colorado, graciously conducted a keyword search for me of their Resumix database and brought up the following criteria from two different hiring managers for the same job title. These are keywords extracted from real job requisitions written by hiring managers.

FINANCIAL ANALYST/SENIOR ACCOUNTANT:

REQUIRED:
- BS in finance or accounting with 4 years of experience or
- MBA in related field with 2 years of relevant experience
- certified public accountant
- forecasting

REQUIRED:
- BS in finance or accounting with 4 years of experience or
- MBA in related field with 2 years of relevant experience
- accounting
- financial reporting
- financial statement
- Excel

DESIRED:
- accounting
- financial
- trend analysis
- financial statement
- results analysis
- trends
- strategic planning
- develop trends
- financial modeling
- personal computer
- microcomputers
- DCF
- presentation skills
- team player

DESIRED:
- ability
- customer
- new business
- financial analysis
- financial
- forecasting
- process improvement
- policy development
- business policies
- PowerPoint
- Microsoft Word
- analytical ability

■ *Sample Résumés with Keywords Highlighted*

Let me show you how keywords can be extracted from an actual résumé. In the examples on the following pages, each résumé has possible keywords highlighted using bold and italic letters. As you can see, résumés for different industries generate completely different keywords. The only keywords that might be the same are ones for "soft" skills.

Just because I've highlighted all possible keywords in a résumé doesn't mean that the hiring manager will write each one of them in a job requisition. Instead, this exercise is meant to help you become more aware of the nouns, adjectives, and sometimes verbs that *might* become keywords in a résumé database search, whether it is at Monster.com or in a company's private database of résumés.

You will also notice that I've only highlighted the word the first time it appears. To applicant tracking software, the number of times a word appears in a résumé or its position at the top, middle, or bottom of a résumé doesn't increase its importance. Relevance is more important than keyword density to these applications. For instance, your résumé will rank higher if you have more years of experience than someone's who doesn't have as much. The software extracts that information using the "from" and "to" dates on your job titles.

NOTE: Do not highlight keywords on your own résumé! They are highlighted on these examples solely as a tool to help you understand the concept of which words become keywords in a search.

Jaime M. Bond

Permanent Address: 1234 Park Road ♦ Vienna, Virginia 22182 ♦ Message: (703) 555-1234
Present Address: Jan Luykenstraat 1234 ♦ 11071 CR Amsterdam ♦ The Netherlands
Home: (+31) 20-555-1234 ♦ Work: (+31) 44-555-1234 ♦ E-mail: jbond@protype.nl

PROFESSIONAL BACKGROUND

♦ Highly motivated *senior manager* with more than ten years of experience in all facets of *global telecommunications networking*.
♦ Instrumental in several phases of the development of a new European telecommunications provider that competed with an entrenched *monopoly* for the first time on the continent; succeeded by working smarter and faster with limited resources.
♦ Background in *business development*, *strategic planning*, *start-up* processes, *product marketing*, *sales*, and *contract negotiations* in the global arena.
♦ Directed the design of *managed voice and data networks* that produced significant cost benefits for customers.
♦ Developed and successfully sold value propositions for complex *frame relay* and *Internet applications*.

PERSONAL PROFILE

♦ Adept at building trust and turning around troubled *client relationships*.
♦ Able to simplify complex ideas and present them effectively at the highest executive level.
♦ Exceptional motivator who is able to build enlightened teams with a strong *customer focus*.
♦ Comfortable working in *cross-cultural* environments; lived and worked in The *Netherlands*.

Experience

SENIOR MANAGER, CUSTOMER *NETWORK DESIGN* (8/01 to present)
Telfort Networks and Systems, Amsterdam, The Netherlands (on temporary assignment from MCI)
Developed a customer-focused *design team* to meet the needs of the sales group for this new European telecommunications provider. Recruited, trained, and managed a team of 14 technical sales support professionals responsible for advanced *telecom design* and *application consulting* in support of a $150 million *account base*. Uncovered *high-end applications* and found solutions that effectively focused on customer needs. Advised the CIO on the feasibility of designs, developed *business plans*, and made high-level executive *presentations*. Prepared and administered $700,000 *budgets*.

Key Accomplishments

♦ Directed the integrated (voice/data) network design, *proposal development*, and *implementation planning process* that was instrumental in securing $10 million in annual new revenues from customers such as Shell, World On Line, and NLNet.
♦ Consulted with sales account teams and assisted them in presenting *business application proposals* to Philips and Akzo Nobel, securing *managed data network* contracts valued at $7 million in annual new revenues.
♦ Saved $5 million in network operating expenses by reorganizing the *backbone network structure* and consolidating *third-party maintenance* under one master contract.

SENIOR NATIONAL ACCOUNT MANAGER (5/99 to 8/01)
MCI National Accounts, San Francisco, California, and Atlanta, Georgia
Managed a team of six sales and *technical support* professionals responsible for business communication application development and consulting to a Fortune 500 global account base with an $18 million annual revenue quota.

Key Accomplishments

♦ Achieved exclusive vendor status with Fireman's Fund Insurance by executing a four-year, $20 million contract for MCI HyperStream frame relay, *Vnet*, *toll free*, and *video conferencing* services. Turned around a bad relationship, reinvigorating the staff and *rebuilding trust* at the highest client level before convincing the client of the compelling benefits of a managed data network.
♦ Implemented a fully managed, 200-node frame relay network for Fireman's Fund, including an *alliance sale* of $700,000 in Cisco routers, saving the client more than $300,000 through a *multivendor partnership*.
♦ Restructured the *implementation plan* for a fully managed, 25-node global frame relay network for Turner Broadcasting which resulted in a three-year, $3 million contract.

♦ Negotiated a very complex and creative contract with Fujitsu that generated $10 million in revenue during a two-year period, taking the client from AT&T even though it had Fijitsu's business on price. Developed the plan for the global application of a Pacific Rim 45-megabit *Internet backbone network*.

♦ Received the Director's Chair Award for exceptional service; exceeded quotas by as much as 180 percent.

PARTNERSHIP DEVELOPMENT MANAGER, MCI Business Markets, Atlanta, Georgia (6/98 to 5/99)

Directed a team of three *marketing* and *finance* professionals responsible for developing *reciprocal sales partnerships* with retailers who sold to mid-sized customers. Negotiated with corporate executives in order to increase director-level support.

Key Accomplishments

♦ Saved the Staples sales partnership by redesigning the *marketing plan* and *operating agreement*, which produced a 100 percent increase in revenue and customer base.

♦ Designed and implemented a successful OfficeMax partnership centered around *joint catalog mailings*, *newsletter delivery*, and an *in-store kiosk* trial.

GLOBAL ACCOUNT MANAGER, MCI Global Accounts, Atlanta, Georgia (12/95 to 6/98)

Responsible for network design, *implementation consulting*, and strategic planning for a Fortune 500 global account base with a $14 million annual revenue quota. Managed a team of three sales and technical support professionals.

Key Accomplishments

♦ Replaced AT&T by selling Syncordia a three-year, $11 million contract covering a wide range of MCI services, including a 35-megabit global *IDNX/Ericsson backbone network* that ultimately produced more than $20 million in revenue.

♦ Secured a global MCI Vnet and toll free service network for Syncordia valued at $1.5 million annually.

♦ Established the first global *financial broker network* within Robinson Humphrey under a two-year, $1.5 million contract for MCI Vnet and toll free service.

♦ Achieved the Chairman's Inner Circle in 1993 for the top one percent of sales people.

PRODUCT MARKETING MANAGER, MCI Global Marketing, McLean, Virginia (10/94 to 12/95)

Managed MCI's $50 million global *leased line business*, including, *service development*, *field support*, and *portfolio business management*. Supervised a team of three marketing and finance professionals. Negotiated operating agreements with *foreign carriers*.

Key Accomplishments

♦ Developed and implemented MCI network service arrangements and MCI *multiline service*, which produced $7.5 million in incremental revenue between 1990 and 1991.

♦ Managed the *business model development* and *product marketing strategy integration* of MCI's $20 million acquisition of Overseas Telecom, a niche provider of *satellite telecommunications services* to South America.

♦ Directed the complete restructuring of MCI's leased line *pricing* format, simplifying the pricing structure by consolidating five *tariffs* into one and *building models* for the impact on the installed revenue base.

♦ Honored with the MCI Excellence in Service Award for the top one percent of MCI staffers.

DESIGN ENGINEER, MCI Switched Network Engineering, McLean, Virginia (6/92 to 10/94)

Responsible for backbone planning and implementation *project management*, including a $20 million fiber expansion for The Home Shopping Network. Planned and implemented a $45 million *backbone migration* from *analog radio* to fiber optics. Designed and implemented *infrastructure support plans* for three DMS-250 *switch installations*.

——————— Education ———————

BACHELOR OF SCIENCE, TECHNOLOGY EDUCATION (1986)
Virginia Polytechnic Institute and State University

CONTINUING EDUCATION

Global *Account Management* (40 hours), *Advanced Technical Marketing* (80 hours), *Executive Presentation* Forum (24 hours), Simplifying *LAN/WAN* Interconnection (24 hours), Professional *Data Selling* Skills (40 hours)

Daniel DeVito

SUMMARY

- Friendly and giving *speech therapist* with a recent degree in *speech language disorders*.
- Proven leader with a *strong work ethic* and a deep commitment to helping others.
- *Personable* and *articulate* with excellent *interpersonal* and *communication skills*.
- Well organized, able to balance priorities and *work independently*.

EDUCATION

BACHELOR OF SCIENCE, **SPEECH LANGUAGE PATHOLOGY** (May 1998)
Abilene Christian University, Abilene, Texas

- Trained in language and speech disorders, with an emphasis on *etiology*, *diagnosis*, and *clinical management* of these disorders.
- Mastered the *international phonetic alphabet* and learned to identify the sounds of English and to *transcribe* and *translate*.
- Learned the *components*, *stages*, and *differences* between how human beings use and acquire language.
- Gained a comprehension of *articulation* and *fluency disorders* and *treatments*.
- Studied the theory and practice of *rehabilitative audiology* and *hearing*.
- Learned how to conduct *basic hearing assessments* on *children* and *adults*.
- Also studied Advanced *Speech-Language Pathology*, *Sign Language I-II*, *Acoustics* and *Voice Science*, Normal *Language Development*, *Whole Language* and *Pragmaticism*, *Linguistics*, *Language* and *Learning Disabilities*, and *Anatomical* and *Physiological Processes of Communication*.

EXPERIENCE

CLINICAL PRACTICUM, Abilene Christian University, Abilene, Texas (1998)

- Wrote *lesson plans* for the treatment of adults, children, and *Down's syndrome* clients in a two-semester *practicum* that provided hands-on experience in speech language pathology.
- Worked closely with three children with articulation, *dysphonia*, and *language disorders*.
- Set long-term and short-term *goals* and made recommendations for *treatment* and *follow-up*.
- Maintained reports for each patient that included *evaluation, diagnosis, treatment plan*, procedures, and *methods*.

YOUTH INTERN, **Hillcrest Church of Christ**, Abilene, Texas (1997 – 1998)

- Taught classes for *middle school* and *high school students* and provided *counseling* for members of the *youth group*.
- Attended weekly *strategic planning* meetings with the *youth minister* and other *interns*.
- Planned *retreats*, *mission trips*, and *youth activities*.

ACTIVITIES & HONORS

- Recipient of the Audra Cobb Memorial Scholarship, 1997.
- Member of the Texas Speech-Language Hearing Association.
- Member of the Speech Pathology Organization (1 year).
- Member of the Students' Association Senate; Co-chair of the Special Friends Committee (2 years), which planned activities to enable student interaction with *mentally and physically handicapped adults*.

ADDRESSES

Until May 2004: ACU Box 12345, Abilene, Texas 79699   Phone: (915) 555-1234
Permanent: 1234 Ruidoso Drive, Fort Worth, Texas 76179   Message: (817) 555-1234

SHAY BAKER

12 Quicksilver Drive
Colorado Springs, Colorado 80922
Telephone: (719) 555-1234

STRENGTHS

- Dedicated *teacher* with the desire to instill in children the passion to be life-long learners.
- Able to set and maintain *high expectations* with the belief that children will rise to them and be *reliable*, *respectful*, *responsible*, and ready to learn.
- *Outgoing* and *patient instructor* who enjoys working with children.
- Effective *team player* with strong *interpersonal*, *communication*, and *presentation skills*.
- Knowledge of *Hyperstudio*, *Storyweavers*, *Corel WordPerfect*, *MS Word*, *Windows*, *MS Publisher*, and the *Internet*.

BACKGROUND

Teaching

- Taught *academic*, *social*, and *motor skills* to *elementary* students.
- Experienced in *team teaching* (5-member team), *combination* and *multi-age classes* (*kindergarten* through *fifth grades*).
- Prepared *objectives* and *outlines* for *courses* and assisted in developing *curriculum*.
- Designed *learning environments* to meet *development objectives* and *state standards*.
- Adapted *lesson plans* for students with *special needs*, including those with *learning disabilities* and *ADHD*.
- Developed a *cooperative learning foundation* using *partners* and the *buddy system*.
- Integrated *reading*, *science*, *social studies*, *writing*, and *math* into *skills-based* and *structured learning environments*.
- Developed a skills-based *reading unit* using a wide variety of materials.
- Created and taught lessons about Germany and Australia in order to help children think with open minds and understand *other cultures* as well as their own.
- *Tutor*ed individual students in reading and math.
- Prepared, administered, and corrected *tests*; kept *attendance* and *grade records*.

Communications

- *Counsel*ed students when *adjustment* and *academic problems* arose.
- Facilitated *student-led conferences* with *parents*.
- Recruited parents to assist with *field trips*.
- Recorded observations of *child development*.

EDUCATION

BACHELOR OF ARTS   May 1997
University of Colorado, Colorado Springs

- Major: *Psychology*
- Minor: *English*
- Completed an additional 11-month Teacher Education Program (TEP)
- *Colorado Elementary Education Certificate*

TEACHING EXPERIENCE

Student Teacher, Jackson Elementary, Colorado Springs, Colorado	2004
Teaching Associate, Jackson Elementary, Colorado Springs, Colorado	2003
Teaching Associate, Steele Elementary, Colorado Springs, Colorado	2002
Teaching Associate, Penrose Elementary, Colorado Springs, Colorado	2002
Teaching Observations, 30 classrooms, Colorado Springs, Colorado	2002
Junior Achievement, Jordahl Elementary, Colorado Springs, Colorado	2001

KEISHA SINGER

1234 East Platte Avenue
Colorado Springs, CO 80903

Telephone: (719) 555-1234
E-mail: ksinger@adrinc.com

PROFILE
- Goal-oriented *recent graduate* with a degree in *geography* and *environmental sciences*.
- High achiever with a *strong work ethic* and effective *problem solving* skills.
- Selected to train as an Olympic athlete at the U.S. Olympic Training Center.
- Works well under pressure; *outgoing* personality with *strong communication skills*.
- Experience with *Windows NT, UNIX, Intergraph Imager, IRAS/C, VI Editor, PhotoScan PS1, ArcInfo, ArcView, ArcPlot, ArcEdit, Idrisi, AML, MS Word, Excel, PowerPoint, Access, Aldus Freehand*, and other software.

EDUCATION

BACHELOR OF LIBERAL ARTS AND SCIENCES (May 1999)
University of Colorado, Colorado Springs
- Major in Geography and Environmental Sciences
- Course work in major: Analysis of *Environmental Systems*, Advanced Geography, *Chemistry*, *Quantitative and Qualitative Reasoning*, Principles of *Geomorphology*, Introduction to *GIS*, Environmental Systems, Geography of *Climate Change*, Advanced *Remote Sensing*, *Cartography*, *Geology* of *National Parks*, *Land Forms*, Environmental Geology, *Regional Geography*, *Physics*, *Calculus*, *Human Geography*, and *Solar Energy*.
- Business courses: *Human Resources Development*, Composition, Psychology, and Macroeconomics.
- GIS project: Assessed the potential *avalanche impact* on *transportation routes* in the Silverton, Colorado, area.
- GIS project: Planning for the construction of a small *research laboratory*, including *land use*, *soil suitability*, *size* (2,000 square meters), and *buffers* (300 meters from sewers, *20 meters from surrounding streams*).
- ArcView project: Researched and developed a *map* for the local *police* department that showed the correlation between *crimes* and convenience stores.

EXPERIENCE

DIGITAL ORTHOPHOTO TECHNICIAN (1999 – Present)
BAE Systems, ADR, Colorado Springs, Colorado
- *Scan mapping diapositives*, perform *quality control* on the *tiles* and *mosaic orthophotos*.
- Perform *raster conversion*, *archive JPEG* files to *tape*, and create *CD*s.
- Write *UNIX scripts* using the *VI editor* for *batching*, *processing*, and *interactive file conversions*.
- Gained familiarity with *USGS* and non-USGS *DOQ workflow*.

AMATEUR ATHLETE (1989 – 1997)
U.S. Olympic Training Center, Colorado Springs, Colorado
- Selected as one of the top three *badminton* players in the U.S. in 1997.
- Achieved top ten ranking during most of career.
- Lettered in varsity badminton during freshman year in high school.
- Won the state championships while a junior and senior in high school.
- Made the Junior National Team for four years straight.
- Selected for the Adult National Team for two years.
- Accepted as a resident athlete at the U.S. Olympic Training Center.
- Participated in two Olympic Festivals (1995 and 1996).
- Trained for one month in Thailand.

HONORS
- Awarded two grants from the U.S. Olympic Committee for ranking and potential.

RANDALL R. FLOURNOY

1234 Rancheros Lane • Denver, Colorado 80922 • Home: (719) 555-1234 • Cell: (303) 555-1234

PROFILE

- Demonstrated success in *materials management* positions for more than 12 years, including:
  - *Cost control/cash flow*
  - *Administration*
  - *Operations*
  - *Contract negotiations*
  - *Purchasing/receiving*
  - *Inventory systems*
  - *Distribution*
  - *Managed care*
  - *Medical/surgical*
  - *Pharmacy*
  - *IV infusion therapy*
  - *Home health care*
- Self-motivated *leader* with strong *interpersonal*, *communication*, and *motivation* skills.
- Able to organize and prioritize multiple *projects* with divergent needs; love challenges.
- Knowledge of *Excel*, *PowerPoint*, *MS Word*, *Windows*, *Matkon*, *Enterprise Systems*, and **Legacy**.
- Certified Senior Material Management, *American Hospital Association*.
- *Certified Registered Central Service Technician*, Purdue University, Indianapolis, Indiana.

EXPERIENCE

CORAM HEALTHCARE, Denver, Colorado
National Director, Materials Management (2002 – 2004)
- Responsible for the general operations of the Material Management Department for a *national home health/IV infusion company*, including the *coordination*, *implementation*, *installation*, and *training* for a *major national infusion pump conversion* saving more than $4 million.
- Maintained and set up *national contracts* for $110 million in *pharmacy* and $20 million in *med/surg*, personally saving Coram $12 million through effective *negotiations*.
- Provided *instruction* and *guidance* for 112 *branches nationwide*, ensuring 98% compliance with the *purchasing program*.
- Worked with *senior management* in the *field* to ensure appropriate *articulation* in all branches.
- Presently converting all med/surg *inventories* to *consignment* and changing the *cash flow pattern* to provide *extended vendor payment* of only the product used and allowing for *reimbursement* closer to the time of product payment to improve cash flow.
- Set up a *preferred provider relationship* with Coram's *resource network*.
- Coordinated the contracts for a *mail order prescription service*; chair of the *formulary/standards committee*.

CENTURA HEALTH, Colorado Springs, Colorado
Director, Materials Management (2000 – 2002)
- Accountable for the overall management of the materials management division, including *purchasing* contracts, *central services*, *processing*, and the *hiring* and *supervision* of 44 full-time *employees*.
- Managed the *distribution of supplies* to more than 51 *separate sites* totaling 1,000 *acute care* beds and 1,000+ *long-term care* beds.
- Maintained at least a 90% national *contract compliance rate* at all locations.
- Implemented a *patient-procedure-based supply delivery system* for *reduction of inventory* and *waste*.
- Coordinated a successful department *re-engineering* to *reduce overhead*, including writing new *job descriptions*, changing *department hours*, *downsizing* employees, *expanding services*, and co-managing an *operating room instrumentation program*.
- Implemented a *managed care supply program* to further drive down health care costs within the *hospital*.
- Served as a member of the *implementation team* to align all Sisters of Charity institutions into a *regionally managed organization* with initial savings of $15 million over five years.

PENROSE ST. FRANCIS HEALTHCARE SYSTEM, Colorado Springs, Colorado (1992 – 2000)
Manager, *Supply, Processing, and Distribution* (1998 – 2000)
- Regional Manager of the *SPD material management* departments with responsibility for *patient supply revenue* exceeding $30 million per year, *budgeting*, and *compliance*.
- Supervised the *acquisition* of *supplies*, *services*, and *equipment*.
- Responsible for *supply processing* and *distribution*, including *surgical processing*, *sterilization*, *instrumentation control*, and *transportation*.
- Maintained a *point-of-use stockless inventory program*, saving $2.5 million per year.
- Developed the concept for a *centralized processing plant* to service the two regions.
- Achieved a 90% *contract compliance* rating with the system's *group purchasing* organization.

EXPERIENCE (continued)

PENROSE ST. FRANCIS HEALTHCARE SYSTEM, Colorado Springs, Colorado (continued)
Surgical Stores Manager (1997 – 1998)
- Supervised the surgical stores, two *buyers*, and one *purchasing assistant* involved in the *acquisition* of all **med/surg needs**, including **supplies** and **capital equipment** for *surgery, heart cath lab, emergency, cardiology, birth center, ICU, CCU*, and *central services* department.
- Planned and implemented a central distribution department.
- Constructed an *automated* system that increased *picking efficiency* by more than 400%.

Surgical Stores Coordinator (1996 – 1997)
- Developed and implemented the surgical stores *inventory control system*.
- Controlled and reduced both official and unofficial inventories by more than $1 million.

Medical/Surgical Buyer (1996)
- Reorganized *work flow*, instilled *leadership* and *accountability* among the *staff*, and improved the *working environment*.
- One of the first *acute care* facilities in the U.S. to discontinue the use of *ETO sterilizing gas* and move to *alternative sterilization* of surgical products.
- Purchased supplies and capital equipment for the surgery, hearth cath lab, respiratory, emergency, and trauma departments.

Health Care Buyer (1995 – 1996)
- Built a new department to reduce surgical inventory; designed and built a low unit of measure *storeroom*.
- Reduced *surgical inventory* by more than $.5 million and improved *service efficiency* by 400%.
- Purchased supplies and *capital equipment* for the *nursing, administration, information services, radiology, rehabilitation*, and *cardiology* departments.

SISTERS OF CHARITY HEALTHCARE SYSTEM, Colorado Springs, Colorado
Manager, Reprographic Facility (1992 – 1995)
- Built a *reprographics* center from the ground up to service seven acute and five long-term care facilities.
- Implemented the *architectural design* and equipped the facility to fulfill the goals set by the region.
- Generated an average of $2 million per year in revenue, with an annual budget of more than $500,000.
- Managed the daily operations and supervised a staff of 14.
- Interfaced with large hospital systems to develop specific goals and a marketing plan to attract patients.

EDUCATION

REGIS UNIVERSITY, Colorado Springs, Colorado
- 58 credits toward a *Bachelor of Business Administration*

PIKES PEAK COMMUNITY COLLEGE, Colorado Springs, Colorado
- *Associate of Industrial Arts Degree*

AFFILIATIONS

- Member of the *American Hospital Association* (AHA)
- President of the local chapter of the *American Society of Healthcare Materials Managers* (ASHMM)
- Member of the *Advisory Board* for School District 11, Regis University, University of Phoenix, and Pikes Peak Community College

CHRISTOPHER ACKERMAN

1234 North Prospect Street • Pueblo, Colorado 80903
Phone: (719) 555-1234 • Cellular: (719) 555-5678 • E-mail: kip4@protypeltd.com

PROFILE
- Experienced *project* and *program manager* with a strong background in:
  - *Requirements analysis* and *design*
  - *Management* and *supervision*
  - *Budgeting* and *resource allocation*
  - *Strategic planning*
  - *Computer-based design*
  - *Object-oriented design*
  - *Systems implementation*
  - *Analysis and testing*
- Proven *team player* with a talent for fostering group *communication* and *team effectiveness*.
- Well-organized professional with experience in *long-range planning*.
- *Cross-culturally sensitive international* traveler with a working knowledge of *Russian* and *German*, proficiency in *Spanish*, and a knowledge of *Japanese*.

EXPERIENCE

Management and Supervision
- Served as *project manager* for the design and *development* of *HySIDE*, a *software modeling tool* used to build and manage complex systems in an *integrated design environment*.
- Managed an international *operations* group of 24 team members responsible for *production control* and operations of the new *data center* for Morrison-Knudsen in *South America*.
- Assisted in planning the *IBM mainframe data center hardware* for this $2 billion project.
- Developed the *telecommunications plan* to support the project, including the *satellite link* to U.S. operations and physical *networking* of the *computers*.
- Responsible for *staff planning*, *hiring*, *personnel evaluations*, and *mobilizing operations* from the U.S. to *Colombia*.
- Successfully developed and managed an $8 million *budget*.
- Implemented a *service monitoring* and *capacity planning program* for the data center.
- Managed a staff of 24 during the last year of the development and *installation* of a *mainframe computer system* to support the *infrastructure development* for a new city of 70,000 occupants in *Saudi Arabia*.

Communication
- Made both formal and information *presentations* of *research findings* to and interacted closely with *government, military, NASA*, and *corporate project monitors*.
- Presented *research results* at *AIAA* conferences and to project monitors.
- Published papers in AIAA *technical journals*.

Technology
- Installed and implemented a *computer-based accounting applications* and *project scheduling system*, and *trained* staff to operate it.
- Installed a *payroll* and *general ledger* application at the University of Petroleum and Minerals in Dhahran, Saudi Arabia.
- Languages: *COBOL, Object Pascal, FORTRAN, OS JCL*.
- Tools: *SRGULL, RJPA, Post, OTIS, UML, TCL, Rational Rose*.
- Operating Systems: *Windows 2000, Windows NT, MVS/JES2, UNIX*.
- Applications: *MS Word, PowerPoint, Excel, Borland Delphi, Microsoft Project, FORTRAN, Tecplot, Latex, Tex, Bibtex, Forehelp, Vorstab, HAVDAC, HySIDE, SIDE, Rhinoceros, TSO, CICS*.
- Hardware: *3270 terminal, IBM Series I computer, IBM 3031 mainframe, PCs, Sun workstation, laptops*.
- Aerospace Engineering: *hypersonic aircraft design, advanced propulsion concepts, off-design analysis, computer simulation, systems testing, object-oriented design, SSTO, TSTO, air breathing launch vehicles, trajectory analysis, boundary layer analysis, rockets, RBCC, multidisciplinary design and optimization, advanced space transportation, DoD / NASA systems, SBIR, SLI, ASTP*.

Research and Analysis
- Used HySIDE to analyze and predict the performance of a proprietary, *single-stage-to-orbit vehicle* as part of the NASA *ABLV (Air Breathing Launch Vehicle)* study.
- Performed *RBCC-SSTO (Rocket-Based-Combined-Cycle, Single-Stage-to-Orbit)* vehicle mission *analysis* using *SRGULL* and *trajectory analysis codes* for the *third-generation space shuttle*, a NASA *MSFC* and *LaRC* project.

EXPERIENCE

Research and Analysis (continued)
- Conducted *tribody missile analysis* for the *Naval Air Warfare Center*'s *Weapons Division* at *China Lake*.
- Analyzed the *second-stage* of a *transatmospheric vehicle concept* for the *AFRL* (*Air Force Research Lab*) at Wright-Patterson Air Force Base.
- Performed *off-design analysis* of a *hypersonic aircraft* for the AFRL.
- Analyzed the *stability* and *control* of NASA's *dual-fuel hypersonic vehicle* in collaboration with *McDonnell-Douglas* Corporation.
- Researched *hypersonic waverider optimization*, stability and control for the University of Maryland.

HISTORY

ASTROX CORPORATION WEST, Colorado Springs, CO (2000 – present)
Division Manager

UNIVERSITY OF MARYLAND, College Park, MD (1996 – 2000)
Research Assistant, Hypersonic Research Group

MORRISON-KNUDSEN COMPANY, Boise, ID (1980 – 1991)
Data Center Manager, **Cerrejon Coal Project**, Colombia, South America (1986 – 1991)
Data Processing Manager, **Washington Public Power Steam Supply Project**, Tumwater, WA (1986)
Computer Operations Manager, **King Khalid Military City Project**, Saudi Arabia (1983 – 1986)
Corporate Data Processing, Boise, ID (1980 – 1983)

EDUCATION

UNIVERSITY OF MARYLAND, College Park, Maryland
Ph.D. in *Aerospace Engineering* (May 2000)
- Dissertation: *The Optimization of* **Engine-Integrated Hypersonic Waveriders** *with* **Steady State Flight** *and Static Margin Constraints*
- Received a four-year postgraduate research assistantship in the Hypersonic Research Group

Master of Science in Aerospace Engineering (May 1996)
- Received a two-year graduate school *fellowship* beginning Fall 1994

Bachelor of Science in Aerospace Engineering (May 1994)
- Graduated *magna cum laude* with a GPA of 3.81
- Recipient of the Robert M. Rivello Scholarship Award, Spring 1993
- Recipient of the Morton Thiokol-Elkton Division Scholarship Award, Spring 1992

AFFILIATIONS
- Senior Member, *American Institute of Aeronautics and Astronautics* (AIAA)
- Member, *Project Management Institute*
- Member, Aerospace Engineering Department, University of Maryland (Member of the Chairperson Search Committee in 1998)

Michael Anderson

123 West Highway 24 • P.O. Box 12 • Cascade, Colorado 80809 • (719) 555-1234 • badger@protypeltd.com

PROFILE

- Dedicated *manager* with a strong background in the *hospitality* industry.
- Experienced in *operations management*, *staffing*, *quality assurance*, and *cost control*.
- Self-motivated and focused; comfortable working independently or as part of a team.
- Adept at communicating effectively with guests, *vendors*, and *staff*.

EXPERIENCE

Achievements

- Turned around an unprofitable operation in less than one year by developing and implementing new *processes and procedures*, *upgrading food service*, and improving *customer service*.
- Maintained *expenses* below *budget* through accurate *planning*, *purchasing*, and cost-effective operations.
- Improved *productivity* and *morale* by initiating systems for *accountability* and instituting *training programs*.
- Designed and coordinated the *tenant finish*, *theme*, *menus*, and *staffing* for a new *bar and grill* seating 60.
- Coordinated Don Johnson's class reunion in his hometown of Wichita, Kansas, with a *banquet* for 380 guests.
- Worked my way up from *waiter* to *bartender*, *cook*, *assistant manager*, and then *general manager*.

Food and Beverage Operations

- Successfully managed the *food and beverage operations* of *elite country clubs*, *upscale hotels*, *family restaurants*, and full-service *casual restaurants/bars* in highly competitive markets.
- Accountable for cost control, budgeting, *profit and loss*, *payroll*, and *record keeping*.
- Designed innovative *marketing campaigns* and *promotions* (*contests*, *giveaways*, *happy hour events*, etc.).
- Responsible for *hiring* and *motivating* a staff of up to 70 *seasonal employees* and 10 *supervisors*.
- Revised *employee manuals* to reduce the possibility of *litigation*.
- Planned *menus*, estimated food and beverage costs, *purchased supplies*, and controlled *inventory*.
- Investigated and resolved food/beverage *quality and service complaints*, ensuring *customer satisfaction*.
- Planned and coordinated *special events* and banquets, including *sales*, *menu development*, *entertainment*, *decorations*, etc.

Country Club Operations

- Managed the operations of a 27-hole *golf course*, *pro shop*, *recreation center*, junior *Olympic swimming pool*, *tennis courts*, *facility and grounds maintenance*, *youth recreation program*, full-service restaurant, *bar, and banquet facility*, *laundry*, and *housekeeping services*.
- Ensured customer satisfaction for an *elite membership* of 2,000 *executives*, *professionals*, and their *families*.
- Developed a new *youth program* that revitalized participation in *recreation center activities*.
- Planned and coordinated *tournaments* and *private/group tennis* and *golf* lessons.
- Served as *Safety* Chairman: conducted monthly safety meetings, instituted programs to reduce *injuries*, and supervised *workers' compensation*, *risk analysis*, *material safety data sheets*, and periodic *safety inspections*.
- Member of the Club Managers Association of America (CMAA) from 1997 through 2000.

WORK HISTORY

Co-Owner, ColoradoDining.com, Colorado Springs, Colorado	2000 – present
Manager, Kissing Camel Club, Colorado Springs, Colorado (summers)	1992 – 2000
Assistant Manager, Garden of the Gods Club, Colorado Springs, Colorado (off seasons)	1992 – 2000
Assistant Manager, Longbranch Saloon, Overland Park, Kansas	1991 – 1992
General Manager, JC's Bar and Grill, Salina, Kansas	1988 – 1990
General Manager, Red Coach Restaurant, Salina, Kansas	1988
Food and Beverage Director, Wichita Royale Hotel, Wichita, Kansas	1987
General Manager, Bombay Bicycle Club, Wichita, Kansas	1982 – 1986

TRAINING

- Earned numerous continuing education credits to maintain membership in CMAA
- Attended the 1998 CMAA World Conference in San Francisco (1 week)
- Participated in monthly CMAA chapter meetings and annual mini conferences (2 days per year)
- The Bullet-Proof Manager Series, Crestcom International (half-day sessions once a monthly for a year)
- Conducting Effective Employee Orientations (1 day)

FRED WOLOCH

1234 Vanreen Drive • Hillsborough, New Jersey 08844 • (719) 555-1234

SUMMARY

- Experienced *maintenance manager* proficient in *electrical* and *mechanical systems*, *equipment repairs*, and quality *facility operations*.
- Effective *team builder* with experience supervising diverse, *multi-disciplinary teams*.
- Certified in *Electrical Safety* and *Machine Condition Monitoring*.
- Exceptional communication skills—fluent in *English*, *Spanish*, *Ukrainian*, and *Polish*.
- Knowledge of *Windows*, *MS Word*, and *WordPerfect computer software*.
- Eligible for *Veteran's preferences*—honorable discharge from the U.S. Army.

EXPERIENCE

CONTRACTOR (2002 – present)
R Properties, Homer Glen, Illinois

- Own and operate a company providing maintenance and *repair services* to local *small businesses*, *restaurants*, and *residences*.
- Review work to be performed, calculate *estimates*, and present *proposals* to *customers*.
- Perform hands-on maintenance of *HVAC*, *swimming pools*, *electrical (110 to 440 volt)*, *plumbing*, *decks*, *appliances*, and other *equipment*.
- Responsible for *preventive and predictive maintenance*, *cleaning*, *painting*, and *interior repairs*.
- Repair and replace *motors* and *controls* in restaurant equipment.

FACILITY MAINTENANCE MANAGER (1987 – 2002)
Tibor Machine Products, Chicago Ridge, Illinois

- Managed all maintenance operations and provided *production support*.
- Serviced, repaired, and *calibrated* all equipment for three *manufacturing* facilities.
- Established and implemented preventive and predictive maintenance programs.
- Evaluated *equipment life expectancy* and implemented methods to improve *machine reliability and capacity* and to *reduce downtime*.
- Reduced operating expenses and improved *inventory control* of *supplies* and *parts*.
- *Negotiated* with *subcontractors* to *set schedules*, *establish needs*, and *make changes*.
- *Estimated project costs* and planned *future project requirements*.
- Inspected *interiors* and *exteriors* of buildings, *fire extinguishers*, plumbing, electrical, HVAC, and related systems and initiated necessary repairs.
- Maintained equipment and maintenance *reports* and *certifications*.
- Served as a *liaison* between maintenance and other operating departments.
- Interviewed and *hired staff* and *contractors*, assigned work, and evaluated *performance* of both English and non-English speaking employees.

SUPERVISOR OF MAINTENANCE (1980 – 1987)
Regal Tube Company, Bedford Park, Illinois

- Coordinated all aspects of machine and *building maintenance*, and performed standard electrical and mechanical repairs.
- Developed *maintenance schedules* and assigned all associated tasks.
- Analyzed *equipment failures*, *cost of repairs*, and *online capability*.
- Established *safety programs* and maintenance *procedures*.

EDUCATION

CONTINUING EDUCATION

- Electrical Safety, National Technology Transfer, Inc.
- *Electrician* Trainee, ICS Intext, National Education Corporation
- How to be the Best Possible Boss, Padgett-Thompson
- Preventing *Discrimination* and *Sexual Harassment*, John Deere Industrial Training
- *Entrepreneurship* Training Program, Institute of Economic Technology

ASSOCIATE OF SCIENCE, *PERSONNEL MANAGEMENT* AND *JOB ANALYSIS*
Moraine Valley Community College, Palos Park, Illinois

ADVANCED *MATHEMATICS*
Daley Community College, Chicago, Illinois

CERTIFICATION IN *ELECTRONICS* AND *MECHANICS*
University of Buenos Aires, Argentina

■ Sample Keywords

You can see why it is so difficult to give definitive lists of keywords and concepts. However, it is possible to give you samples of actual keyword searches used by the recruiters at StorageTek to give you some ideas.

Let me emphasize again that you should list only experience you actually have gained. Do not include the keywords on the following pages in your résumé just because they are listed here.

ACCOUNT EXECUTIVE

REQUIRED:
- BS degree
- 3 years technical selling experience
- Fortune 500 account management experience
- sales
- storage industry
- solution selling

DESIRED:
- Siebel
- quota levels
- VAD
- VAR

ACCOUNTING ANALYST

REQUIRED:
- BA or MBA
- 2–4 years of experience
- asset management
- SAP
- accounting

DESIRED:
- fixed assets
- capital assets
- corporate tax
- US GAAP

BASE SALES REPRESENTATIVE

REQUIRED:
- 2–4 years of sales or contract management experience
- 2+ years of telemarketing or telesales experience

DESIRED:
- Siebel
- storage industry

BUSINESS MANAGER, CENTRAL ARCHIVE MANAGEMENT

REQUIRED:
- BS in engineering or computer science
- 10 years of related engineering and/or manufacturing experience
- strategic planning
- network
- product management
- program management

DESIRED:
- business plan
- line management
- pricing
- team player
- CAM
- marketing
- product strategy
- vendor
- general management
- OEM
- profit and loss

BUSINESS OPERATIONS SPECIALIST

REQUIRED:
- bachelor's degree
- 4 years of directly related experience
- production schedule
- project planning

DESIRED:
- ability to implement
- CList
- data analysis
- off-shift
- team player
- automation
- ability to plan
- customer interaction
- VM
- CMS
- JCL
- REXX
- MVS
- UNIX
- analytical ability
- customer interface
- network
- skills analysis
- automatic tools

DEVELOPMENT ENGINEER, ADVISORY

REQUIRED:
- BS/BA, Masters desired
- 5–10 years mechanical engineering experience
- 10+ years experience in hardware design
- EMC/EMI debug
- mechanical design
- tape drive

DESIRED:
- DFSS (Design for Six Sigma)
- ANSYS or Metlab
- mechanisms design
- shock
- vibration
- NARTE
- tape library
- data storage

FINANCIAL ANALYST, STAFF

REQUIRED:
- BS in Finance or Accounting
- 1–2 years related experience
- customer-focused experience
- excellent written communication skills
- collection
- financial forecast
- financial modeling
- financial reporting
- financial consolidation
- reconciliation

DESIRED:
- international finance
- hyperion consolidation software
- channel experience

ORDER SPECIALIST

REQUIRED:
- BS degree
- 1–3 years experience
- order administration
- order fulfillment
- invoice processing
- Microsoft Word
- Excel

DESIRED:
- database

PROJECT MANAGER, HUMAN RESOURCES

REQUIRED:
- bachelor's degree in human resources, business, or related field
- 6 years broad experience

DESIRED:
- communications
- project management
- milestone development
- time management
- credibility
- recruiting
- long-range planning
- sourcing

SECRETARY III

REQUIRED:
- high school education or equivalent
- 5 years of experience
- typing skill of 55–60 wpm
- interpersonal skills
- oral communication

DESIRED:
- administrative assistance
- clerical
- data analysis
- file maintenance
- material repair
- PowerPoint
- project planning
- reports
- screen calls
- troubleshoot
- answer phones
- communication skills
- document distribution
- mail sorting
- Microsoft Word
- presentation
- publication
- schedule calendar
- secretarial
- appointments
- confidential
- edit

- material
- policies and procedures
- problem solving
- records management
- schedule conference
- telephone interview

SOFTWARE ENGINEER—EMBEDDED, ADVISORY LEVEL

REQUIRED:
- BS or MS degree in one of the computer sciences or engineering
- 12–14 years of experience minimum
- controller architecture design experience
- disk controller
- fiber channel
- SCSI design
- embedded systems

DESIRED:
- open systems
- product development

SOFTWARE ENGINEER—EMBEDDED, STAFF

REQUIRED:
- BS or MS degree in one of the computer sciences or engineering
- 3–5 years of experience minimum
- C
- embedded systems
- realtime

DESIRED:
- pSOS
- iCLinux

SOFTWARE ENGINEER, SENIOR

REQUIRED:
- BS/MS in engineering, computer science or closely related field
- 8 to 9 years of experience

DESIRED:
- C
- customer
- hiring/firing
- prototype
- structured design
- code development
- DASD

- methodology
- real time
- supervision
- communication skills
- experiment design
- problem solving
- software design
- testing

SYSTEMS ENGINEER, SENIOR

REQUIRED:
- BS degree in related field
- 8–10 years of experience
- pre-sales
- systems engineering
- MVS
- data storage

DESIRED:
- systems configuration
- capacity planning
- DFHSM
- HSC
- presentation skills

4 The Journey of the Scannable Résumé

As mentioned in the introduction to the concept of scannable résumés in Chapter 1, employers are being flooded with résumés from very qualified applicants, sometimes receiving as many as 100,000 unsolicited résumés a month. In the last decade of the twentieth century, as companies downsized and human resource departments became smaller, they could no longer afford to hand sort résumés. In order to manage this deluge of paper, these companies turned to computers and scanners.

In order to give you some insight into this technology, this chapter will be devoted to walking you through the journey your paper résumé takes from the moment it is received in a human resource department until you are hired. At the end of this chapter you will find a list of some of the companies that use the most popular résumé scanning and applicant tracking systems, which will help you determine whether creating a scannable résumé is really a necessity for you. Don't be hesitant to call a company's human resource department to ask if they scan résumés. It is the only way to be absolutely certain that your résumé needs to be scannable.

■ Optical Character Recognition

When your paper résumé is received by a human resource department that uses a computerized applicant tracking system, your résumé must first be transferred into binary information that a computer can read before it can be stored in the résumé database. This is accomplished with a scanner that is connected to a computer running a special kind of software that can examine the dots of ink on your printed page and determine by their shapes which letters they represent. This is called optical character recognition, or OCR for short.

This software matches patterns with sets of characters stored in its memory, which is one of the reasons why it is important to choose a type style (or font) for your résumé that conforms to normal letter shapes. If you use a highly decorative type style, the OCR software will have difficulty making matches and will misinterpret letters. This means your words won't be spelled correctly, which of course means that a keyword search for the word *bookkeeping* will never turn up your résumé if the OCR thought you typed *bmkkeepmg.* The next chapter will guide you through designing your résumé with this in mind.

For now, let's assume that you have designed a résumé that the scanner can read. First, depending on the company's procedures, your paper résumé may be received directly by the recruiter assigned to fill a certain position (if the job was advertised) or by the human resource department in general (if you have sent your résumé unsolicited).

When the recruiter has finished reviewing your information, your paper résumé is added to the stacks of résumés to be processed by the computer that day or your résumé is sent to an outsourcing agency to be scanned later (which can delay the processing of your résumé by as much as six weeks).

A staffing professional will then put your cover letter (sometimes) and résumé into the feeder bin of a flatbed scanner, separating your résumé from the ones above and below it with a blank piece of paper. Most companies scan only the résumés, but those that do scan the cover letters generally do not extract information from them for their résumé databases. Why? Because people generally go into detail about what they want in their cover letters and not just what they have done. This confuses the applicant tracking systems and adds qualifications that you don't have.

Within seconds, the scanner has passed its light over your pieces of paper and the computer begins extracting information to fill in its electronic form, which will become part of your e-résumé. There are actually three versions of your résumé created in this step. One is a snapshot of your paper résumé so the hiring manager can actually view your résumé in the format in which it arrived. The second is a generic text version of your résumé. This is the result of the optical character recognition. The pretty formatting is deleted and all that is left is your text. This one looks fairly messy, but the words are all there. The third is an electronic form that the applicant tracking software completes after it extracts bits of information from your résumé. In Yahoo! Resumix's *Hiring Gateway*, this summary form would look something like the screen shot at the top of the next page.

This electronic form contains information that can be used to keep track of you from the moment you are called for an interview to years after you are hired. There are spaces to record the date your résumé was received, where you heard about the job, test results, interview dates, correspondence, comments, contact tracking, and much more.

After the computer has finished creating your electronic résumé, a clerk will verify some of the information. This person usually spends only about five minutes checking your name, phone number, and address and making sure that important information isn't missing. Seldom will the verifier spend much more time reviewing your summary form, skills, or résumé.

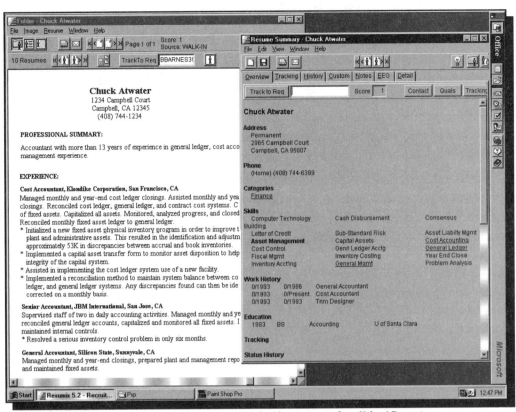

Screen shot of Hiring Gateway reprinted with permission from Yahoo! Resumix.

The computer can automatically generate a letter acknowledging that your résumé was received and let you know how long it will be retained in the résumé database. As already mentioned, this can vary from 90 days to a year to forever if you have skills that are in short supply. Some candidate management systems will even allow a company to use a voice response system where applicants can call a special telephone number to verify that their résumés were received and to provide dates of receipt. The letter from the company will indicate whether this option is available.

Now your résumé is sitting in cyberspace waiting for a hiring manager to find it in a search. Before addressing what happens to your résumé from this point on, you should know that there is another way for your résumé to enter this database.

■ Faxed Résumés That Never See Paper

When a classified advertisement publishes a fax number and you send your résumé via a facsimile machine, you have bypassed the U.S. Postal Service and the job of the scanner. As you probably know, a fax machine is simply a specialized computer, scanner, and printer combined into one device. The scanner part of the fax machine translates your text into binary data that is then transferred over the phone lines to a machine at the other end of the connection. If the machine at the other end is a computer instead of a fax machine, your data is stored on a hard drive until someone chooses to print it on paper.

Companies using computerized applicant tracking systems to store résumés in a database rarely print the résumés received via fax. Instead, they leave your résumé in a queue until a clerk can process your file and extract the information for the same electronic form used to summarize the paper résumés. The quality of the fax is often not as good as a scanned paper résumé, so I usually advise my clients to mail a hard copy of their résumé and cover letter in addition to faxing them whenever possible. This gives your résumé double exposure and helps to ensure that a more accurate version of your résumé ends up in the résumé database.

Actually, either e-mailing your ASCII text file or entering your résumé directly at an Internet site (or at a kiosk in a company's human resource department) is your best choice since you have total control over what ends up in your file. Chapters 6 and 7 will talk more about these options.

■ *Applicant Tracking Systems*

What happens next? Your résumé has been successfully scanned, faxed, or e-mailed into a company's résumé database. The data is floating in cyberspace just waiting for someone to discover it. Now it is time for a hiring manager to write a "job requisition" for an open position. This document contains the absolute requirements for the job, including the level of education and experience required, necessary and optional skills, and a written job description. This job description contains the keywords that will be used by the software to find your résumé (see the screen shot below).

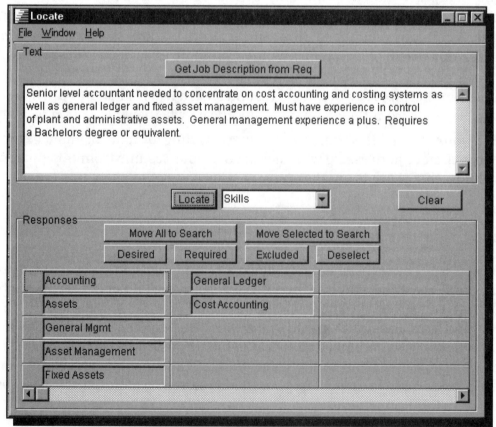

Screen shot of Hiring Gateway reprinted with permission from Yahoo! Resumix.

Staffing professionals can weight these keywords, depending on how much importance they want the words to have. For instance, if knowledge of Microsoft Word is more critical to a job than knowledge of PowerPoint, then Microsoft Word can be assigned more weight.

Once the criteria for the search have been set, the computer searches the database and chooses the candidates whose résumés contain the chosen keywords (see the screen shot from *Hiring Gateway* below). The résumés are ranked on the screen by how many matches the computer found. Résumés that match the criteria with 100 percent accuracy—which is rare, by the way—will be listed first, with subsequent résumés ranked in descending order.

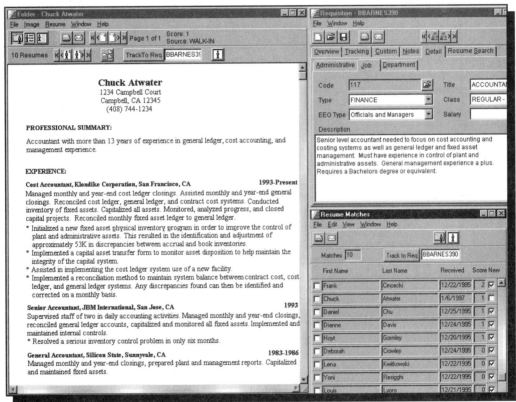

Screen shot of Hiring Gateway reprinted with permission from Yahoo! Resumis.

Once a set of résumés has been selected using the initial keywords, it is often necessary to shorten the list. The first keyword search can turn up 1,000 résumés or more, depending on the size of the database, so the hiring manager must decide whether to make some of the "desired" keywords "required" and try again or to narrow the search by adding criteria. This can be accomplished by searching for a job title in your past experience or by the name of a well-known company for whom you might have worked or by the particular university you attended. It might even mean a search for your professional affiliations to see if you are making a difference.

Which criterion is the most important to the hiring manager depends a great deal on the industry. For instance, a research facility or university would be more interested in the name of the school where you studied. A company that develops software, on the other hand, would want to know about your programming skills instead. An accounting firm might be more interested in whether you worked for a well-known firm at some time in your past.

The selected résumés can be viewed on screen, printed, faxed, or e-mailed as required. This sometimes includes a snapshot of your résumé exactly as you presented it, although this usually depends on whether the recruiter wishes to wait the few minutes it can sometimes take for the image to appear on the screen (see the screen shot below).

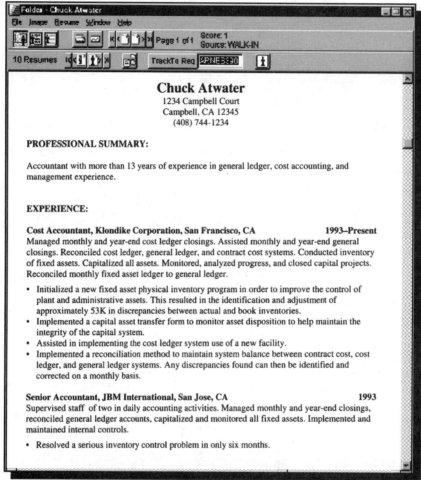

Screen shot of Hiring Gateway reprinted with permission from Yahoo! Resumix.

■ *Which Companies Scan Résumés?*

If you are sending your résumé to a large company with more than 1,000 employees (see the list at the end of this chapter), you can be almost certain that the company is using some type of computerized candidate management system. These companies are accepting electronic résumés from their Internet sites and via e-mail, then integrating the pure electronic versions with the paper résumés they receive via the Postal Service and fax. Once the paper résumés are scanned, all of the résumés are then stored in one massive computer database.

This process is expensive and generally not cost effective for smaller companies—"smaller" meaning companies with fewer than 1,000 employees. These smaller companies, however, often outsource the scanning of their paper résumés, sometimes to as far away as India, which can delay the time it takes your résumé to enter the company's database by more than a month, another good reason for e-mailing your résumé or entering into an e-form at a company's Web site.

There are some exceptions to the 1,000-employee rule, however. High-tech companies usually have the infrastructure in place to make implementing programs such as this less expensive, and they tend to have higher turnover, which means more advertised job openings and more résumés to process. In fact, the average high-tech business experiences 100 percent turnover of its IT staff every five years.

Recruiters are another exception to the rule of 1,000 employees or more. Recruiting firms might have small staffs themselves, but they process incredible numbers of résumés. Assume that your résumé will be scanned into a computerized database if you are sending it to a large recruiting firm.

Even federal, state, county, and large city governments are turning to applicant tracking systems in order to make their hiring processes more efficient. For instance, many U.S. Government agencies use Yahoo! Resumix's *Hiring Gateway* to manage applicants. Federal applications generally require more than just a résumé, too. Statements of knowledge, skills, and abilities (KSAs) are often part of the process, as are long application forms completed either online or on paper.

Here are just some of the companies that scan résumés and use computerized candidate management systems. This list doesn't even pretend to be all inclusive, so I encourage you to call human resource departments before submitting your résumé, or just send a scannable résumé by default to any large company. Remember what I said in Chapter 1—only 24 percent of companies in the United States scan résumés.

As discussed on page 13, you also have the option of printing a copy of your ASCII text résumé and sending it along with your formatted résumé. In that case, you don't have to worry about whether or not your formatted résumé is scannable. Instead, the clerks who scan the résumés will pick the version that will scan the best, based on their experience with the software.

Abbott Laboratories	Amerada Hess
Ace Hardware	American Brands
Advanced Micro Devices	American Electric Power
Aetna Life & Casualty	American Express
AFLAC	American Financial Group
Aid Association for Lutherans	American General
Air Products & Chemicals	American Home Products
Albertson's	American International Group
Alco Standard	American President
Alcoa	American Standard
Allegheny Power System	American Stores
AlliedSignal	Amerisource Health
Allmerica Financial	Ameritech
Allstate	Amoco
Alltel	AMP
Alumax	AMR
Amdahl Corporation	Amway

Anheuser-Busch
AON
Apple Computer
Applied Materials
Aramark
Archer Daniels Midland
Arizona State Government
Armstrong World Ind.
Arrow Electronics
Asarco
Ashland
Associated Insurance
AST Research
AT&T
Atlantic Richfield
Automatic Data Processing
Avery Dennison
Avnet
Avon Products
Baker Hughes
Ball
Baltimore Gas & Electric
Banc One Corporation
Bank of America
Bank of Boston Corporation
Bank of New York Company
Bankamerica Corporation
Bankers Trust N.Y. Corporation
Barnett Banks
Baxter International
Bear Stearns
Becton Dickinson
Bell Atlantic
Bell Helicopter
Bellsouth
Bergen Brunswig
Berkshire Hathaway
Best Buy
Bethlehem Steel
Beverly Enterprises
Bindley Western
Black & Decker
Boatmen's Bancshares
Boeing
Boise Cascade
Bristol-Myers Squibb
Browning-Ferris Industries
Bruno's
Brunswick
Burlington Northern Santa Fe
Caliber Systems

Campbell Soup
Canadian Tire Corporation
Cardinal Health
Carolina Power & Light
Case
Caterpillar
Centerior Energy
Centex
Champion International
Chase Manhattan Corporation
Chemical Banking Corporation
Chevron
Chiquita Brands International
Chrysler
Chubb
CIGNA
Cinergy
Circle K
Circuit City Stores
Cisco Systems
Citicorp
Clorox Company
CMS Energy
Coastal
Coca-Cola
Coca-Cola Enterprises
Colgate-Palmolive
College Ret. Equities Fund
Columbia Gas System
Columbia/HCA Healthcare
Comcast
Comerica
Compaq Computer Corporation
CompUSA
Computer Associates International
Computer Sciences
ConAgra
Conrail
Conseco
Consolidated Edison of N.Y.
Consolidated Freightways
Consolidated Natural Gas
Continental Airlines
Cooper Industries
Corestates Financial Corporation
Cornell University
Corning
Cotter
CPC International
Crown Cork & Seal
CSX

Cummins Engine
Cyprus Amax Minerals
Dana
Dayton Hudson
Dean Foods
Dean Witter Discover
Deere
Dell Computer
Delta Air Lines
Dial
Diamond Shamrock
Digital Equipment
Dillard Department Stores
DMR Group, Inc.
Dole Food
Dominion Resources
Dover
Dow Chemical
Dresser Industries
DTE Energy
Duke Power
Dun & Bradstreet
E.I. DuPont de Nemours
Eastman Chemical
Eastman Kodak
Eaton
Echlin
Eckerd
Edison International
Electronic Data Systems
Eli Lilly
Emerson Electric
Engelhard
Enron
Entergy
Estée Lauder
Exxon
Farmland Industries
Federal Express
Federal Home Loan Mtg.
Federal National Mortgage Association
Federated Department Stores
FHP International
Fidelity Investments
First Bank System
First Chicago NDB Corporation
First Data
First Interstate Bancorp
First Union Corporation
Flagstar
Fleet Financial Group

Fleetwood Enterprises
Fleming
Florida Progress
Fluor
FMC
Food 4 Less Holdings
Ford Motor Company
Foster Wheeler
Foundation Health
Foxmeyer Health
FPL Group
Fred Meyer
Gannett
Gap
Gateway 2000
Geico
General Dynamics
General Electric
General Instrument
General Mills
General Motors
General Public Utilities
General RE
Genuine Parts
Georgia-Pacific
Giant Food
Gillette
Glaxo, Inc.
Golden West Financial Corporation
Goodyear Tire & Rubber
Graybar Electric
Great Western Financial Corporation
GTE
Guardian Life of America
H. F. Ahmanson
H. J. Heinz
Halliburton
Hannaford Bros.
Harcourt General
Harris
Hasbro
Health Systems International
Hershey Foods
Hewlett-Packard
Home Depot
Honeywell
Hormel Foods
Household International
Houston Industries
Humana
IBP

Illinois Tool Works
Ingersoll-Rand
Inland Steel Industries
Intel
Intelligent Electronics
International Business Machines
International Paper
ITT
ITT Hartford Group
ITT Industries
J.C. Penney
J.P. Morgan & Co.
James River Corporation of Virginia
Jefferson Smurfit
John Hancock Mutual Life Insurance
Johnson & Johnson
Johnson Controls
K-Mart
Kaiser Permanente
Kellogg
Kelly Services
Kerr-McGee
Keycorp
Kimberly-Clark
Knight-Ridder
Kroger
Lear Seating
Lehman Brothers Holdings
Levi Strauss Associates
Liberty Mutual Insurance Group Ltd.
Lincoln National
Litton Industries
Lockheed Martin
Loews
Logica
Long Island Power Authority
Longs Drug Stores
Loral
Louisiana-Pacific
Lowe's
LTV
Lyondell Petrochemical
Manpower
Manville
Mapco
Maricopa County, Arizona
Marriott International
Marsh & McLennan
Masco
Massachusetts Mutual Life Insurance
Mattel

Maxxam
May Department Stores
Maytag
MBNA
McDonald's
McDonnell Douglas
McGraw-Hill
MCI Worldcom
McKesson
Mead
Mellon Bank Corporation
Melville
Memorial Sloan-Kettering Cancer Center
Mercantile Stores
Merck
Merisel
Merrill Lynch
Metropolitan Life Insurance
Microage
Micron Technology
Microsoft
Minnesota Mining & Mfg.
Mobil
Monsanto
Morgan Stanley Group
Morrison Knudsen
Morton International
Motorola
Mutual of Omaha Insurance
Nash Finch
National City Corporation
Nationsbank Corporation
Nationwide Insurance Enterprise
Navistar International
New York Life Insurance
Newell
NGC
Niagara Mohawk Power
Nike
Noram Energy
Nordstrom
Norfolk Southern
Northeast Utilities
Northern States Power
Northrop Grumman
Northwest Airlines
Northwestern Mutual Life
Norwest Corporation
Nucor
NYNEX
Occidental Petroleum

Office Depot
OfficeMax
Ohio Edison
Olin
Olsten
Oracle
Overnite Transportation Company
Owens & Minor
Owens-Corning
Owens-Illinois
Paccar
Pacific Gas & Electric
Pacific Mutual Life Insurance
Pacific Telesis Group
Pacificare Health Systems
Pacificorp
Paine Webber Group
Panenergy
Parker Hannifin
Payless Cashways
Peco Energy
Penn Traffic
Pennzoil
PeopleSoft
Pepsico
Peter Kiewit Sons
Pfizer
Pharmacia & Upjohn
Phelps Dodge
Philip Morris
Phillips Petroleum
Pitney Bowes
Pittston
PNC Bank Corporation
PP&L Resources
PPG Industries
Praxair
Premark International
Price Costco
Principal Mutual Life Insurance
Procter & Gamble
Progressive
Provident Cos.
Providian
Prudential Insurance of America
Public Service Entr. Group
Publix Super Markets
Quaker Oats
Quantum
Qwest
R.R. Donnelley & Sons

Ralston Purina
Raytheon
Reader's Digest Association
Recruiters (most large firms)
Reebok International
Reliance Group Holdings
Republic New York Corporation
Revco D.S.
Reynolds Metals
Rite Aid
RJR Nabisco Holdings
Rockwell International
Rohm & Haas
Roundy's
Ryder System
Safeco
Safeway
Salomon
Sara Lee
SBC Communications
Schering-Plough
SCI Systems
Seagate Technology
Sears Roebuck
Service Merchandise
ServiceMaster
Sharp HealthCare
Shaw Industries
Sherwin-Williams
Smith's Food & Drug Centers
Sonoco Products
Southern
Southern Pacific Rail
Southwest Airlines
Spartan Stores
Sprint
St. Paul Cos.
Stanley Works
Staples
State Farm Group
State Street Boston Corporation
Stone Container
Stop & Shop
Student Loan Marketing Association
Sun
Sun Microsystems
Suntrust Banks
Supermarkets General Holdings
Supervalu
Sysco
Tandy

Teachers Ins. & Annuity
Tech Data
Tele-Communications
Teledyne
Temple-Inland
Tenet Healthcare
Tenneco
Texaco
Texas Instruments
Texas Utilities
Textron
Thrifty Payless Holdings
Time Warner
Times Mirror
TJX
Tosco
Toys 'R Us
Transamerica
Travelers Group
Tribune
TRW
Turner Broadcasting
Turner Corporation
Tyco International
Tyson Foods
U.S. Bancorp
U.S. Healthcare
U.S. Industries
UAL
Ultramar
Unicom
Union Camp
Union Carbide
Union Pacific
Unisys
United Healthcare
United Parcel Service
United Services Automobile Association

United Technologies
Universal
Unocal
Unum
USAIR Group
USF&G
USG
USX
Utilicorp United
Valero Energy
VF
Viacom
Vons
W. R. Grace
W. W. Grainger
Waban
Wachovia Corporation
Wal-Mart Stores
Walgreen
Walt Disney, Inc.
Warner-Lambert
Wellpoint Health Networks
Wells Fargo & Co.
Westinghouse Electric
Westvaco
Weyerhaeuser
Whirlpool
Whitman
Willamette Industries
Williams
Winn-Dixie Stores
WMX Technologies
Woolworth
Worldcom
Xerox
Yellow
York International

5 Designing the Perfect Scannable Résumé

In all of my interviews with companies that scan résumés, the staffing professionals emphasized the importance of a résumé designed with scannability in mind. Your paper résumé must be formatted in such a way that a scanner can read it or the words won't be spelled right. And, if the words aren't spelled right, a keyword search will never turn up your résumé.

This chapter is devoted to helping you avoid the pitfalls that commonly cause a résumé to scan poorly. This includes choosing the right fonts, laying out the text of your résumé so it is scanner friendly, selecting the right paper color, and so on. At the end of the chapter are some samples of résumés that made it through the scanning process with flying colors. With these guidelines, your résumé will be ripe picking for the hiring manager's computerized keyword search.

■ The Complete Guide to Style, Fonts, Paper, and So On

Let's start at the top of your résumé and work our way down. Since your résumé is basically an advertisement for you and your skills, you should think about the design of your résumé from a marketing standpoint. When you see a well-designed ad, what is the first thing you notice (besides a picture of the product)? The product name, of course. Since you *are* the product, your name should be the first thing a reader sees and remembers.

❑ Your Name

The size and boldness of the type of your name should be larger than the largest font used in your text, but for a scannable résumé it should be no larger than 20-point type. You may use all capital letters, a combination of upper and lower case, or capitals combined with small capitals (LIKE THIS). On the following is an example of a Times Roman Bold font in a few good point sizes for the name on a scannable résumé:

- **14-POINT NAME**
- **16-POINT NAME**
- **18-POINT NAME**
- **20-POINT NAME**

Avoid using decorative fonts like these for either your name or your text:

- **Bodini Poster**
- **Broadway Engraved**
- Bard
- *Commercial Script*
- COTTONWOOD

- *Crazed*
- *Freestyle Script*
- *Lalique*
- *Kaufmann*
- Linotext

Using reverse boxes to print white type on a black (or gray shaded) background is another mistake. Scanners can't read them and your name will be missing from your résumé! Here is a sample of a reverse boxed name:

PAT CRISCITO

Lastly, make certain your name is at the top of each page of your résumé. The clerks who scan résumés are often dealing with hundreds of pieces of paper every day. It is not a good idea to staple a scannable résumé, so it is very easy for the pages of your résumé to become separated from each other.

❏ *Address*

Next comes your contact information. It isn't always necessary to put your address at the top of your scannable résumé. Today's sophisticated applicant tracking systems know by more than position on the résumé whether the text is an address or phone number. It doesn't matter whether you put your contact information at the top or bottom of your résumé; this is your personal preference. However, always list your e-mail address in addition to your home and cellular telephone numbers and postal information.

❏ *Fonts*

Use popular fonts that are not overly decorative in order to ensure optimum scannability.

This sentence is typeset in a decorative font that is known to cause problems with résumé scannability (Sanvito).

So is this sentence (AGaramond Italic).

Following are some samples of good fonts for a scannable résumé:

Serif Fonts *(traditional fonts with little "feet" on the edges of the letters)*

Bookman . . . . The quick brown fox jumps over a lazy dog
THE QUICK BROWN FOX JUMPS OVER A LAZY DOG

Candida . . . . The quick brown fox jumps over a lazy dog
THE QUICK BROWN FOX JUMPS OVER A LAZY DOG

Century Schoolbook . . . . The quick brown fox jumps over a lazy dog
THE QUICK BROWN FOX JUMPS OVER A LAZY DOG

Charter . . . . The quick brown fox jumps over a lazy dog
THE QUICK BROWN FOX JUMPS OVER A LAZY DOG

Garamond . . . . The quick brown fox jumps over a lazy dog
THE QUICK BROWN FOX JUMPS OVER A LAZY DOG

Palatino . . . . The quick brown fox jumps over a lazy dog
THE QUICK BROWN FOX JUMPS OVER A LAZY DOG

Times Roman . . . . The quick brown fox jumps over a lazy dog
THE QUICK BROWN FOX JUMPS OVER A LAZY DOG

Utopia . . . . The quick brown fox jumps over a lazy dog
THE QUICK BROWN FOX JUMPS OVER A LAZY DOG

Sans Serif *(contemporary fonts with no decorative "feet")*

Antique Olive . . . . **The quick brown fox jumps over a lazy dog**
THE QUICK BROWN FOX JUMPS OVER A LAZY DOG

Arial (Helvetica) . . . . The quick brown fox jumps over a lazy dog
THE QUICK BROWN FOX JUMPS OVER A LAZY DOG

Arial (Helvetica) Narrow . . . . The quick brown fox jumps over a lazy dog
THE QUICK BROWN FOX JUMPS OVER A LAZY DOG

Avant Garde . . . . The quick brown fox jumps over a lazy dog
THE QUICK BROWN FOX JUMPS OVER A LAZY DOG

Myriad Roman . . . . The quick brown fox jumps over a lazy dog
THE QUICK BROWN FOX JUMPS OVER A LAZY DOG

News Gothic . . . . The quick brown fox jumps over a lazy dog
THE QUICK BROWN FOX JUMPS OVER A LAZY DOG

Optima (Humanist, CG Omega) . . . . The quick brown fox jumps over a lazy dog
THE QUICK BROWN FOX JUMPS OVER A LAZY DOG

It doesn't make any difference whether you choose a serif or a sans serif font, but the font size should be no smaller than 9 or 10 points and no larger than 12 points for the text. Having said that, you will notice that the fonts in the examples above are all slightly different in size even though they are exactly the same point size. Every font has its own designer and its own personality, which means that no two typefaces are exactly the same. Look at the difference between the 9-point Avant Garde and the 9-point Times Roman fonts below:

- Times Roman—9 point

- Avant Garde—9 point

You will notice that the Times Roman appears considerably smaller and could potentially cause problems with a scanner, while the 9-point Avant Garde (and the other sans serif fonts above) scanned fine in all of our tests.

The key to choosing a font for a scannable résumé is that none of the letters touch one another at any time. This can be caused by poor font design, by adjusting the kerning (the spacing between letters) in your word processor, or by printing your résumé with a low-quality printer. Even some ink-jet printers can cause the ink to run together between letters with the wrong kind of paper.

Any time one letter touches another, a scanner will have a difficult time distinguishing the shapes of the letters and you can end up with misspellings on your résumé. A keyword search looks for words that are spelled correctly, so a misspelled word is as good as no word.

Don't use underlining on your résumé for the same reason. Underlines touch the descenders on letters like g, j, p, q, and y and make it difficult for an OCR program to interpret their shapes. Take a look at these words and see if you can tell where a scanner would have trouble:

- The quick brown fox jumps over a lazy dog

- *The quick brown fox jumps over a lazy dog*

- The quick brown fox jumps over a lazy dog

- The quick brown fox jumps over a lazy dog

Related to fonts are bullets—special characters used at the beginning of indented short sentences to call attention to individual items on a résumé. These characters should be round and solid (•) for a scannable résumé. Scanners interpret hollow bullets (○) as the letter "o." Don't use any unusually shaped bullets (□, ✛) that the scanner will try to interpret as letters.

While we are on the topic of special characters, the percent (%) and ampersand (&) signs used to cause problems for some OCR software, but that isn't a problem anymore. From the perspective of good writing, however, you should always spell out the word *and,* except in cases where the ampersand appears in the name of a company. Foreign accents and letters that are not part of the English alphabet can be misinterpreted by optical character recognition.

Even though you have probably heard that italics are a no-no on a scannable résumé, today's more sophisticated optical character recognition software can read italics without difficulty, provided one letter does not touch another. The engineers

I spoke with who designed résumé scanning software all stated that their software has no problem reading italics, and my staff has confirmed that with tests. We have even scanned résumés typeset in all italics without a problem, although I don't recommend that simply from a readability standpoint. The key is to choose a font that is easy to read, is not overly decorative, and does not have one letter touching another. The italic typefaces of any of the samples in this chapter would be fine to use as accents on your résumé.

❑ *Format*

Rely on white space to define sections. Scanners like white space. They use it to determine when one section has ended and the next has begun. Horizontal lines can also be used to define sections since they are usually ignored by OCR software, provided they do not touch any of the letters on the page. However, avoid the use of short, vertical lines or small boxes since scanners try to interpret these as letters.

Don't use columns (like a newspaper) on your résumé. Scanners read from left to right and often have difficulty determining how to arrange text that was originally set in columns. Although the keywords will be intact, your résumé may end up looking like garbage in the ASCII text version created during the OCR process.

In today's job market, résumés (whether electronic or paper) don't have to be limited to one page. Craig MacDonald, in a special report for the *Seattle Post-Intelligencer*, says, "The cold, hard truth is, writing a résumés is just like advertising. Effective advertising means capturing the audience's attention quickly, concisely describing why someone should want to buy the product (you), and then closing the sale by suggesting a means of rapidly making the purchase. This has nothing to do with length, but a lot to do with format, language, tone, and style."

With e-résumés in particular, the more keywords and synonyms you are able to use, the better your chances of being selected in a keyword search. Therefore, it is better to have a two-page résumé with all your skills and qualifications listed than to have a one-page résumé with information missing because you tried to conserve space. Here is the general rule for a résumé today.

- New graduates—one page
- Most people—one or two pages
- Senior executives—two or three pages

One caution, however. The reader sees only one screen at a time and may decide to stop reading after the first screen if something doesn't entice him or her to read on. Therefore, you should make certain that the meat of your résumé is on the first half of the first page. This can be accomplished with a profile or keyword summary, followed by a list of your achievements (see the screen shot on the next page for a good example).

Remember to keep your sentences powerful and interesting to read. Cyberspace doesn't negate the need for good writing. You still want a human being to read your résumé sooner or later!

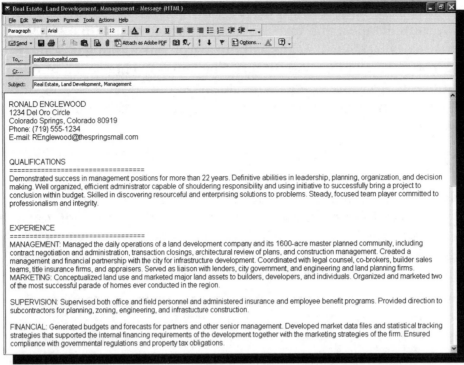

Screen shot of Microsoft Outlook used with permission of Microsoft Corporation.

❏ *Paper*

Print your résumé on a high-quality, light-colored paper (white, off-white, or *very* light gray). Never use papers with a background (pictures, marble shades, or speckles). The scanner tries to interpret the patterns and dots as letters. This is a good rule to follow even for paper résumés that will never be scanned. Often, companies will photocopy your résumé to hand to a hiring manager, and dark colors or patterns will simply turn into dark masses that make your résumé difficult to read. If a company has multiple locations, the original résumé may even get faxed from one site to another and the same thing would happen.

Avoid using photocopies of your résumé unless you have access to a high-quality copier. Original laser printed masters are best, although a high-quality ink-jet printer is acceptable.

Print on only one side of the page and use standard-size 8½" × 11" paper. The scanner cannot turn your page over, so the reverse side might be missed when the clerk puts your résumé into the automatic document feeder. That same process is the reason why you should not use 11" × 17" size paper. The pages would have to be cut into 8½" × 11" sheets and the printing on the reverse side would not get scanned.

Don't fold your résumé, since the creases make it harder to scan. It is much better to invest in flat 9" × 12" envelopes and an extra two bits of postage to make a good first impression. Laser print and copier toner tend to crack off the page when creased, making the letters on the fold line less than solid, which a scanner could easily misinterpret. Staple holes can cause the pages of a résumé to stick together, so never put a staple in a résumé you know will be scanned.

Now that you know all the secrets for designing a résumé that will pass the scannability test, let's look at some sample résumés that scanned well.

KEVIN BERRIE

(719) 555-1234	*123 Sand Road, Woodland Park, Colorado 80863*	*berrie@aol.com*

PROFILE
- Ambitious sales professional with more than ten years of proven sales experience.
- Strong background in building territories and using creative marketing approaches.
- Respected for powerful negotiating and closing abilities.
- Self-motivated and focused; comfortable working independently with little supervision.
- Computer literate in Windows, MS Word, MS Office, and the Internet.

EXPERIENCE

SALES REPRESENTATIVE (2002 – present)
Russ Berrie Company, Colorado Springs, Colorado
- Sold giftware to wholesale accounts for the largest distributor in the United States
- Consistently exceeded sales goals; increased new accounts by 20 percent and sales volume by 35 percent in first three months.
- Gained extensive experience in cold calling and getting to the decision maker.
- Made courtesy calls to existing customers to ensure satisfaction and customer retention.

OWNER/MANAGER (1992 – 2002)
Sierra Distributing, Colorado Springs, Colorado
- Owned and operated a company that manufactured and distributed leather goods, jewelry, and other items to major clients in the motorcycle industry, including Harley-Davidson and the Motorcycle Warehouse.
- Developed new customers through trade shows and effective sales and marketing campaigns.
- Managed all aspects of administration, purchasing, inventory management, manufacturing, quality control, cost controls, importing, and achieving revenue objectives.

ACCOUNT EXECUTIVE (1999 – 2001)
Western Distributing, Colorado Springs, Colorado
- Opened new accounts for the area's largest beverage distributor.
- Achieved a minimum of 30 percent monthly growth in an established territory.
- Awarded salesman of the month within the first three months.
- Earned a bonus every month for exceptional sales volume.
- Written up in corporate newsletters for sales achievements.

PLANT MANAGER/PRODUCTION MANAGER (1996 – 1999)
Coulson of Texas, Dale Electronics, and *Hyer Boot Company*, El Paso, Texas
- Coordinated and supervised all phases of production, including plant engineering and layout, research and development, quality control, shipping and receiving, inventory control, warehousing, security, maintenance, and budgeting.
- Directed as many as 250 plant personnel, including 14 supervisors.
- Increased production by 30 percent, substantially upgraded product quality, cut production costs by 10 percent, and reduced overtime.

EDUCATION

BACHELOR OF SCIENCE IN BIOLOGY (1987)
University of Texas, El Paso, Texas
- Minor in Geology.

CONTINUING EDUCATION
- Extensive sales training through corporate seminars and independent study.

Ken E. Kearney

1234 Traverse Court • Colorado Springs, Colorado 80916 • (719) 555-1234 • kek@hotmail.com

QUALIFICATIONS

- Skilled assembler with 15 years of diverse experience
- Background in quality control and new product startup
- Results-oriented professional who gets the job done
- Effective team player with strong communication and facilitation skills

EXPERIENCE

Technical

- Developed "Saturn" disk drives for Quantum and supported engineering with process development.
- Established manufacturing production for new 4-gigabyte disk drives in a state-of-the-art 100K clean room.
- Served as lead facilitator for the disk drive rework room.
- Set up all work stations and obtained certifications in over 95 percent of them.
- Built 7/8 platter disk drives as an Assembler III; performed failure analysis.
- Traveled to Sequel in San Jose to set up the 8X line purchased from DEC.
- Served as liaison between line workers and management.
- Produced master valves for Eaton within 3/10,000[th] of customer specifications.

Quality Control

- Tested disk drives in an evaluation laboratory to assure compatibility.
- Checked valves—both visually and using a Pentrex booth—for surface metallurgical defects.
- Set tolerances on the production lines, gauges, and dial indicators to assure quality.
- Calibrated micrometers and calipers; tested and maintained various equipment.
- Corrected machine problems on the manufacturing floor and performed parts review for blueprint changes.

Inventory Management

- Implemented a just-in-time manufacturing/pull system.
- Simplified ordering parts by setting up a Kanban system and changing the layout to match the clean room.
- Maintained inventory and ordered parts to match the build schedule.

Training and Supervision

- Supervised up to eighteen workers in clean-room assembly; audited and completed time cards.
- Trained staff in assembly, quality control, and inventory control concepts.

EMPLOYMENT HISTORY

2003–2004	**Assembler III**	Quantum Corporation	Colorado Springs, CO
2001–2003	**Assembler III**	Digital Equipment Corporation	Colorado Springs, CO
1999–2001	**Clean-Room Facilitator**	Digital Equipment Corporation	Colorado Springs, CO
1996–1999	**Material Controller**	Digital Equipment Corporation	Colorado Springs, CO
1993–1996	**Material Handler**	Digital Equipment Corporation	Colorado Springs, CO
1993–1996	**Material Handler**	Talent Tree Temporaries	Denver, CO

EDUCATION

University of South Dakota, Springfield, South Dakota
3 credits short of an Associate Degree in Diesel Technology

U.S. Navy, Memphis, Tennessee
Aviation Hydraulics Class "A"

JEFFREY A. MCENTIRE

PROFILE

- Dynamic public speaker with a strong background in the food, beverage, and travel industries.
- Demonstrated success in a broad range of management positions for more than 11 years.
- Self-motivated and focused; comfortable working independently or as part of an integrated team.
- Adept at communicating effectively with people of diverse interests and levels of authority.

PHILOSOPHY

Guest obsession is the act of taking exceptional customer service to the next level. Inside every conscious being is the simple "Wow!" sensation. It is a universal feeling that crosses language barriers, cultures, and genders. Everyone has it! If you can make customers think, feel, or even say "Wow!" because of something you have done to service them, they will be your customers for life.

EXPERIENCE
Training

- Designed and presented "The Wow Factor" seminar to numerous service-based companies. Part one of the seminar is for managers and supervisors and is designed to help them internalize The Wow Factor, making it a part of their lives and allowing them to train their workers. Part two is for employees. It teaches them how to believe in The Wow Factor and how the concept can put money in their pockets.
- Presented monthly seminars to Macaroni Grill staff members to promote guest obsession and personal development.
- Trained and developed restaurant managers through the management development program.
- Instructed more than 70 Disney bartenders in guest service and flair as part of a mandatory course.
- Created a regular "personal challenge day" for employees, a day dedicated to team building exercises and group events, ending with a personal challenge (bungee jumping or hang gliding).
- Guest speaker for a 125-member luncheon of the Osceola Chamber of Commerce.
- Invited to speak for the graduation ceremonies of the Kissimmee Culinary Institute.

Management

- Successfully opened and managed various high-profile restaurants throughout the Southeast.
- Assumed the management of a large-volume Macaroni Grill restaurant, increasing sales in just under two months to $4.6 million, moving the store from number four to number two in the area.
- Recruited, hired, supervised, and motivated assistant managers, chefs, and up to 250 staff.
- Accountable for budgeting, profit and loss, and full business planning.

Walt Disney

- Assisted in the development of the concept for the Beach Club at Walt Disney World and in implementing the conversion to a $6.2 million operation; stayed on as General Manager.
- Devised and executed profitable promotions never before attempted by Walt Disney World, including the Venus Swimwear Pageant and the Pleasure Island Jet Ski Tournament.
- Coordinated service staff, nightly promotions, and tours for celebrities such as Tom Cruise, Warren Beatty, Michael Jackson, and Steven Spielberg, among others.
- Assisted in the pre-opening development of Pleasure Island and managed the operations of the Comedy Warehouse, Adventurers Club, and Neon Armadillo with a staff of 250 (gained experience in labor union contracts and negotiations).
- Planned and placed the initial $600,000 liquor order for all of Pleasure Island.
- Managed the Steermans Quarters Restaurant on the Empress Lilly Riverboat with full-service breakfast, lunch, and dinner, and two seatings of 500 per day for the Disney character breakfast.

Entrepreneurial

- Created a successful company that was designed to take guest obsession to a new level with high-profile travelers, allowing travelers to maximize their travel time through the use of a personal itinerary specialist who traveled with them and coordinated every detail.
- Raised capital through research and development of a detailed business plan.
- Handled clients such as Reba McEntire, Ricky Skaggs, Robin Leach, etc.
- Established detailed network of contacts throughout Florida and the Caribbean, including restaurants, hotels, golf courses, boat charters, and other travel organizations.
- Successfully negotiated a contract for the design and development of a country music nightclub for The Shooters Corporation, including everything from interior design to merchandise sales.
- Owned and operated Success Analysis, a company that sent secret shoppers into restaurants to critique the operation, providing a detailed report to enhance customer service.

ADDRESS

123 Turkey Point Drive, Melbourne, Florida 32932   Pager (800) 555-1234, Phone (407) 555-1234

WORK HISTORY

General Manager, Romano's Macaroni Grill, Dunwoody, Georgia   2002 – present
General Manager, Romano's Macaroni Grill, Kissimmee, Florida   2002
Manager, Romano's Macaroni Grill, Altamonte Springs, Florida   2000 – 2002
Entrepreneur, Travel Itineraries, Inc., and Success Analysis   1998 – 2000
Walt Disney Management Development Program   1995 – 1998
Beach Club, Pleasure Island, Empress Lilly Riverboat
Associate General Manager, Safari Bar and Restaurant, Houston, Texas   1992 – 1995
Promoted from various positions, including Assistant Manager, Bar Manager,
Head Music Programmer, and Front Door Manager in six different locations

EDUCATION

WALT DISNEY MANAGEMENT DEVELOPMENT PROGRAM   1995
- Completed six-month program in only four months.
- Learned every facet of the Disney organization, from in-depth culinary skills to financial controls.

UNIVERSITY OF SOUTH ALABAMA   1990 – 1992
- Concentration in business management.

COMMUNITY SERVICE

- Member of the Chamber of Commerce Board of Directors, Kissimmee, Florida   2002 – 2003
- Board Member and Counselor for Central Florida Martial Arts and Boxing Academy (a not-for-profit prison youth release program)   1998 – 2001

COMPUTERS

- Knowledge of both Windows and Macintosh computer environments
- Skilled in Internet communications, MS Word, Excel, PageMaker, Adobe Photoshop, Filemaker Pro, Daytimer, Quicken, and MacWrite

KENNETH MELBOURNE

123 Potomac Avenue • University Park, Texas 75205 • (214) 555-1234 • melbourne@thespringsmall.com

PROFILE

- Highly motivated, confident, and energetic sales professional with a background in high-tech industries.
- Award-winning history of building new territories and using creative marketing approaches.
- Experience with international marketing, competitive strategy, strategic business planning, re-engineering, case studies/data driven models, telecommunications, and information technology.
- Proficient in PC, Windows NT, Windows XP, UNIX, and Macintosh computer environments; extensive experience with Access, PowerPoint, MS Word, Excel, and programming languages.

EDUCATION

SOUTHERN METHODIST UNIVERSITY, Cox School of Business, Dallas, Texas   2000 – 2002
UNIVERSITY OF TEXAS, Arlington, Texas   1998 – 2000
Bachelor of Business Administration, May 2002
- Major in Management Information Services; Minor in International Business
- SMU Scholarship, Who's Who Among Students in American Universities and Colleges
- Financial Management Association National Honor Society, Alpha Chi National Honor Society
- Beta Gamma Sigma National Honor Society for Collegiate Schools of Business, Golden Key Honor Society

EXPERIENCE

Southern Methodist University, Dallas, Texas   *Systems Administrator*   2000 – present
Improved efficiency by identifying areas requiring change and specifically developing, testing, and implementing new practices and procedures. Streamlined an automated network-based database that maintains records in excess of $1.3 million within the External Relations Office. Analyzed, designed, and supported the faculty information system for the Cox School of Business. Created and maintained HTML web pages for the Dean's Council. Work/study program for 30 hours per week while carrying a full-time academic schedule.

Interstate Battery Systems of America, Dallas, Texas   *National Sales Representative*   1993 – 1995
Performed quantitative analyses and evaluations of distributor business reports at corporate headquarters. Prepared, summarized, and presented findings to senior management. Promoted to National Sales Representative after only six months of employment. Traveled extensively to establish new business opportunities for distributors. Maintained 100+ local client accounts. Managed point-of-sale merchandising systems. Received awards for yearly top sales and most new accounts generated (52 percent cold-call closing ratio).

IDD Products, Irving, Texas   *Sole Proprietor*   1989 – 1993
Developed market entry strategy for home-building-related consumer goods products for the Dallas/Fort Worth metroplex. Implemented promotional strategy and sold to a 200+ customer base, providing comparative market research of cost savings to customers. Buyer in the World Trade Center and Dallas Trade Mart and Design Center.

Lanier Business Products, Dallas, Texas   *Electronic Technician*   1988 – 1989
Maintained client accounts for 300+ corporations within a 200-mile radius of the Dallas/Fort Worth metroplex. Analyzed and serviced 3M copy machines and sold maintenance contracts for equipment. Recognized by Atlanta headquarters for generating highest yearly sales volume in the Western Region following first six months of employment. Eight-time recipient of top production award for monthly volume.

ADDITIONAL EXPERIENCE

- Gained extensive teamwork experience through membership in university committees, including Presidential, Student Advisory, Missions and Objectives, Marketing Task Force, Appeals, Rules, Recruitment, and Affairs.
- Used strong presentation skills to address North Texas Articulation Council Advisor's Conference.
- President and founding officer of the University Club; negotiated contract with Texas Rangers baseball club and sports food management; raised more than $30,000 within six months.

Molly Fitch

PROFILE
- Experienced advertising account executive with a diverse background.
- Dedicated professional who works until the job is done.
- Well-organized but flexible problem solver who enjoys being challenged.
- Effective team player with strong interpersonal and communication skills.

EXPERIENCE

ACCOUNT EXECUTIVE (1/04 – present)
RPM Advertising (formerly Graham Advertising), Colorado Springs, Colorado
- Plan, coordinate, and direct advertising campaigns for clients.
- Responsible for more than $2.5 million in total advertising budgets, focusing on the automotive industry.
- Confer with clients to determine advertising requirements and budget limitations, utilizing knowledge of products, media capabilities, and audience characteristics.
- Work with agency artists and other media production specialists to select media type and cost, and to determine media timing.
- Negotiate contracts with newspapers and billboard advertisers.
- Coordinate activities of workers engaged in market research, copy writing, artwork layout, media buys, development of special displays and promotional items, and other production activities as needed to carry out approved campaign.
- Design preliminary newspaper ad layouts and write scripts for television and radio advertising.

MANAGER IN TRAINING (9/03 – 12/03)
Abercrombie and Fitch, Denver, Colorado
- Responsible for opening and closing the store, regulating saleable and damaged merchandise, collecting money for sales, and researching/collecting returned checks.
- Input payroll for more than 50 sales associates and balanced the books.
- Provided customer service in a retail environment and ensured customer satisfaction.

ASSISTANT MANAGER (5/02 – 9/03)
Cook's Nook, Fort Worth, Texas
- Assisted customers with purchases and maintained inventory of merchandise.
- Opened and closed the store each day, and balanced cash register receipts.

MARKETING INTERNSHIP (5/02 – 7/02)
The Marketing Group, Dallas, Texas
- Organized, edited, and distributed mass mailings for promotional campaigns.

RECEPTIONIST (Summers 1999, 2000, 2001)
Vidmar Motor Company, Pueblo, Colorado
- Contacted newspaper and radio stations to schedule advertising, make recommendations, and monitor trafficking.
- Assisted in editing television commercial promotions.
- Regulated telephone calls for 60 associates and maintained mail correspondence.

SALES REPRESENTATIVE (8/00 – 12/00)
Texas Christian University Skiff, Fort Worth, Texas
- Marketed advertisements for TCU's newspaper, *The Skiff*.
- Assisted in the design and layout of advertisements.

EDUCATION

BACHELOR OF ARTS, ADVERTISING/PUBLIC RELATIONS (5/03)
Texas Christian University, Fort Worth, Texas
- Emphasis in Business

ADDRESS

1234 Samuel Point, Colorado Springs, Colorado 80906, Cellular (719) 555-1234

ROGER LE BARON

(719) 555-1234   *123 Plainview Place, Manitou Springs, Colorado 80829*   *lebaron@cs.com*

PROFILE

- Dedicated fire chief and inspector with more than 20 years of firefighting experience.
- Background includes management, fire inspection, firefighting, and emergency treatment.
- Experienced in the application of the Uniform Fire Code, field supervision, personnel training, community relations, and public education.
- Effective team player with strong interpersonal and communication skills.
- Adept at working under pressure and handling emergency situations.

CERTIFICATION

- Colorado State Certified Firefighter II
- Colorado State Certified Fire Suppression Systems Inspector
- Colorado State Certified Code Enforcement Officer
- Scheduled to take ICBO Fire Inspector exam, November 2004
- Certified Emergency Medical Technician, 1977 – 1997

EXPERIENCE

Fire Chief

- Ensured the preservation of life, property, and safety through direction of proper emergency scene management.
- Supervised fire suppression, emergency medical treatment, and rescue operations.
- Investigated fire origins and wrote fire reports.
- Recruited and screened volunteer firefighters.
- Provided classroom and field training in strategies of fire suppression, ground hose lays, use and maintenance of equipment, safety and first aid, and rural and wildland firefighting.
- Coordinated activities with other fire departments in overlapping jurisdictions, ensuring smooth working relationships.
- Instrumental in the formation of the Northeast Teller County Fire Protection District.

Fire Inspector

- Inspected commercial/residential buildings and fire detection/suppression systems in order to detect hazardous conditions and to ensure compliance with city ordinances and fire codes.
- Consulted with architects, engineers, and contractors to expedite construction; conducted on-site inspections and plans reviews of construction in progress.
- Used long-term planning, conflict resolution, and follow-up skills to ensure that existing facilities were in compliance with code.
- Implemented a successful fire prevention program in the Manitou Springs schools through site visits, open houses, and building inspections.

Firefighting

- More than 20 years of firefighting experience.
- Received alarms, dispatched volunteers, and responded to fire scenes.
- Provided emergency medical care for the sick and injured, and assisted in rescues during fire and nonfire situations.

Zoning Ordinance

- Conducted extensive field investigations of properties, structures, and signs and enforced violations of the city zoning and land use ordinances.
- Evaluated and categorized violations and determined the appropriate course of action.
- Made presentations before the City Council, Planning Commission, and Hearing Officer on variances, appeals, ordinance amendments, and other enforcement-related matters.

Administration

- Responsible for six ambulances and a crew of twelve with Schaefer Ambulance Service.
- Supervised field operations, trained new drivers, and maintained vehicles and equipment.
- Helped the ambulance company grow to Santa Ana's largest ambulance service.
- Managed budgets, inventoried equipment, and ordered supplies.

WORK HISTORY

Fire Code Inspector, City of Colorado Springs, Colorado	2003 – present
Firefighter (Volunteer), Manitou Springs Fire Department, Colorado	1994 – present
Zoning Inspector, City of Colorado Springs, Colorado	1994 – 1997
Fire Chief, Northeast Teller County Fire Protection District, Colorado	1993 – 1994
Captain/Firefighter, Northeast Teller County Fire Protection District, Colorado	1990 – 1993
Fire Inspector, City of Manitou Springs, Colorado	1989 – 1990
Driver/Engineer, Ivywild/Cheyenne Cañon Fire Protection District, Colorado	1985 – 1990
Captain (Volunteer), Ivywild/Cheyenne Cañon Fire Protection District, Colorado	1985 – 1990
Field Supervisor/Crew Chief, Schaefer Ambulance Service, Santa Ana, California	1980 – 1985

TRAINING

Fire Inspection Principles (two weeks), National Fire Academy, Emmettsburg, Maryland	2001
Annual ICBO Conference (one week)	2000, 2001
Alarm Systems (four days), National Fire Protection Association	2001
Firefighter Safety and Survival, National Fire Academy, Emmettsburg, Maryland	1991
Arson Investigation Seminar, EMTAC Conference	1989
High Rise Firefighting Seminar (two days), International Society of Fire Service Instructors	1987
Rural Firefighting Tactics Seminar (two days), State of Colorado	1987
Basic Auto Extrication (three days), Emergency Squad Training Institute	1985
Various Other Courses with local fire departments throughout career	

HOLLY D. FIDELIO

123 Spring Grove Terrace • Colorado Springs, Colorado 80906 • (719) 555-1234 • hdfidelio@juno.com

PROFILE
- Goal-directed hotel professional with a background in sales/marketing, project management, public relations, customer service, training, and supervision.
- Adept at managing multiple complex tasks simultaneously.
- Respected for effective problem-solving and decision-making skills.
- Articulate and persuasive with strong interpersonal and communication skills.

EXPERIENCE

RADISSON INN NORTH, Colorado Springs, Colorado   2000 – present
Director of Sales (May 2001 – present)

Sales/Marketing
- Maximized customer satisfaction and revenue goals by developing and implementing effective sales and marketing strategies for regional and national sales accounts.
- Increased sales volume and profitability by formulating and executing projects for all markets.
- Maintained and built local corporate accounts by designing programs to meet client needs.
- Established sales goals and coordinated the development of the marketing plan and budget.
- Implemented strategies to improve market penetration and developed alternatives.

Administration
- Controlled the date, availability, and rate of guest rooms and function space.
- Reviewed market analysis to determine client needs, occupancy potential, desired rates, etc.
- Coordinated transient and group room commitments to ensure proper market mix.
- Qualified prospective leads and analyzed sales statistics to maximize profitability.
- Negotiated with clients to achieve maximum profit while ensuring customer satisfaction.

Supervision
- Selected qualified employees, conducted orientations and Radisson's "Yes I Can" training, evaluated performance, and recommended salary increases as appropriate.
- Utilized leadership skills and motivation techniques to optimize employee productivity.

Associate Director of Sales (November 2000 – May 2001)

Sales/Marketing
- Recruited by Radisson to assist the director of sales with department operations, market research, budgeting, sales planning, goal setting, and staff training.
- Achieved budget by identifying and actively soliciting individual and group business from new and existing local, regional, and national sales accounts.
- Assisted in the formation of the hotel marketing plan.
- Coordinated all bookings with other departments to ensure complete customer satisfaction.

LE BARON HOTEL, Colorado Springs, Colorado   1999 – 2000
Sales Manager

Sales/Marketing
- Negotiated and booked group business to achieve revenue and customer satisfaction goals.
- Achieved budgeted goals by making outside sales calls to solicit new and existing business from social, military, education, religious, fraternal, and association market segments.
- Assisted in the development of annual sales goals and room revenue budget.
- Entertained clients weekly and conducted on-site inspections.
- Serviced in-house customers to foster additional business, repeat bookings, and referrals.

FIGURE SKATING PROFESSIONAL, Colorado Springs, Colorado   1999 – present

Instruction
- Taught figure skating, choreographed routines, and evaluated student performance.
- Motivated and assisted students in setting and achieving objectives.

Honors/Awards
- World-class figure skater and former national and international competitor.
- Gold medalist in ice dancing, 1989 World Junior Team Member, Sarajevo, Yugoslavia.
- Participated in USFSA seminar for elite American ice dancers and in the Olympic Training Center's sports science programs.
- National recipient of NutraSweet's "Giving it 100 percent" Award in 1988.
- Guest star on various ice shows throughout the United States.

MEDIA PLAY, Colorado Springs, Colorado   1998 – 1999
Manager

Management
- Actively involved in the design and start-up of a 50,000 sq. ft. retail outlet store.
- Responsible for merchandising, public relations, advertising, sales promotions, and book signings.
- Implemented human resource, cash control, and customer service procedures.
- Interviewed and hired employees; conducted performance evaluations.
- Managed load balancing and statistics for inventory, ordering, and sales databases.

91

EXPERIENCE
(continued)

PLAZA ICE CHALET, Colorado Springs, Colorado   1994 – 1998
Head Figure Skating Coach
- Served as head coach; supervised and managed coaching staff.
- Provided individual and group instruction; implemented off-ice ballet, jazz, conditioning, and strength training programs.
- Directed the annual Springspree and Festival of Lights ice shows, including choreography, music selection, publicity, advertising, and scheduling.

EDUCATION

BACHELOR OF ARTS, PSYCHOLOGY, *Summa Cum Laude*, GPA 4.0   1998
University of Colorado, Colorado Springs, Colorado
- Recognized as the Outstanding Social Sciences Undergraduate
- University of Colorado Regent Scholar
- Recipient of Colorado Scholastic Scholarship
- Participated in the Psychology Honor Program
- Member of the American Psychological Association, Psi Chi National Honor Society, Business Club, and Society for Human Resource Management

COMPUTERS

Experience with WordPerfect, MS Word, Windows, SPSS, Fidelio, Lotus 1-2-3, e-mail, and database management for local and network file systems

VOLUNTEER

- Teach marketing to university business classes as a guest speaker
- Research Assistant to University of Colorado psychology professor
- Assisted in homeless shelters and soup kitchens
- Fund-raising volunteer for the United States Figure Skating Association

AFFILIATIONS

- Southern Colorado Business Travel Association, Board of Directors, 1997
- Society of Government Meeting Planners
- United States Figure Skating Association
- Professional Skaters Guild of America
- National Strength and Conditioning Association
- University of Colorado Alumni Association

SANDRA K. FRANCIS

12 Dolphin Circle • Colorado Springs, Colorado 80918 • (719) 555-1234 • skf@hotmail.com

PROFILE

- Experienced Critical Care Nurse dedicated to providing excellence in patient care
- Detail oriented, thorough, and accurate working under pressure
- Adept at managing multiple and diverse tasks simultaneously
- Outstanding communication and interpersonal skills
- An empathetic, professional caregiver who is able to quickly establish and maintain rapport with patients

PROFESSIONAL EXPERIENCE

STAFF NURSE/CHARGE NURSE (July 1997 – present)
St. Francis Hospital/Penrose Hospital, Intensive Care Unit, Colorado Springs, Colorado
- Assess, plan, and implement primary care of the critical medical, surgical, pediatric, and trauma patients and perform charge nurse functions.
- Monitor and troubleshoot ventilators, invasive hemodynamic catheters, and intra-cerebral pressure lines.
- Operate as primary fluid resuscitation nurse for trauma team and perform Code Blue functions according to ACLS protocols.

STAFF NURSE (RN) (October 1992 – July 1997)
Sacred Heart Hospital, Adult and Pediatric Intensive Care Unit, Pensacola, Florida
- Served as staff nurse in Pediatric ICU for the first four years, providing ongoing assessment, analysis, planning, evaluation, and problem solving.
- Provided primary care to critical pediatric patients, including medical, surgical, trauma, acute, and chronic care.
- Responsible for ventilators, intracerebral pressure lines, invasive hemodynamic cathe-ters, and electrocardiograms.
- Rotated between adult and pediatric ICU during the last year.
- Responded to adult and pediatric traumas and Code Blues.

STAFF NURSE (LPN) (October 1989 – May 1992)
Sacred Heart Hospital, Orthopedic Floor, Pensacola, Florida
- Team nurse responsible for half of patients under direct supervision of a Registered Nurse while working toward an undergraduate degree in nursing.
- Gained experienced with total knee surgery, back surgery, back pain, trauma, and general overflow patients from other floors.
- Administered all medications except intravenous ones.

EDUCATION/ TRAINING

UNIVERSITY OF COLORADO, Colorado Springs, Colorado (2003)
Completed Pre-Med Requirements: general chemistry, physics, biology, organic chemistry, calculus, genetics, biochemistry

UNIVERSITY OF SOUTH ALABAMA, Mobile, Alabama (1999)
Bachelor of Science in Nursing

PENSACOLA JUNIOR COLLEGE, Pensacola, Florida (1992)
Associate of Science in Registered Nursing

OTHER TRAINING
- 16-week Critical Care Course (October 1995), Florida Hospital, Orlando, Florida
- Certificate of Occupation Proficiency in Practical Nursing (August 1989), Pensacola Junior College, Pensacola, Florida

PROFESSIONAL ACCOMPLISHMENTS

- CCRN certification by American Association of Critical Care Nurses (Since 2000)
- Advanced Cardiac Life Support (ACLS) (Since 1996)
- Trauma Nursing Core Course (TNCC) (November 2004)
- Proposed and implemented pediatric protocols and pediatric trauma cart at St. Francis Hospital ICU (2001)
- St. Elizabeth Ann Seton Nursing Award for Excellence (2000)

Anne K. Ferrer

1234 Camfield Circle • Phoenix, Arizona 80920 • (602) 555-1234 • E-mail: anneferrer@thespringsmall.com

PROFILE

- Eleven years of diverse clinical experience as a speech-language pathologist
- Graduate degree in speech-language pathology with a GPA of 4.6/5.0
- Certified as clinically competent in speech pathology by the American Speech-Language-Hearing Association
- Team player with an infectious positive attitude and strong communication skills
- Highly self-motivated and confident problem solver who continually seeks ways to expand clinical knowledge

EXPERIENCE

Clinical Speech-Language Pathology

- Provided speech-language diagnostics and therapy to neurologically impaired adults in acute care hospital, rehabilitation, nursing home, and home health care settings.
- Interfaced with interdisciplinary team to develop functional outcome goals, returning adults and adolescents to previously held jobs with a 90 percent success rate by providing speech-language diagnostics and therapy in a mild traumatic brain injury rehabilitation program.
- Experienced in working with children (ages birth to three years) in an early intervention community program and with adults with neurogenic disorders and head/neck cancers.
- Experienced in providing therapy for dysphagia, aphasia, dysarthria, verbal apraxia, head trauma, voice disorders, fluency disorders, right hemisphere brain injuries, and articulation/phonology.
- Background in computer-assisted cognitive rehabilitation, diagnosis of swallowing disorders using the modified barium swallow procedure, and feeding groups.

Program Development

- Developed a mild head injury screening tool and informal cognitive evaluation criteria.
- Assisted in developing an Activities of Daily Living questionnaire to assess cognitive functional limitations.
- Met with team members weekly to develop programs for assisting patients in successfully returning to daily living functions.
- Initiated and implemented a sucking/swallowing intervention program for infants in a neonatal intensive care unit.
- Developed and implemented programs in tracheoesophageal puncture (TEP), cognitive retraining using a computer, and evaluation and treatment of swallowing disorders.

Supervision and Training

- Supervised speech-language pathology graduate students in diagnostics and therapy.
- Provided patient and family education to assist patients in achieving functional goals.
- Taught in-service and cross-training classes to peers and other medical staff.
- Served as in-service coordinator for a rehabilitation department for two years.

WORK HISTORY

CLINICAL SPEECH-LANGUAGE PATHOLOGIST

The Penrose-St. Francis Healthcare System, Colorado Springs, Colorado	2000 – present
Patti McGowan-Ferrer, MS, CCC, Colorado Springs, Colorado	2003 – present
Symphony Home Care Services, Colorado Springs, Colorado	2002 – present
Marquette General Hospital, Marquette, Michigan	1998 – 2000
Speech-Language-Hearing Center, Lubbock, Texas	1988 – 1998
Texas Tech University, Lubbock, Texas	Summer 1988

EDUCATION

MASTER OF SCIENCE IN SPEECH AND LANGUAGE PATHOLOGY	1995
BACHELOR OF SCIENCE IN SPEECH AND HEARING SCIENCE	1993
University of Illinois, Champaign, Illinois	

GARY D. BELLEVUE

P.O. Box 123456 ▸ Peterson, CO 80914 ▸ Home: (719) 555-1234 ▸ Cell: (719) 555-5678 ▸ E-mail: garydb@protypeltd.com

OBJECTIVE   A challenging position in computer electronics.

PROFILE
- ▸ **EXPERIENCE** – Three years of in-depth experience as a computer and switching systems specialist.
- ▸ **EDUCATION** – Undergraduate degree in computer information systems. Associate degree in electronic systems technology.
- ▸ **TRAINING** – Extensive on-site computer training with Lockheed Martin, Digital Equipment Corporation (DEC), IBM, and the United States Air Force (USAF).
- ▸ **SKILLS** – Well organized, detail oriented, and analytical problem solver; able to pinpoint problems and initiate creative solutions in a timely and efficient manner.
- ▸ **LEADERSHIP** – Outstanding leader with a proven record of accomplishments.
- ▸ **TEAMWORK** – Member of the Unit Advisory Council and Work Center Quality Air Force team.
- ▸ **COMPUTERS** – Knowledge of IBM PC and mainframe computer systems, DOS, Windows, UNIX, MVS, VMS, Silicon Graphics, DEC hardware, and Netex networks.

EXPERIENCE   **ELECTRONICS SPECIALIST** (2003 – Present)
United States Air Force, NORAD, Cheyenne Mountain, Colorado Springs, Colorado
- ▸ Performed troubleshooting and repair on more than 200 printed circuit modules, power supplies, switch panels, keyboards, peripherals, and other repairable components of computer systems.
- ▸ Provided support for the logistical transition, troubleshooting, and repair of the new Space Defense Operations Center (SPADOC) computer system.
- ▸ Skilled in the use of diagnostic programs, oscilloscopes, I/O prom burners, logic analyzers, Genrad 1792D automatic test equipment, computer test beds, and other precision measuring equipment to diagnose problems.
- ▸ Supervised and trained five technicians, ensuring quality and productivity and prioritizing the workload to meet or exceed established milestones.
- ▸ Personally developed a simplified training program for the NOVA 1220 test bed, decreasing qualification time by more than 30 percent.
- ▸ Created more efficient programs for monitoring benchstock, fire prevention, tools, remote network security, and ground safety by reorganizing guidelines and procedures.
- ▸ Personally created a new method of isolating diagnostic subroutine failures by using a complex logic analyzer test set, identifying several undetected failures and increasing test bed reliability 20 percent.
- ▸ Was recognized by the Air Force for saving $25 to $75 per integrated circuit by using EPROM programmer expertise to program integrated circuits, allowing re-use of firmware.

EDUCATION   **MASTER OF SCIENCE, COMPUTER INFORMATION SYSTEMS** (2001 – present)
University of Colorado, Colorado Springs, Colorado

BACHELOR OF SCIENCE, COMPUTER INFORMATION SYSTEMS (2001)
Bellevue University, Bellevue, Nebraska
- ▸ Minor in Business Administration

ASSOCIATE OF SCIENCE, ELECTRONIC SYSTEMS TECHNOLOGY (1996)
Community College of the Air Force, Maxwell Air Force Base, Montgomery, Alabama

TRAINING   **CIVILIAN ON-SITE TRAINING:** Lockheed Martin SPADOC 4C Hardware Maintenance Training (240 hours) ▸ Digital SPADOC 4C Hardware Maintenance Training (200 hours) ▸ IBM SPADOC 4C Hardware Maintenance Training (320 hours) ▸ IBM I/O System Training ▸ Digital VAX 4000 Diagnostic and Module Level Repair, DSSI Subsystems, Baseband Ethernet Hardware, and Magtape Maintenance

U.S. AIR FORCE TRAINING: High Reliability Soldering (40 hours) ▸ Apprentice Electronic Computer and Switching Systems Specialist (413 hours) ▸ Computer and Switching Principles (574 hours) ▸ Fiber Optics (32 hours) ▸ Quality Awareness (16 hours)

JAN T. CAMFIELD

SUMMARY OF QUALIFICATIONS

- Reliable and committed sales and marketing professional with 15 years of experience in the telecommunications industry.
- Proven track record of success in positions of increasing responsibility.
- Outstanding organizational and management skills; talent for seeing "the big picture."
- Adept at establishing effective working relationships with clients, colleagues, and industry associations.
- Highly motivated with a strong commitment to delivering quality service.
- Skilled in contract negotiations; articulate and persuasive in written and verbal presentations.

PROFESSIONAL EXPERIENCE

Sales/Marketing

Member of the sales team responsible for launching two cable television networks—Cable Health Network and Lifetime Television:

- Established network affiliates in the Central Region through analysis of the marketplace, cold calling, and exceptional after-sale service.
- Positioned niche network, negotiated contracts, and effected ongoing affiliate support with local ad sales, promotions, and community outreach programs.
- Consistently exceeded annual goals by 20 percent; recipient of four "Region of the Year" awards.

As Manager, Special Markets for Lifetime Television:

- Negotiated more than 200 new client agreements, expanding national distribution and revenue.
- Collaborated with marketing department to create targeted marketing campaigns for new distribution outlets, resulting in increased value, awareness, and sales.
- Organized participation in and worked trade shows.
- Developed and conducted product training seminars for client staff.

Management

As Manager, Special Markets for Lifetime Television (a newly created position and division of the company), developed and implemented sales and marketing strategies to increase distribution for the cable television network through alternate technologies, increasing annual revenue stream by $10M:

- Developed strategic plans, competitive analyses, budgets, and a business plan for the division.
- Worked closely with legal department to create form agreements for five distinct distribution outlets and revised agreements based on changing demands of marketplace.
- Acted as internal consultant on government rules and regulations affecting alternate markets.
- Made presentations and participated in panels at industry trade shows, increasing awareness and value of the network in the new marketplace.
- Directed trade association task forces to examine and resolve industry issues.

WORK HISTORY

1998 – 2004	Special Markets Manager	Lifetime Television, Dallas, Texas
1993 – 1998	Regional Account Manager	Lifetime Television, Dallas, Texas
1992 – 1993	Marketing Coordinator	Lifetime Television, Dallas, Texas
1990 – 1992	Marketing Coordinator	Cable Health Network (sold to Lifetime), Dallas, Texas
1988 – 1990	Sales/Marketing Assistant	Frito-Lay, Inc., Dallas, Texas
1986 – 1988	Account Representative	Paramount Pictures, Atlanta, Georgia

1234 Biltmore Court • Aspen, Colorado 80907 • (719) 555-1234 • camfield@juno.com

EDWARD L. PETERSON

1234 Arequa Ridge Drive • Colorado Springs, Colorado 80919 • (719) 555-1234 • ELPeterson@protypeltd.com

QUALIFICATIONS
- Experienced project manager with a background in military logistics and the private sector.
- Profit-oriented, conscientious manager with strong organizational skills.
- Exceptional communication skills; able to motivate others to function as a successful team.

EXPERIENCE

JAMITCH ENTERPRISES, Peterson AFB, Colorado (2002 – present)
Project Manager, Standard Base Supply System Contract
- Responsible for the overall planning, directing, and resource management of a private-sector contract with the U.S. Air Force ($150 million of inventory and 110,000 transactions per month).
- Realized a profit through efficient utilization of resources, cost controls, safety and quality control, problem resolution, and budget programming.
- Selected and managed a work force of approximately 140 personnel at four locations, ensuring effective staffing and union negotiations.

TECOM, INC., Peterson AFB, Colorado (1993 – 2002)
Project Manager, Standard Base Supply System Contract (1997 – 2002)
Project Manager, Transient Alert Services (1996 – 1997)
Consultant (1993 – 1996)
- Responsible for the same duties as above for five years.
- Managed Transient Alert Services, including the provision of appropriate arrival and departure services for 500–600 transient aircraft per month.
- Supervised, trained, and scheduled a staff of 26.
- Served as a consultant for three years in the preparation of proposals for base supply and aircraft maintenance contracts, including staffing, organization, PWS responses, quality control plans, and safety procedures.

USAF ACADEMY AERO CLUB, Colorado (1993 – 1996)
Contract Flight Instructor
- Taught student pilots to commercial/instrument ratings, accumulating 650+ hours.

UNITED STATES AIR FORCE (1978 – 1993)
Assistant to the Deputy Chief of Staff for Logistics, USAF Academy, Colorado
Director of Supply, USAF Academy, Colorado
Deputy Base Commander, RAF Alconbury, England
Supply Squadron Commander, RAF Alconbury, England
Staff Supply Officer, Directorate of Civil Engineering, HQ USAF
- More than 24 years of logistics experience, including materiel management, inventory, supply, budgeting, transportation, fuels, and procurement.
- Assisted the Deputy Chief of Staff with supply, contracting, transportation, logistics plans, and program directorates, including squadron commander responsibilities for more than 325 personnel.
- As Deputy Base Commander, administered the support requirements for 6,000 personnel, including involvement with security police, legal services, personnel, recreation services, civil engineering, and equal opportunity/affirmative action policies.
- Formulated, analyzed, and evaluated policy methods and procedures and implemented directives necessary for facilities management support.
- As Supply Squadron Commander, managed the efforts of more than 250 personnel to provide supply support to three squadrons.
- Developed a new concept for contracting supply support that was employed by a majority of air force bases.

EDUCATION

BACHELOR OF SCIENCE, University of Missouri
U.S. AIR FORCE TRAINING: Industrial College of the Armed Forces, Squadron Officers School, Staff Supply Officer Course

ALBERT JACKSON III

12 S.E. 115th Avenue • Portland, Oregon 97202
Home: (503) 555-1234 • Cell: (503) 555-5679 • E-mail: ajiii@protypeltd.com

EXPERIENCE

CONTRACTS MANAGER, DATA SERVICES DIVISION (1999 – 2004)
Aerotek, Inc., Portland, Oregon, and Colorado Springs, Colorado
- Recruited and qualified technical consultants for job placements within Fortune 500 clients nationwide.
- Negotiated contract parameters on behalf of the consultants to maximize their productivity and suitability for the labor agreement.
- Created a sales team whereby recruiters could develop leadership skills and refine sales techniques for a smooth transition into account management.
- Marketed services to undeveloped territories with a primary focus on network communications.
- Generated $300,000+ in annual net revenues for the company.

FINANCIAL ADVISOR, RETAIL DIVISION (1997 – 1998)
Prudential Securities, Inc., Atlanta, Georgia
- Procured, developed, and managed institutional and private client accounts.
- Consulted with client base on government regulations, market conditions, and securities reports.
- Refined financial sales efforts through the use of seminars, telemarketing, and direct-mail promotions.
- Executed transactions through the New York Stock Exchange, over the counter, and commodity trading desks.

FLOOR SUPERVISOR (1996 – 1997)
J. Crew Group, Inc., Jackson, Wyoming
- Instructed and supervised associates in all sales and operational activities.
- Monitored departmental sales figures and created promotional campaigns to enhance merchandise movement.
- Maintained customer profiles and ensured that customer service standards were met.
- Worked directly with the corporate office to define the needs and goals of the factory outlet.

ASSISTANT PROJECT MANAGER (1995 – 1996)
Central Parking Systems, Washington, D.C.
- Managed the marketing, operation, and maintenance of a 3,000-space parking facility.
- Supervised cash handling, accounts payable, accounts receivable, and inventory control procedures.
- Coordinated the efforts of 29 hourly employees.
- Participated in corporate proposal efforts throughout Maryland, Virginia, and Washington, D.C.
- Compiled internal quality control information for upper management.

RANCH HAND (Summers 1990 – 1995)
A Bar A Ranch, Encampment, Wyoming
- Accounted for financial records and large cash deposits.
- Directed bartending procedures during convention week.
- Greeted and oriented guests to the ranch.
- Supervised operations in the absence of the foreman and general manager.
- Selected as Top Hand for summer 1989.

EDUCATION

BACHELOR OF ARTS IN ECONOMICS (1997)
University of North Carolina, Chapel Hill

INTERESTS

Computers: Lotus 1-2-3, MS Word, PowerPoint, IBM and Macintosh computers
Languages: Working knowledge of French
International: Traveled throughout Western Europe (1983)

ACTIVITIES

Sports: Colorado Outward Bound School, South San Juans, Colorado (1993); Member of the LaCrosse Club and Soccer Teams (1991 – 1992) and Ski Team (1991 – 1994)
Community Service: Volunteer for Big Brother (1986 – 1987); Fund Raiser for American Heart Association (1986); Rush Advisor for Inter-Fraternity Council (1986)

JAMES K. DECKER

123 Buttermere Drive, Denver, Colorado 80906

Cellular: (719) 555-1234

Email: jkd@protypeltd.com

PROFILE
- Dependable manager with the proven ability to relate to clients and build trust.
- Self-motivated and focused; comfortable working independently with little supervision.
- Intuitive communicator who enjoys social interaction and speaking to groups.
- Highly proficient in Windows, MS Word, Excel, WordPerfect, QuickBooks, Dolphin Imaging, email, and the Internet.

EDUCATION

BACHELOR OF ARTS IN COMMUNICATION (2004)
University of Colorado, Boulder, Colorado
- Course work included: Rhetorical Dimensions of Communication, Empirical Research Methods, Human Communication Theory, American Sign Language I/II/III, Contemporary Mass Media, Organizational Communication, Interviewing, Communication in Society, Interpersonal Communication, Principles and Practices of Argumentation, Interaction Skills, Current Issues in Communication (Critical Thinking).

EXPERIENCE

MARKETING INTERNSHIP (2004)
Greater Colorado Springs Chamber of Commerce, Colorado Springs, Colorado
- Completed a four-month internship in marketing, media relations, programs, and event management.
- Prepared and distributed promotional, public relations, and other communication materials.
- Developed and maintained a matrix to track the organization's involvement in the local media.
- Part of the team responsible for pre-event planning, event management (invitations, reservations, facilities, reception, logistics, public relations), and post-event evaluation.
- Served as an ambassador for the organization with Chamber members and the community.
- Assisted with budget review and tracking.
- Served on the Women's Business Council advisory committee.
- Traveled with Chamber management to the annual Colorado Springs Day at the State Legislature.

OFFICE MANAGER / LAB TECHNICIAN (2001 – present)
Dr. James E. Killebrew, LLC, Colorado Springs, Colorado
- Manage the operations of a busy orthodontic practice dedicated to excellence in customer service.
- Recruit, hire, train, and supervise six staff members—an orthodontic assistant, patient coordinator, back office support, and facilities maintenance.
- Fully accountable for profit and loss of the practice, including accounts payable, accounts receivable, insurance billing, collections, payroll, quarterly tax payments, and reconciliation of bank and credit card statements.
- Forecast staffing needs, expenses, and income; prepare and manage annual budgets.
- Meet with patients to present cases and close the sale by selecting the right financing option for each patient's needs.
- Schedule appointments and referrals, prepare patients for treatments, take and develop x-rays (Ceph and Pano), and sterilize equipment.

Key Accomplishments:
- Created a new scheduling system that allowed the staff to see more patients every day, which reduced the work week from 5 days to 3.5 days while at the same time increasing income by 27%.
- Developed Excel spreadsheets to track inventory more accurately, which significantly reduced obsolete inventory and supplies on hand.
- Reduced overhead expenses 49.4% by eliminating an overpriced outside janitorial service and cross-training orthodontic assistants in lab processes.

EXPERIENCE
(continued)

SURGICAL ASSISTANT / FINANCIAL INSURANCE SPECIALIST (2002 – 2003)
Associates in Maxillofacial and Oral Surgery, Colorado Springs, Colorado

- Gained hands-on medical experience while completing training as a surgical assistant, including knowledge of oral surgery concepts, practices, and procedures.
- Managed the financial operations of this multi-million-dollar practice with six offices and a surgery center seeing up to 60 patients per day.
- Responsible for accounts receivable, invoicing, posting, accepting payments, making adjustments to accounts, writing refund checks, and updating accounts as needed.
- Filed insurance claims and updated ADA, CPT, and ICD-9 codes.

MANAGER (1999 – 2001)
Brinker International, Denver, Colorado

- Served as an internal consultant to general managers of company-owned On the Border, Chili's, Maggiano's, Macaroni Grill, and Big Bowl restaurants in Colorado.
- Responsible for improving profitability, overall performance, and customer service of individual stores by creating more efficient operating processes and procedures.
- Audited inventory and developed measuring and inventory systems to lower overhead.
- Oversaw general construction, furnishing, licensing, and opening of new restaurants.
- Created, organized, and maintained employee files; created new positions to better meet the needs of guests and to improve morale.
- Researched and developed training programs to improve the customer service and suggestive selling skills of employees.
- Nominated for the Better Business Bureau's Excellence in Customer Service Award in 2001.

MANAGER (1998 – 1999)
Houston's Restaurant, Dallas, Texas

- Managed the operations of an American-style grill with more than $6 million in annual sales.
- Created, designed, and implemented all marketing, advertising, and promotional campaigns.
- Generated top-of-the-mind awareness through resourceful marketing techniques, which increased volume in all seasons.
- Developed sales contests and promotions that increased per-person sales averages by 30%.
- Created weekly training classes to instruct wait staff in suggestive selling techniques.
- Accountable for maintaining expenses below budget through accurate planning, purchasing, and waste reduction controls.
- Planned menus, estimated food and beverage costs, and purchased supplies.
- Responsible for all accounting, cash handling, reporting, and payroll functions.
- Recruited, supervised, motivated, scheduled, and evaluated a staff of 90 employees.
- Instituted high standards for the wait staff and developed innovative training programs that emphasized the importance of customer satisfaction and going beyond the expected.
- Initiated weekly management meetings with the general manager, kitchen manager, and key employees to discuss the restaurant's weekly objectives, goals, upcoming events, budget, personnel, and customer service issues.
- Worked with the kitchen manager to reduce food costs by developing specials to use food effectively.
- Lowered monthly bar costs from 23.6% to 19% through cost-effective purchasing and by increasing sales, monitoring inventory, and instituting a more accurate pouring system.
- Investigated and resolved food quality and service complaints, ensuring customer satisfaction.

6 Designing the Perfect e-Mailable Résumé

E-mail is a very rapid and cost-effective means of communication, and it makes your information available to potential employers immediately. There is no longer a need to wait for the U.S. Postal Service to get your résumé and cover letter across the country or around the world. With e-mail, your message is there within minutes, giving you a competitive advantage over someone who does not yet feel comfortable with using e-mail.

Don't feel alone if you are one of those who is not accustomed to using e-mail every day in your work and personal lives. According to the latest U.S. Census data, 44 million households have access to the Internet, but that is only 42 percent of American homes. Of those people, only 87.7 percent used e-mail. In Canada, 12.3 million households (64 percent) had at least one member who used the Internet regularly in 2003, either from home, work, school, a public library, or another location. Nearly 75 percent of American businesses use e-mail every day, but not every person in every business has access to a computer to send and receive e-mail.

If you are uncertain how to get an e-mail address or use the software, you should talk with your Internet service provider or online service. It would take an entire book to give you the details of how to operate every kind of software.

However, here are a few generalizations about e-mail addresses that you should know:

1. Try to make your e-mail address as simple as possible. The best address is one that has your last name and either first name or your first and/or middle initials.

2. Avoid "funky" e-mail addresses that are more about your personal preferences than they are about work.

3. Avoid the use of the underscore (_) in your e-mail address. When you type your e-mail address on your letterhead or résumé, MS Word will automatically turn it into a hyperlink, which means it will be

underlined (<u>pat_criscito@protypeltd. com</u>). That underline often obscures the underscore, and people mistake the resulting hole as a space, and you cannot use spaces in e-mail addresses. Choose a dash (-) or period (.) instead, or if you can avoid it, don't use punctuation at all, which is an even better option.

4. Don't use your work e-mail address for your job search. Get a free-mail account (like yahoo.com or hotmail.com) that you can access from any computer with a connection to the Internet.

5. Most e-mail addresses today are not case sensitive, so feel free to mix capital letters and lower-case letters to make your e-mail address easier to read. For instance, *PatCriscito@protypeltd.com*.

6. When privacy is an issue, avoid e-mail addresses that include parts of your name. You can always use your job title as your e-mail address if you are trying to hide your identity online.

7. Avoid using the capital letter O or the digit 0 in an e-mail address since they often look alike when printed. The same goes for lowercase "l," which looks like a capitalized "I." The exception would be if your name includes one of those letters and your name is fairly common.

■ *A Word About Confidentiality*

First of all, there is no such word as *confidential* in cyberspace. Think of your e-mail as a postcard. Once you transmit your words via any electronic means, they are free for all to see. Your boss can read the trail left behind by your e-mail at work any time he or she wishes, even if you delete the message.

Most companies regularly check e-mail messages for fraud, waste, or abuse. In fact, a recent survey indicated that as many as 63 percent of companies audit their employees' e-mail and/or Internet usage. What that means is that you shouldn't say anything in your company e-mail that you wouldn't want your boss to read.

By the way, I don't recommend using your work e-mail account to send and receive job hunting information even if you are using it after work hours. Why? First, for the obvious reason that your employer may discover that you are thinking about leaving your current job. Second, your e-mail header shows potential employers that you are using company equipment for personal business, which is a turn-off. Don't put work phone numbers on your résumé or cover letters for the same reason. A personal e-mail address, cellular telephone number, or voice mailbox is the best addition to your home phone number on a résumé or letterhead.

In addition to the problem with confidentiality at work, on the Internet your e-mail is accessible by anyone with the knowledge of how to filter data from the various networks of computers through which your e-mail must pass. Anyone with system administration access on any of these computers could potentially read your mail. The chances are slim that this will happen—most people just don't have the time or the inclination to read someone else's mail—but there is always a remote possibility that your e-mail could get into the hands of a dishonest person, like an identity thief. It doesn't happen very often, but these crooks have been known to steal a work history, Social Security number (never put one on a résumé!), and other identifying information to assume your identity. Never say anything in an e-mail message that you wouldn't want published on the front page of *The New York Times* or shouted from the top of a building!

When you are posting your résumé into online databases, never give your Social Security number, date of birth, gender, race, medical information, or other sensitive personal information. Most of this information is protected under Title VII of the Civil Rights Act of 1964, which prohibits companies from discriminating on the basis of race, color, religion, sex, or national origin.

If a Web site asks you to specify your gender and/or race, it is generally voluntary, so you can choose not to comply. As a general rule, companies can wait until after your interview to conduct background investigations that would require your Social Security number and birth date. The only exception would be special job application sites like *www.usajobs.opm.gov*, which is the Web site of the United States Office of Personnel Management. Sites like these conduct instant background checks before the interview.

Never, ever give anyone on the Internet a credit card number, bank account number, mother's maiden name, or special identifying characteristics like eye color. No credible employer will ever ask you for this information, even to conduct a background check.

If you think your online identity data has been stolen or that a job search site has violated its posted privacy policy, you can file a consumer complaint with the Federal Trade Commission (FTC) by calling 877-FTC-HELP or using the FTC's online filing system at *http://www.ftc.gov*, "File Complaint Online."

If you are concerned that your résumé will be seen online by your current employer, there are some things you can do to improve confidentiality. First, many career Web sites offer the option of making your résumé anonymous or let you exclude certain companies from seeing your résumé.

You can choose not to post your résumé to a career site's résumé database and use the site simply to search for jobs. When you reply to a job posting and send your résumé, it generally goes directly to the company and not into the career site's database.

If you want to use all of the benefits of a career Web site, there are some other options for making your résumé confidential:

1. Remove your current employer's name on your résumé and replace it with a general description of its industry (i.e., a software development firm in the Silicon Valley).

2. Make your job title more generic.

3. Delete your name and use something like "Confidential Candidate" instead.

4. Create an e-mail address that doesn't include your name.

5. Place an alternate contact phone number on your résumé so someone can screen calls for you. This can be done with a private voice mailbox or an answering service.

6. Use a Post Office box to receive mail and job-related correspondence, or delete all contact information altogether except your special e-mail address.

7. If you are planning to attach your MS Word résumé, make sure that you have removed all personal identifiers from the file. To find these hidden identifiers, select the "File" menu, then "Properties," and then "Summary."

If you want an e-mail address that is portable and free, try some of the free-mail services available on the Web. These services allow you to access your e-mail from any Internet connection, and you can keep the same e-mail forever—or for as long as these services exist! Check *http://www.refdesk.com/freemail.html* for a list of free e-mail services or try a few of these:

- *http://www.juno.com*
- *http://www.hotmail.com*
- *https://www.netaddress.com*
- *http://www.graffiti.net*
- *http://mail.yahoo.com*
- *http://www.mail.com*
- *http://www.excite.com*
- *http://www.eudora.com*

There are even anonymous services that will make your e-mail anonymous for you. They strip your name, e-mail address, and other revealing information from any message you send. Check the EmailPrivacy.info Web site for a list of remailers (*http://www.emailprivacy.info/remailers*). Here are a few for starters:

- *http://www.jobmail.net*
- *http://www.anonymizer.com*
- *http://www.gilc.org/speech/anonymous/remailer.html*
- *http://www.makmo.com/php/mail/inviamaileng.php*

■ *The Equipment*

Before you can receive or send e-mail, you need a computer, a modem and phone line or a cable connection, and computer software that will allow you to connect and communicate with another computer. Don't get nervous about the technical details here. Think of your computer as you would your microwave oven; you don't have to know how it works in order to use it effectively.

When it comes to your Internet connection, the faster, the better. A modem is a piece of computer hardware that connects your computer to a phone line, allowing you to communicate with another computer. *Modem* stands for *modulate–demodu-late*, which is the converting of digital signals from your computer to the analog signals of your telephone line and then back into digital signals at the other end of the line.

The faster your modem, the faster you can receive and send data through the telephone line. Speeds range from 2,400 bps to 56,000 bps, although you can reach speeds of 128 kbps if you have a DSL or ISDN telephone line, which doesn't require a modem at all since the telephone line itself is digital. All you need is a network-style adapter card in your computer.

Speaking of telephone lines, more than 21 million Internet connections don't even use telephone lines anymore. Cable television service providers have taken 20 million customers away from the telephone companies. Another 500,000 connections are through satellites, and broadband wireless accounts for 537,000 connections. You will can now surf the Internet at up to 768 kpbs and receive an incoming voice call at the same time. You may still pay a premium for these services, but it is well worth it for the speed. Most e-commerce sites are designed with faster access speeds in mind, which means you will experience a much longer wait if you connect from a standard telephone line.

If you are limited to a telephone line for now but intend to surf the Net often, it pays to have a dedicated telephone line installed for your modem. Otherwise, the other members of your family may hate you, especially if you have teenagers who don't appreciate your tying up "their" telephone line. If you have only one telephone line and it has call waiting, you must turn off call waiting before logging onto your Internet service provider or online service.

■ *The Software*

In order to access the Internet, you must establish an account with either an Internet service provider (a company dedicated to offering customers direct access to the Internet and a few basic services) or a commercial online service like America Online, CompuServe, Prodigy, MSN, Earthlink, and Netzero, among others.

Commercial online services offer broad packages of value-added services that include everything from e-mail to Internet access, home page space on their servers, forums for real-time chatting with other members, and an incredible array of information resources. You pay a flat rate for unlimited access, and the software is free with a simple phone call to a toll-free number. The main advantage of using commercial online services is that they are easy to set up (essentially "plug and play") and easy to use. This is a quick solution to accessing the Internet and setting up an e-mail account, and most people start here.

Besides the wealth of value-added benefits that commercial online services provide, you can access your account from almost anywhere in the country with a local or toll-free telephone number. If you travel, being able to access your e-mail and the Internet without paying long-distance charges from anywhere in the world is a real benefit.

If you find yourself using your commercial online service primarily to access the Internet, are using very little of its value-added services, and rarely use the Internet outside of your local area, a local Internet Service Provider (ISP) may be the best way to access the Internet. You can find an ISP that offers unlimited hours of online time for free or for as little as $9 per month, and the software to get you started is usually free.

ISPs that offer free access (no charge) usually offer very limited service. It's like being invited to a free buffet where all they serve is mashed potatoes. Since most free ISPs are supported by advertisers, you will probably have to put up with banner ads, which reduce the viewable size of your Internet browser. It is sometimes better to pay for a full-service ISP and avoid getting busy signals when you dial in.

Simply look for providers in your local telephone book or in the free computer magazines you will find in the racks at your local grocery store or office supply outlet. All of the major long-distance telephone companies offer Internet access, and cable television companies offer cable modems and Web TV.

If you already have access to the Internet, here are some online ISP lists:

- *http://www.isps.com*
- *http://thelist.internet.com*
- *http://www.lowermybills.com/internet/internet.html*
- *http://www.addlebrain.com*
- *http://www.freedomlist.com*
- *http://www.freei.com*
- *http://www.netzero.com*
- *http://www.juno.com*
- *http://www.internet4free.net*
- *http://www.access-4-free.com*

Look for an ISP that is dependable and offers high-speed access. Make certain it offers technical support at least during normal business hours, preferably 24 hours a day. Most ISPs will meet your needs, but some are often overloaded, which means you may have trouble gaining access to the Internet at certain peak times of the day. Look for an ISP with a user-to-modem ratio of no more than ten to one—five to one is ideal.

One major advantage an ISP has over a commercial online service is the speed of data transfer. When America Online, MSN, CompuServe or other commercial online service is experiencing heavy usage, your data transfer is slowed down considerably. ISPs, on the other hand, usually don't have that problem.

■ *How to Find e-Mail Addresses*

Unfortunately, there is no quick and easy method of finding e-mail addresses. There are no "White Pages" listing every e-mail address on the Internet, although there are several sites that list millions. Often, the most reliable means of discovering an e-mail address is to call the person and ask. If you can't do that, there are some sites on the Internet that can help you find someone's e-mail address.

- Yahoo! People Search lists millions of e-mail addresses (including celebrities!) *http://people.yahoo.com/*

- Lycos' People Search, a list of both e-mail addresses and more than 90 million U.S. residential phone listings and addresses—*http://www.whowhere.com/*

- Global white pages and e-mail forwarding service—*http://www.bigfoot.com/*

- E-mail Finder—*http://emailfinder.com*

- Internet Address Finder with more than 5 million names—*http://www.iaf.net*

- Infospace.com includes both reverse lookup and hundreds of ways to track people down—*http://www.infospace.com*

- World E-mail Directory with more than 12 million e-mail addresses and 140+ million business and phone addresses worldwide—*http://worldemail.com*

- U.S. Search—*http://www.ussearch.com/consumer/index.jsp*

- AT&T Anywho Info for both businesses and individuals, including a reverse look-up service where you enter a phone number and it tells you who owns it—*http://www.anywho.com*

- 555-1212.com is the old, familiar telephone directory assistance but now via computer—*http://www.555-1212.com*

- PeopleSearch.net offers reverse lookup for e-mail and street addresses as well as for telephone numbers—*http://www.peoplesearch.net*

- Find mE-Mail allows you to register your old and new e-mail addresses so your friends and business contacts can find you when you change your e-mail address—*http://www.findmemail.com/*

- Like Find mE-Mail, FreshAddress.com helps people find you when you change your address—*http://www.freshaddress.com*

- Internet Address Finder—*http://www.iaf.net/*

- MESA, a meta e-mail search agent that searches other sites, including Big Foot, IAF, WhoWhere, Switchboard, Yahoo! People Search, Populus, and Usenet—*http://mesa.rrzn.uni-hannover.de/*

- Search the Usenet Addresses Database—*http://usenet-addresses.mit.edu/*

- Switchboard, a Web-based telephone directory—*http://www.switchboard.com/*

Don't neglect to check the membership directory of your commercial online service. If you have an AOL, CompuServe, Prodigy, MSN, Earthlink, or other account, you have access to millions of e-mail addresses of fellow subscribers simply by looking in the member directory.

To find e-mail addresses for specific companies, you can use some of the resources listed above or the search engines discussed in Chapter 12 to hunt down their home pages, or you can turn to the online Yellow Pages. Following are some of the resources for finding e-mail addresses for companies:

- Qwest Dex Yellow Pages on the Internet—*http://www.qwestdex.com*

- More than 16 million U.S. businesses, street-level maps for each entry, and third-party reviews of restaurants and hotels—*http://www.bigbook.com/*

- Profiles of public companies—*http://www.hoovers.com*

- The Securities and Exchange Commission's EDGAR Database of Corporate Information—*http://www.sec.gov/edgarhp.htm*

- Kompass allows access to basic business addresses free but charges for information on revenue and other subjects—*http://www1.kompass.com/kinl/en/*

- Metacrawler's Yellow Pages, White Pages, and dot.com directories—*http://www.metacrawler.com/index.html*

■ *How Can I Be Sure My e-Mail Was Read?*

Once you have sent an e-mail message, how do you know if your e-mail was received? Well, you will never know for sure, although some online service providers allow confirmation of an e-mail sent from one of their subscribers to another (for instance, AOL to AOL). The recipient may be one of those people who only checks her e-mail once a week or once a month, so you won't be sure your message was received. Once you have sent an e-mail message, it is irretrievable. You can't get it back!

Occasionally, however, an e-mail message you have sent will be returned to you like unopened mail. You will receive a rather cryptic message from the MAILER-DAEMON or POSTMASTER telling you that your mail could not be delivered as addressed. There are usually two possible reasons for this.

First, the site you were mailing to may not exist. When that happens, you get a "host unknown" message from the MAILER-DAEMON. The site part of the e-mail address (after the @ sign) must be a valid Internet site and it must be spelled correctly and sometimes must be in the right case (lower case, all capital letters, or a combination). If the host you specified in the e-mail address can't be found, your message will be bounced back to you. Double-check the address, make any changes, and try it again.

Second, the problem may be that the user name part of the e-mail address (before the @ sign) is either not spelled correctly, is in the wrong case, or the person doesn't exist. The message in this case would be "user unknown." Again, double-check the address and try again.

Occasionally, there might be a third reason for returned mail. It is possible that the receiving end is having computer problems. In that case, simply try again later. If you don't get a message from the MAILER-DAEMON or POSTMASTER, you can assume that your mail reached its destination.

There is a difference between an e-mail address and an URL (Universal Resource Locator—pronounced "earl"). An e-mail address *(pcriscito@protypeltd.com)* allows you to send a message to someone else's computer. An URL is a physical address where something is located on the Internet; you cannot send a message to an URL. The first part of an URL *(http://, ftp://, gopher://)* tells the computer what type of Internet resource you want to access:

- *http://* is a Web site

- *ftp://* is a file transfer protocol site

- *gopher://* is a Gopher search engine site

The second part of an URL is the specific type of system where the account is located *(www* for *World Wide Web)*. Depending on the structure of the network, this part may not be present.

Third is the site of the network—the school or the company or the organization *(.yahoo)*. The domain is the top-level Internet directory where the site is registered *(.com)*. The complete URL would look something like this: *http://www.yahoo.com.* This would take you to Yahoo!'s home page. To get more specific, after the *.com*, an URL can direct you to a specific file you would like to access once you reach the computer. For instance, *http://www.yahoo.com/economy* takes you immediately to the page that focuses on the economy. To read an Internet address out loud to someone, you would say, "http, colon, slash, slash, www, dot, yahoo, dot, com, slash, economy."

■ *Steps for Creating an ASCII Text File of Your Résumé*

To make sense of this topic, you must first understand the difference between a native word processing format and an ASCII text file. ASCII (pronounced "askee") is an abbreviation for American Standard Code for Information Interchange. It is a universal code that nearly all computers understand, and most e-mail messages are sent in this format. ASCII text files are very generic—they have no special fonts, margins, tabs, bold, italic, or other formatting codes added. When you create a file in a word processor (like Microsoft Word), on the other hand, the program automatically formats and saves its files in a "native" format. This native format includes codes that not all computers or software programs can read.

Don't use any special bells and whistles when you type your ASCII text résumé in a word processing program. That means don't use boldface, underline, italics, fonts, font size, margin settings, etc. Tabs will disappear when you convert your file to text, so use your spacebar to move words over instead of tabs.

Also be careful of the "smart quotes" that many word processing programs automatically place when you press the " key on your keyboard. These special characters will not translate when you save your file as ASCII text. That includes mathematical symbols, em-dashes, en-dashes, and any character that does not appear on your keyboard.

Your choices for bullets are also limited to the characters on your keyboard. Some of the better symbol choices to highlight lines of text are ~, *, +, but I recommend using paragraphs and generous white space on an ASCII résumé instead of trying to force lines into bulleted phrases. You can use special characters from your keyboard to create dividers, like a series of ~~~~ or ----------- or ===== or ********.

Do not set full justification on an ASCII résumé. Instead left justify all lines so the right margin in jagged.

Many browsers and e-mail readers are set to 60-character line lengths, but you can't control how someone else's e-mail software will format your message at the other end. If you force lines in your e-mail message to end at 60 characters, they won't display properly on someone else's smaller screen. When you type your résumé text, let your sentences "wrap" to a new line so the pasted text will adjust itself to the width of the e-mail message screen or electronic form on the Internet. Use the enter key to add extra white space between paragraphs and sections but not at the end of lines within a paragraph. That way, you can be sure the lines will break correctly and your ASCII résumé will look neat on the screen.

Don't worry about the page breaks that your word processor shows you. They won't matter once the text is pasted into your e-mail or into an electronic form on the Internet, since the text adjusts itself to fit the available space.

An ASCII résumé can be longer than one page, but remember that you have one screenful of space (about 15 lines) to grab your reader's attention and motivate him or her to click down to the next screen. You should start with a summary of your qualifications and achievements at the top of your résumé and then list your chronology of experience.

If you have already created a neat, formatted paper résumé and have saved it on your computer, it is easy to strip it of all the codes by saving it as an ASCII text file. In most word processing software, you can select "Save As" from the "File" menu and choose "ASCII Text" (or "MS DOS Text"). Remember to save the file under a new name with a "txt" extension. You don't want to save over your formatted paper résumé and lose all that hard work! See the screen shot below for the process in Microsoft Word.

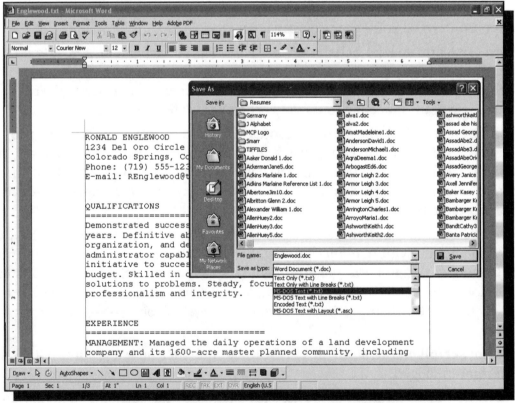

Screen shot of Microsoft Word used with permission of Microsoft Corporation.

110

In Corel WordPerfect, the best file type to select is "ASCII (DOS) Generic Word Processor," which maintains the wrap at the end of lines. If you choose "ASCII DOS Text," the file will be saved with hard returns at the end of every line of text and it won't wrap correctly when pasted into an e-mail or e-form on the Internet. Just as in Microsoft Word, after you have saved the file as a "txt" file, you must then open it again and clean up the text.

Now that you have a generic file on your computer screen, you need to be careful how you save that file, or your word processor will still add hidden codes that will make your file jumbled on the Internet. You must always remember to "Save As" from the "File" menu or your word processor's default format will take over. Repeat the instructions above for saving the file as an "ASCII (DOS) Generic Word Processor" in Corel WordPerfect or "MS DOS Text" in Microsoft Word.

On the following pages are sample résumés created in word processing programs but saved as ASCII text files. You will notice that they are nothing special to look at and are more than one page long, but hiring managers are accustomed to seeing these generic files and aren't expecting beauty. Their e-mail software will add its own font (which you can't control), so your résumé won't look quite as bad as it does on your screen.

This "ugly" ASCII résumé serves a specific purpose, and that is to get your words into a computerized résumé database or across the Internet in the body of an e-mail message. Always cut this text file from your word processor or Microsoft Notepad and paste it into the body of the e-mail message even when you are attaching a Microsoft Word document to the e-mail. We'll talk more about that on page 118.

RENA D. SMITH
1234 Wild Trap Drive
Colorado Springs, Colorado 80925
Home: (719) 555-1234
Cell: (719) 555-5678
E-mail: rena.smith@protypeltd.com

PROFILE
~~~~~~

Proven team leader with a strong background in telecommunications customer service. High-energy professional who enjoys the challenge of solving complex problems. Experienced supervisor with a reputation for team building, coaching, and mentoring. Strengths: detail oriented, flexible, analytical, self-motivated, and articulate. Experienced in Windows, MS Word, Excel, Netscape, Internet Explorer, and Vision software.

EXPERIENCE
~~~~~~

QWEST (Formerly US WEST Communications), Denver, Colorado
Excelled in supervisory positions for this telecommunications leader over a 25+ year career. Awarded numerous certificates, stock options, and bonuses for excellence in service. Achieved President's Club twice, an honor reserved for the top 10 percent of employees nationwide.

LEAD PROCESS ANALYST
Federal Government Division, Colorado Springs, Colorado (2001 to present)
Provide tier-two technical support to sales personnel in all 50 states. Handle escalated and chronic problems for federal government customers, including missed deadlines, facility issues, and special projects. Required to respond within one hour of being contacted and to provide constant feedback to all parties involved. Collaborate with internal departments and nationwide customers to manage large projects. Serve as a member of the Emergency Response Team for 14 states in the Qwest network on call 24/7 received recognition for exceptional service. Fill in for supervisors and peers during absences. Assist in coaching customer relations managers in the Federal Government Customer Care Group. Received a Certificate of Appreciation for coordinating the NATO project in 2003.

PROCESS MANAGER
Construction/Engineering Staff, Denver, Colorado (1999 to 2001)
Evaluated whether the Perigon initiative (a legacy system upgrade) and its four component projects will improve productivity, cost effectiveness, contractor accountability, accuracy and quality of work, and the ability to interface with current systems. Created 30 user guides to provide standard methods and procedures for each type of user. Assisted in deploying the new systems in 14 states, including user demonstrations and training programs. Worked closely with creative services to develop a training video to educate users on new systems; responsible for scripting, editing, music and graphic selection, and content. Collaborated with field,

construction, and engineering staff to ensure a smooth transition of work and to develop productivity measures for system users.

CONSTRUCTION MANAGEMENT CENTER SUPERVISOR
Colorado Springs, Colorado (1997 to 1999)
Supervised the Construction Management Center for the southern and western Colorado territories. Processed 400 to 500 construction jobs a month, including scheduling, monitoring, updating, tracking, and ordering of materials for the office and outside plant cable. Supervised 10 analytical associates, 2 clerical contractors, an administrative assistant, network technician, and job force manager. Worked closely with engineers, senior executives, and other internal/external customers to maintain work flow and certification standards. Responsible for reports, held orders, designed services, and database maintenance. Served as management's representative to the union; responded to discrimination, performance, and attendance issues.

CENTRAL OFFICE MANAGER
Colorado Springs, Colorado (1990 to 1997)
Managed the daily operations of a 1,500 square-mile territory with 24 offices and 3 area codes that included Colorado Springs, Glenwood Springs, and Idaho Springs. Supervised, coached, and trained 17 technicians, ensuring safety, productivity, and quality performance. Coordinated the scheduling and completion of all central office jobs. Responsible for meeting design service and delayed order commitments. Managed several projects to convert switches from analog to digital and to upgrade, add, or remove central office and power equipment. Succeeded in reducing staff overtime by changing work schedules to better meet customer demand and by cross-training technicians.

NAC/MPAC MANAGER
Colorado Springs, Colorado (1989 to 1990)
Managed the Number Assignment Center (NAC) and the Machine Performance Assignment Center (MPAC). Supervised a system support group of 15 employees responsible for assigning telephone numbers and tracking central office equipment. Collaborated with engineers to add or replace central office equipment.

NETWORK AND SWITCH OPERATIONS MANAGER
Colorado Springs, Colorado (1988 to 1989)
Investigated and resolved held order and customers complaints that had been escalated to the CEO/executive level or Public Utilities Commission. Resolved up to 90 major complaints monthly from businesses and consumers. Analyzed and improved administrative, personnel, and customer service processes. Gathered information to support the expense budget for the southern Colorado district. Coordinated training and rewrote job descriptions to increase productivity.

HELD ORDER MANAGER
Colorado Springs, Colorado (1986 to 1988)
Supervised the daily operations of five employees in the Line Network Operations Department and resolved labor/legal personnel issues. Resolved customer complaints and reduced held orders by coordinating network capacity. Interfaced with the Public

Utilities Commission on customer complaints and established a win-win relationship. Previous positions with US WEST Business Office Manager (Sales, Billing, and Ordering), Service Representative, Administrative Assistant, and Directory Assistant Operator

EDUCATION
~~~~~~
REGIS UNIVERSITY, Colorado Springs, Colorado (1980 to 1981)
Courses in business management

TRAINING
~~~~~~
Computers: Microsoft Word, Netscape

Leadership: Quality Team, Leadership Renewal, Team Problem Solving, Initial Management Course, Team Building, Project Management, Labor Relations

Training: Train the Trainer, Detailed Quality Engineering

Systems: DACSII/ISX, DMS100/200, 5ESS, NECTAS System, Special Services, Dedicated Internet Access

VOLUNTEER
~~~~~~
Coordinated Operation Back to School for five years raised more than $10,000 of school supplies for two years in a row. Falcon School District raising funds to build a life-sized sculpture for the Venetucci Tribute.

AFFILIATIONS
~~~~~~
Executive Women International, Vice President and various committees. Coordinated the national conference hosted by the Denver chapter. Selected the location, lodging, meals, hospitality room, and conference agenda.

Telephone Pioneers Group, 15 years.

Silver Key, Board of Directors, 7 years.

Pikes Peak Community College, Marketing Committee.

City of Colorado Springs, Telecommunications Policy Action Committee, 3 years.

MATTHEW C. GELLER
1234 Knoll Lane, Apt. 123
Colorado Springs, Colorado 80917
Home: (719) 555-1234
Cellular: (719) 555-5678
E-mail: mcgeller@protypeltd.com

BACKGROUND
===
Experienced Engineer with a strong background in:
* Electro-mechanical systems
* Research and development
* Hydraulics and pneumatics
* Robots and robotic controllers
* Lasers
* Optics
* Servo systems
* Precision measuring instruments
* Extremely close tolerances
Eight years of experience servicing medical equipment in the
field and factory, including x-ray, mammography, hematology, and
immunoassay systems. Experienced with FDA inspections and regula-
tions for the inspection of prototype medical equipment. Exten-
sive expertise in module integration at the system level. Collab-
orated with R&D engineers to build and test prototyped enhance-
ments to existing systems.

STRENGTHS
===
Adaptable engineer who can readily transfer skills and bring a
fresh perspective to any industry. Effective communicator with
the ability to provide exceptional customer service at all
levels. Experienced trainer with extensive hands-on and classroom
technical experience. Proficient in Windows, MS Word, Excel,
PowerPoint, Outlook, and Internet Explorer.

MEDICAL EXPERIENCE
===
ENGINEERING SERVICE TECHNICIAN (1992 to 1995)
Lorad, Inc., Danbury, Connecticut
Directed a team of eight electro-mechanical technicians in the
construction and testing of mammography and x-ray equipment.
Spent 50 percent of time providing field service to downed
equipment in a large territory with ten hospitals. Collaborated
with R&D engineers on design improvements and prototype enhance-
ments for new product lines. Met with customers to determine
liability for warranty problems and negotiated settlements.
Trained new technicians, field engineers, and customers on
equipment and tool repair. Helped write assembly and repair
procedures for factory and field service personnel. Installed and
monitored systems at hospital beta test sites. Provided technical
phone assistance to service engineers. Performed system upgrades
in both field and factory settings.

SENIOR ENGINEERING SERVICE TECHNICIAN (1987 to 1992)
Miles, Inc., Tarrytown, New York
Led a team of 15 electro-mechanical, electrical, and test technicians in the research and development of hematology and immuno-assay systems. Conducted quality control inspections of in-production and finished modules. Managed materials and production control for the entire product line. Worked closely with design engineers on product improvements and prototype development. Responsible for troubleshooting and repairing all electro-mechanical, cable, hydraulic, and pneumatic problems. Wrote all training manuals for new electro-mechanical assemblies. Trained domestic and international field engineers on electro-mechanical systems and served as an expert resource for field service engineers. Transferred systems from an R&D environment to the production plant in Puerto Rico—trained, installed, and retrofit legacy systems. Accountable for controlling inventory of parts and maintaining repair logs of systems. Installed systems at beta testing sites for FDA approval; collaborated with FDA inspectors on revisions to new systems before production release.

TECHNOLOGY EXPERIENCE
==
SENIOR FIELD SERVICE ENGINEER (1995 to 2003)
SVG Lithography, Wilton, Connecticut / ASML, Tempe, Arizona
Stationed at an Intel chip-manufacturing site in Colorado Springs in order to troubleshoot and maintain SVG lithography equipment (valued at $10 million) from component to system levels. Installed new tools as they arrived at the site, and performed lithographic testing to ensure tools meet customer specifications. Performed system upgrades and modifications at the request of customer and/or factory. Provided technical phone assistance to other sites and managed all warranty issues. Diagnosed and repaired computerized electro-mechanical systems. Maintained and tracked precision-calibrated tools used for system repairs. Trained new employees on all tool phases from module replacement to troubleshooting down to the component level. Interviewed, made hiring recommendations, supervised, and evaluated 10 engineering technicians. Prepared daily and weekly site reports and part repair logs; met with senior customer engineers daily. Wrote training manuals for certain modules and documented repair procedures. Developed an automated journal system that tracked weekly repair time using Excel.

Key Accomplishments: Helped identify a duct work error that was costing Intel $100,000 per shift because of contamination blowing up from the sub-fab. Saved Intel $250,000 by changing motor coils in the system rather than replacing the entire module. Cleaned vacuum ports, which prevented replacement of the system, saving Intel an additional $250,000. Received a Silicon Valley Group award in recognition of outstanding contributions to the MSX and REA build process.

COMPUTER TECHNICIAN / ENGINEERING TECHNICIAN (1983 to 1987)
TAD Technical Services, Poughkeepsie, New York

116

Assigned to IBM to manage a team of five electro-mechanical technicians in cabling and power supply installation on million-dollar mainframe computer systems. Served as a repair technician for all electro-mechanical, cabling, and power supply issues. Collaborated with design engineers on product improvements. Performed quality control inspections on cabling with a 98 percent defect-free rate for the entire group. Rewrote assembly procedures, enabling a reduction in build time from eight hours to four hours or less. Responsible for materials management and production control in designated area. Trained new employees on cabling and power supply system installation and quality control.

EDUCATION
==
UNDERGRADUATE STUDIES (1990 to 1993)
Duchess Community College, Poughkeepsie, New York

PROFESSIONAL DEVELOPMENT
General Industry Safety and Health (10 hours, 2001)
* OSHA/SVG Safety
* Lockout/Tag Out
* Walking and Working Surfaces
* Physical Hazards
* Job Hazard Analysis
* Chemical Hazards
* Hazardous Energies
* Egress and Fire Protection
* Electrical Safety
* Personal Protection/PPE

Micrascan Training (2001):
* Computerized Electro-Mechanical Systems
* Environmental Control Systems
* Preventive Maintenance
* Reticle Handling
* Wafer Handling
* Lithography
* Beam Delivery System
* Robotic Handling

■ *How to Compose and Send an e-Mailed Résumé*

You may be thinking, "I can do that. I'll just skip this section." Don't! Even though the process itself is pretty basic, there are a few tricks of the trade that you shouldn't miss, so please read this section completely.

You can type your entire résumé into an e-mail message from scratch, but why would you do that when you have already typed it, spell checked it, and used your word processor's grammar function? When you are composing a cover letter and/or résumé for e-mail, it is always much better to start with your word processor since you can use its powerful grammar and spell check features to make certain your document is perfect before e-mailing it to a potential employer.

After you have created this perfect résumé in your word processor and saved it in ASCII format, open the ASCII file again in your word processor. Click on "Edit" and choose "Select All." Then click on "Edit" and choose "Copy."

Open your e-mail software. After you have typed in the address where you will be sending your message and added your subject line, click on the message box so your cursor is active in the large white space. Then select "Edit" and choose "Paste." Your text will appear in the message box.

Now you are ready to attach your Microsoft Word file and click on "Send." Most e-mail programs will automatically log on for you and send your message, or you can schedule it to send later.

Here are some screen shots from MS Word and America Online to walk you through the process.

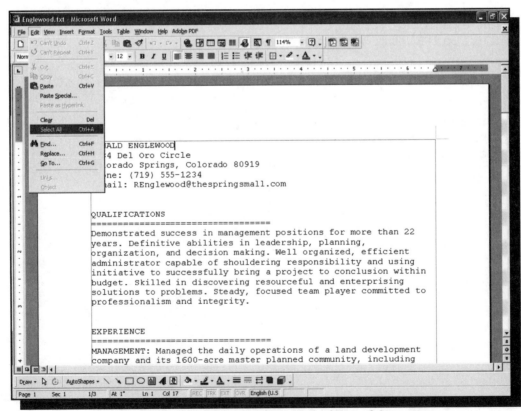

Screen shot of Microsoft Word used with permission of Microsoft Corporation.

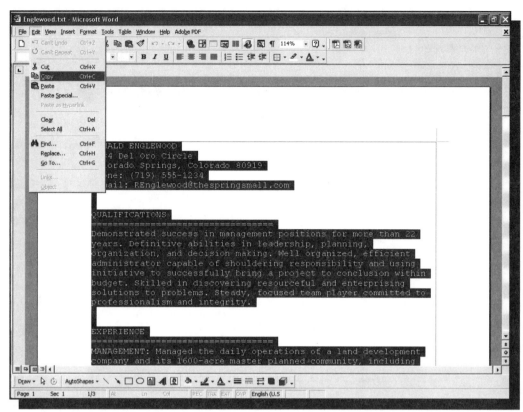

Screen shot of Microsoft Office used with permission of Microsoft Corporation.

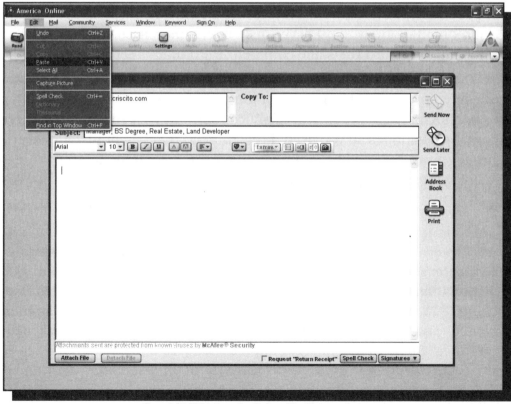

Copyright 2004, America Online. Used by permission.

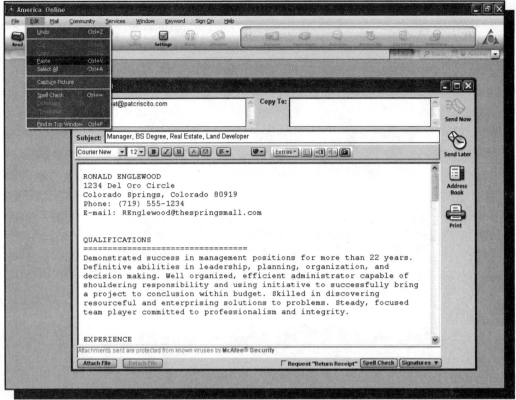

The subject line is a valuable tool for introducing who you are and what you do. Don't neglect this line. You can use it for your objective statement, to reference the job opening for which you are applying, or to show that you are updating a résumé you have sent previously. Never leave a subject line blank, since that is the hallmark of spam (or junk mail). I know that I never open e-mail messages sent to me without a subject line, and I've heard the same comment from many recruiters.

What about a cover letter? Remember that e-mail is intended to be quick, so don't precede your pasted résumé with a long-winded cover letter. A simple paragraph or two that highlights your best qualifications and tells your reader where you heard about the position is all you need. I recommend that you limit your cover letter to no more than two paragraphs, although there are exceptions to every rule in the career business. Here's a sample cover letter that you can paste before your résumé in an e-mail:

I found your posting for a Customer Service Manager (Job #12343) on the Internet at Monster.com and would appreciate your serious consideration of my qualifications. I have more than thirteen years of operations management experience that included budget analysis and tracking ($13 million), expense control, staffing, training, and customer service. I have succeeded in significantly controlling costs and maximizing productivity in all my jobs. I could also bring to this position my team spirit, ability to manage multiple priorities with time-sensitive deadlines, and strong communication skills.

Pasted below is the text version of my résumé and attached is the MS Word document as your advertisement requested. I look forward to hearing from you soon.

Sincerely, Jane Doe

Do not attach the Microsoft Word file of your cover letter to the e-mail. Always paste the text of your cover letter into the body of the e-mail message. Why? You should send only one attachment to each e-mail, and that file should be your résumé. There are still e-mail software packages that have difficulty with "zipped" (compressed) files. When you attach more than one file to any e-mail, it is automatically compressed into a single file for transmission over the Internet. At your recipient's end, you have to be confident that the person's e-mail software will automatically "unzip" the files. Although it is becoming more likely that the decompression will be automatic, I can't guarantee it in every case. For that reason, I recommend that you send only one file attached to your e-mail—your MS Word résumé. It's better to be safe than sorry.

Now, experiment. Send the résumé to yourself or a friend, print it, and see what it looks like. Also look at it on your computer screen. If the text and spacing didn't translate correctly, this is the time to fix it. Save it again and then try the e-mail one more time. Once it is perfect, you are ready to use the file in e-mail and on the Internet.

■ Sending a Binary File

You may be asking why you can't just attach a Microsoft Word file to the e-mail message and forget about this cut and paste thing. First of all, when you attach a file to an e-mail message, the recipient of your e-mail will see only what you have typed in the subject line and your brief cover letter in the message box saying that your résumé is attached. When he clicks on the icon to "Download Now," your résumé will be saved on his hard drive. Later, he will have to remember that he has a file to view, recall where he saved it on the hard drive, and then open a word processor like Microsoft Word in order to view your résumé. Wouldn't you much rather have him begin reading the text of your résumé the minute he opens his e-mail? If he wants to see the formatted version, he can always download your MS Word document and look at it later.

There is also the chance that the recipient won't have the right software to open your file, either. For many years, I have known a small, niche recruiter without a large office staff. He never invested in the Microsoft Office software, so every time he received an attached MS Word file, he would send it to me to print and then he would collect the paper printouts once a week or so. He didn't have Adobe Acrobat on his system until just last week, even though it's free at *www.adobe.com*!

Speaking of Acrobat files, many large recruiters do not like to receive PDF (Adobe Acrobat) files because they can't automatically save them in their applicant tracking software. This will eventually change as more of these software packages become capable of importing PDF files. Yahoo! Resumix will have this feature by the end of 2005.

Another reason not to send PDF files to executive recruiters is that they like to change things on résumés before they are submitted to their client companies, which they can't do with Acrobat files since they are more like a photograph of your paper résumé than a word processed file.

Sending ASCII text e-mail across the Internet is relatively painless, but attaching binary files can get complicated. First, both you and your recipient must have the same (or newer) version of the software used to create your "pretty" résumé. For instance, if you created a résumé in Microsoft Word XP and your recipient has Word 95, she won't be able to open the file at all.

What if you use WordPerfect but your recipient uses Word? The file might convert, but the format will be scrambled in many places.

What if you used a unique font to design your Word résumé, but your recipient's computer doesn't support that font? Then your résumé will adjust to a new default font, and your résumé will look different from how you created it.

These are things you can't control. You also can't control how your recipient's e-mail software decodes your MS Word file. In order to send files across the network of computers that make up the Internet, binary files must be encoded in a special way before they are sent and then decoded when they are received at the other end. Each file is broken into tiny packets of information and sent across various parts of the Web. At the recipient's end, those packets must be put back together again . . . and in the right order!

Most e-mail software will automatically encode an attached file, so it is invisible to you. However, sending between different platforms (PCs, Macintosh, UNIX) can sometimes cause problems with decoding.

There are so many things that you can't control when sending binary files across the Internet that you want to take the safest route possible. And that route is to cut and paste your ASCII text file into the e-mail message screen. Then it is okay to attach an MS Word document to the e-mail. Your reader can choose to download it or not, but you haven't lost anything because your résumé is being read right on the screen.

Let's take a look at how you attach a file in Microsoft Outlook on the next page. It is as simple as clicking on the paper clip and telling Outlook where to find the file you want to attach. That file can be stored on your hard drive, a CD-ROM, a floppy disk, or some other digital storage medium. Once you select the file, it is automatically attached to your e-mail message and ready to be sent.

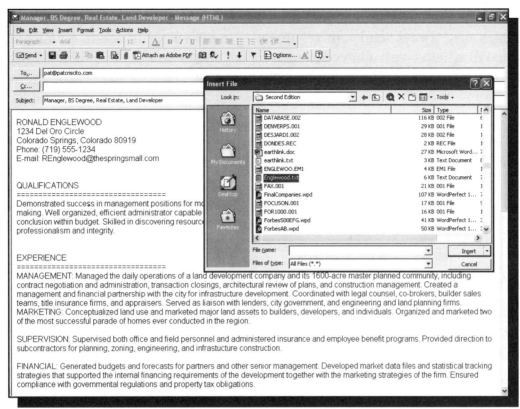

Screen shot of Microsoft Outlook used with permission of Microsoft Corporation.

■ *How to e-Mail Your Résumé Directly to a Company's Recruiter*

The same generic ASCII text file that you created can be used to send your résumé directly to a company's recruiter or human resource department. Many classified advertisements in today's newspapers list e-mail addresses or home page addresses on the Internet. When you access a company's home page and search their database of job openings, there will be a hypertext link (the highlighted text, usually blue, underlined, or made to stand out in some way) that will allow you to send your résumé directly to the company's recruiters or human resource department.

When you see an e-mail address in a newspaper advertisement, simply follow the instructions beginning on page 118 for creating and sending an e-mail message from your online service or Internet service provider. This e-mail message of your résumé is usually received by the recruiter assigned to fill the job opening or sometimes directly by the hiring manager.

After a certain period of time, usually 30 days or less, the file is uploaded to the company's main résumé database (applicant tracking system) where your résumé becomes accessible to any recruiter or hiring manager in the company who is looking to fill a position. Your résumé will remain there for as long as a year before it is purged, which means you can be considered for jobs that you hadn't even thought about during keyword searches, which of course is one of the benefits of a computerized résumé database and applicant tracking system.

Today, you will find e-mail addresses published more often than they were just a few years ago. Always send your résumé via e-mail when you see an e-mail address published in a help-wanted advertisement. This shows you are comfortable with the technology and gives you an advantage over those applicants who choose to mail a paper résumé only.

There is nothing wrong with sending an e-mail message and then following up with a cover letter and a paper copy of your résumé mailed to the address shown in the advertisement. This gives your résumé two chances to be seen, and the paper résumé allows you to show more of your personality than the boring ASCII text of an e-mail message.

■ *How to e-Mail Your Résumé for a U.S. Government Job*

If you applied for a U.S. Government position before the turn of the 21st century, you are probably familiar with an SF-171. Thank goodness that form is now dead! It was a nightmare to complete.

In its place the U.S. Government now accepts a résumé; however, it expects that résumé to have more information than a traditional, private-sector résumé. That additional information is what you once added to an SF-171— things like full mailing address of your employer with Zip code, number of hours worked per week, months and years for dates, supervisor's name and telephone number, and your pay rates.

A government résumé always requires a Social Security number and birth date. Following is an example of one such government résumé that was posted to *www.usajobs.opm.gov*. After the résumé sample, you will find a Knowledge, Skills, and Abilities (KSA) statement (for a different client) that is often required in addition to a résumé. The questions, of course, will be different for every job.

JEFFREY L. BARNES
12 East Yale Avenue #34
Denver, Colorado 80231
Home: (303) 555-1234
Cell: (719) 555-0000
Work: (303) 555-5678
E-mail: jlbarnes@protypeltd.com

SSN: 123-45-6789
Candidate Source: External

QUALIFICATIONS
~~~~~~
Experienced computer professional with a strong background in:
Data center management
Environmental systems
Data center relocation
Networking
Emergency procedures
Database management
Hardware installation
Inventory control
Process engineering

Personable team player who gains immense satisfaction from a job well done. Reliable self-starter who holds herself to very high standards and works well independently. Held a Top Secret security clearance through 2002; Secret clearance in progress.

EXPERIENCE
~~~~~~
DATA CENTER MANAGER
USA.NET Data Center
5350 South Valentia Way
Denver, Colorado 80111
Supervisor: Jane Doe
Phone: (303) 555-1234
August 2001 to present
Salary: $44,000
Hours: 40+ per week
Description: Shut down and secured the Colorado Springs data center and coordinated the disposal or shipment of all equipment to Denver. Assumed control of the Denver Data Center, including 3,200 square feet of space with 100+ racks of equipment valued at more than $10 million. Selected rack and equipment positions inside the data center ensured that power requirements did not exceed 80 percent and that racks did not overheat. Ran cable for the computer equipment SCSI, 25-pair, CAT 5, fiber, console, phone, etc. Developed and maintained an inventory of parts and equipment locations within the building. Helped to plan a proposed move of the data center, including vendor selection, cable tray layouts, power j-box connections, voltage planning, analog lines, racks, and equipment. Assisted in the successful development of a disaster recovery site with associated power configuration. Ensured that proper physical security measures were employed in a tight security environment. Responsible for authorizing either escorted or permanent access of personnel to the center. Created and updated emergency procedures and served on call 24/7 for any

issues arising with the environmental systems or access permissions. Developed and maintained a database (using MySQL, PHP, Solaris 2.8, and HTML) of technical specifications, equipment information and locations, power circuit schedules, requests for access and equipment, personnel access authorizations, incident response handling, change management records, emergency procedures, parts inventory, disposed parts log, equipment history and ticketing system, and other network information.

DATA CENTER MANAGER
USA.NET Data Center
102 S. Tejon, Suite 230
Colorado Springs, Colorado 80903
Supervisor: John Doe
Phone: (719) 555-1234
May 2000 to August 2001
Salary: $36,000 to $39,000
Hours: 40+ per week
Description: Responsible for the Colorado Springs Data Center with 2,900 square feet of space containing more than 80 racks of computer equipment. Planned and supervised the installation of an FM-200 fire system, air conditioning systems, 1800kw generator, and battery backup systems. Managed the electricians and telecom vendors who installed power circuits and phone lines. Developed clear, concise written emergency procedures for the environmental and emergency systems. Changed door codes on the cipher locks and managed access permissions. Built UNIX-based equipment to specification; controlled choice of vendors and locations of equipment to ensure that power and heat limits were not exceeded. Planned and coordinated the shipment of large equipment in and out of the data center; rigged special cabling to hoist equipment using the elevator shaft. Conducted ongoing tests on hardware parts using Solaris VTS testing software and replaced parts as required. Created an efficient inventory system for finding and retrieving hardware and software. Developed a history log of data center events, an information book that provided a centralized location for all information related to equipment in the data center, and a book of technical specifications. Created picture diagrams attached to each rack in order to prevent unnecessary opening of the racks. Maintained and renewed maintenance agreements on the battery backup systems, generators, and air conditioning units. Developed a database like the one in Denver to track technical specifications, equipment locations, etc.

SOFTWARE ANALYST, COMPUTER EMERGENCY RESPONSE TEAM
Colorado Army National Guard
State Headquarters
6848 South Revere Parkway
Centennial, Colorado 80112
Supervisor: MSG Jane Doe
Phone: (303) 555-1234
June 2000 to present
Salary: Pay Grade E-4 to E-5
Hours: 2 days a month, 2 weeks a year
Description: Completed a six-month computer information systems analyst school and continued a part-time career as a noncommissioned officer in the Army National Guard. Provide direct customer support to network users in the Directorate of Computer Security and Information Management (DCSIM). Responsible for training users, resolving system conflicts, and managing the configuration of hardware and software. Install and maintain network hardware devices, operating systems, and client-server software. Load and configure software and critical updates to Windows 2000; configure interfaces and device

drivers; update architecture databases to reflect installations and changes in software; and track software licenses. Create and remove user accounts and change passwords.

COMPUTER INFORMATION SYSTEMS ANALYST
United States Army/Computer Science School
Fort Gordon, Georgia 30905
Supervisor: NCOIC SFC John Doe
Phone: not available
November 1999 to April 2000
Salary: Pay Grade E-4
Hours: 40 per week

ADMINISTRATIVE SPECIALIST
Alabama Army National Guard
Task Force Caribbean Castle
Monte Plata, Dominican Republic
Supervisor: CSM John Doe
Phone: not available
March 1999 to April 2000
Salary: Pay Grade E-4
Hours: 60+ per week
Description: Accepted a one-year, active-duty National Guard position to provide administrative support to Task Force Caribbean Castle and Task Force Sula in Central America. Planned and coordinated morale, welfare, and recreation for all personnel. Responsible for personnel assignments, orientations, evaluations, awards, and benefits.

ADMINISTRATIVE SPECIALIST
Alabama Army National Guard
Task Force Sula
El Progresso, Honduras
Supervisor: John Doe
Phone: not available
January 1999 to March 1999
Salary: Pay Grade E-4
Hours: 60+ per week

TRAINING ADMINISTRATIVE SPECIALIST
Alabama Army National Guard
State Headquarters
P.O. Box 3711
Montgomery, Alabama 36109-0711
Supervisor: MSG Jane Doe
Phone: not available
April 1996 to March 1999
Salary: Pay Grade E-4
Hours: 2 days a month, 2 weeks a year, plus some other miscellaneous time throughout the four years
Description: Transitioned from active duty Army to part-time National Guard. Managed personnel data for 300 soldiers in the Army Physical Fitness Training program. Helped to build the training library database using Access; input more than 1,000 entries.

TELECOMMUNICATIONS OPERATOR
United States Army
Delta Company
201st Military Intelligence Battalion 30905
Ft. Gordon, Georgia
Supervisor: SSgt. John Doe
Phone: not available
August 1994 to April 1996
Salary: Pay Grade E-4
Hours: 40 per week

United States Army
HQ, 21st Theater Area Command (TAACOM)
Attn: AERIM, Unit 23203
APO, AE 09263
Panzer Kaserne
Kaiserslautern, Germany
Supervisor: MSG Jane Doe
Phone: not available
August 1993 to August 1994
Salary: Pay Grade E-3 to E-4
Hours: 40 per week
Description: Completed a four-year tour of active duty that included work with the 201st Military Intelligence Battalion and its secure messaging system, as well as DINAH operations and administrative support. Ran daily backups of the secure messaging system and ensured the proper flow of secure data to avoid system shutdowns. Transmitted, received, and distributed classified and unclassified messages and materials and trained other DINAH operators. Responsible for the destruction and disposal of secure data.

SECURITY ADMINISTRATIVE SPECIALIST
United States Army
HHD 53rd Transportation Battalion
Attn: S-2, Unit 23125
APO, AE 09227
Kleber Kaserne
Kaiserslautern, Germany
Supervisor: MSG John Doe
Phone: not available
August 1992 to August 1993
Salary: Pay Grade E-1 to E-3
Hours: 40 per week
Description: Requested security clearances and managed the daily administrative duties of the Kleber Kaserne Security Office in Kaiserslautern.

TECHNOLOGY
~~~~~~
Operating Environments: UNIX, Windows NT/2000, Solaris 2.8
Applications: MS Word, Excel, PowerPoint, Access, Outlook, Visio, Solaris VTS
Languages: MySQL, HTML, PHP, VI Editor
Hardware: Sun, Cisco routers and switches, HP, Dell, Compaq, PCs, servers, LANs, WANs, wireless networks, environmental systems, tape backups, EMC and Clarion storage arrays

EDUCATION

~~~~~~

BACHELOR OF SCIENCE, COMPUTER INFORMATION SYSTEMS (in process) Auburn University, Auburn, Alabama
Completed two years toward an undergraduate degree. Planning to return to school to finish the degree as soon as possible.

PROFESSIONAL DEVELOPMENT

~~~~~~

UNITED STATES ARMY COMPUTER SCIENCE SCHOOL
Computer Information Systems Analyst (November 1999 to April 2000)
Graduated second in class with a 99.1 percent grade point average
Completed hands-on training in:
+ UNIX and Windows NT system administration
+ Installation, configuration, and maintenance of microcomputer systems and data communication devices.
+ Installation and configuration of hard drives, video interfaces, input/output interfaces, motherboards, CISCO routers, data terminal hardware, and conducted/radiated materials.
+ Signal representation and modulation, asynchronous/synchronous transmission, and data link protocols.
+ Management of users and maintenance of user environments, network architectures, and file servers.
+ Troubleshooting data communication systems.
+ The design, installation, configuration, and initialization of LAN and WAN terminals, network security, and peripheral configurations.
+ Configuration of routers for multiple protocols, packet switching concepts and fundamentals, and LANtastic systems and bridges.
+ Defense Messaging System administration and HTML web development.

UNITED STATES ARMY AND NATIONAL GUARD TRAINING
+ Computer Vulnerability Assessment Program, 40 hours (2003)
+ Incidence Response Handling Course, 40 hours (2002)
+ Primary Leadership Development Course, 80 hours (2002)
+ Information Systems 101 Course, 40 hours (2001)
+ Microsoft Office, Phase I/II, 80 hours (1998)
+ Administrative Specialist Course, 80 hours (1998)
+ ATTRS System Course, 40 hours (1997)
+ Security Management Course, 40 hours (1992)
+ Record Telecommunications Center Operator School, 12 weeks (1992)

ESTHER JAMES
P.O. Box 12345
Colorado Springs, Colorado 80936
Cell Phone: (719) 555-1234
E-mail: esther.james@protypeltd.com

SSN: 123-45-6789

Knowledge, Skills, and Abilities
Announcement Number: OIG-2001-64, Auditor

1. Knowledge of basic accounting and auditing standards, audit procedures, and audit techniques. During my undergraduate studies, my course work included Intermediate Accounting (nine semester hours), Advanced Accounting (nine semester hours), Financial Accounting, Corporate Accounting, Nonprofit Accounting, and nine semester hours of Auditing. I have a strong understand of generally accepted accounting procedures (GAAP). I am currently enrolled in a class with my employer, USAA, on insurance accounting.

2. Ability to conduct and coordinate work in support of the audit process. My education has prepared me to conduct and coordinate work in support of the audit process. I have nearly twenty years of management experience that has required extensive coordination and scheduling of work processes. This background would translate well into the audit process.

3. Ability to collect, organize, and analyze data in logical formats. For two tax seasons, I have helped accountants collect, organize, and analyze data for both individual and corporate tax returns. This required detail-oriented thinking that greatly enhanced my ability to process data logically.

4. Ability to meet and effectively brief higher-level professionals. USAA provides insurance to officers of the uniformed services. During the past two years, I have worked closely with high-level government officials by answering their questions regarding their policies and selling additional services. I have also receive numerous TOPS awards for exceptional customer service. In addition, I conduct weekly unit briefings that include managers from within our department.

5. Skills in oral and written communications. All of my jobs have required strong verbal and written communication skills. As a store manager, telemarketer, and customer service representative, I have been required to relay information to customers and to sell products and services in an effective manner. Recently, I completed a one-year course in Writing at Work with the Insurance Institute.

Qualifications

Bachelor's degree in accounting. I completed my Bachelor of Science degree with a major in Business/Accounting with the University of Phoenix in February of 2001. My course work consisted of 36 semester hours of accounting and auditing.

One year of specialized experience. I worked through two tax seasons with accounting firms in the preparation of individual and corporate tax returns. In my other experience, I have been responsible for preparing payroll, bookkeeping, and reconciling bank statements. As a store manager in two retail businesses, I audited the books and inventory monthly and balanced cash registers nightly.

7 | Using the Internet in Your Job Search

The Internet, World Wide Web, the Web, WWW, Information Superhighway, the Net, Cyberspace—no matter what you call it, millions of employers and potential employees are accessing the Internet every day. As of this writing:

1. 81 percent of organizations with between 250 and 5,000 employees in North America have distinct corporate career sites for recruiting.

2. 96 percent of all medium-sized and large companies use the Internet for their recruitment needs.

3. Employers spend $7 billion on Internet-based recruiting, which accounts for more than one-half of the industry's spending.

4. There are more than three billion Web sites on the Internet today.

5. 16+ million résumés are currently floating online.

6. 30 percent of North American households use the Internet to search for job listings (up from 12 percent in 1998).

7. More than 5 million people search for jobs on the Internet each day.

8. Managerial workers are more likely to use online job sites, but operators and laborers are quickly adopting the use of the Internet for job searching. More than two-thirds of online job seekers are from nontechnical professions.

To grasp how important computers and the Internet have become, think about how your life would be without a telephone. The Internet has become as important to our daily lives as the telephone. Today, you can still choose to use computers or not, but in the near future, your choice will become more like deciding not to have electricity or running water. Cyberspace networking and job searching are already determining whether some people get the job they want or whether they must settle for anything they can find.

■ *What Is the Internet?*

The Internet evolved from a military research program (ARPAnet) in the late 1960s, but the government has almost no role in its operation today. It originally developed out of the tensions of the Cold War when computer networks were considered vulnerable in the event of nuclear war.

Using a set of computer protocols called TCP/IP, the original ARPAnet was created as a self-healing network. Data was placed into tiny packets, each sent with complete addressing information, so that if one route to a destination failed, the packet could be routed to another. Each packet was switched by computers along a path that would take it to its final destination, but no two packets needed to follow the same path. At the end of the path, the packets were reassembled by a destination computer. The Internet of today works in much the same way.

ARPAnet first connected four universities in the United States in 1969—Stanford Research Institute, UCLA, UC Santa Barbara, and the University of Utah. Even though ARPAnet was originally designed to allow scientists to share data and access remote computers, e-mail quickly became the most popular application, but it was still about information exchange and not user experience.

By 1983, TCP/IP had become the universal language of the Internet, and William Gibson coined the term *cyberspace* in his novel *Necromancer*. In the 1980s, the military component became a separate network and the civilian network grew under the sponsorship of the U.S. National Science Foundation, which created the NSFnet, a network of free, high-speed "backbone" lines and supercomputers. Universities, supercomputer sites, NASA, the Department of Energy, and the National Institutes of Health soon joined their networks to this network. This connection of computer networks was called the "Internet" because it interconnected many networks (try to say that fast!). It was at this time that special computers called "gateways" began to act as traffic cops of the Internet, directing messages between networks and translating protocols.

By 1990, business had entered the picture as companies began using the Internet to exchange e-mail and access files. Marc Andreesen and a group of other students at the National Center for Supercomputing Applications (NCSA) wrote the first user-accessible Web browser, called Mosaic, which was released for user platforms in September 1993. Andreesen then left to start a company called Netscape and the Internet race was on.

Today, the Internet is the world's largest computer network. In 1981, there were only 213 host computers on the Internet. Each host could provide access for one person or an entire organization. Today, the Internet links more than 250 million hosts into one massive, international information system, and the Internet has penetrated everyday life in ways no one was able to predict.

What does all this mean to you and your job search? Nearly every kind of business imaginable has established a presence in this fundamental information medium. Like television in the 1940s, the Internet has become an important communication, entertainment, educational, and employment medium. Almost any aspect of business conducted in print, in person, or on the telephone can be conducted through the Internet . . . and that includes hiring.

■ *What Is the World Wide Web?*

According to Webopedia, the World Wide Web (WWW) is "a way of accessing information over the physical computers of the Internet. It is an information-sharing model that is built on top of the Internet. Not all Internet servers are part of the World Wide Web."

The World Wide Web is not synonymous with the Internet. Webopedia says that "the Internet is a massive network of networks, a networking infrastructure. It connects millions of computers together globally, forming a network in which any computer can communicate with any other computer as long as they are both connected to the Internet."

The World Wide Web was created in 1992 at CERN (the European Laboratory for Particle Physics in Geneva), a huge Swiss research laboratory, as a project to link physicists around the world. Because of its intuitive, easy-to-use hypertext design, the Web quickly spread beyond its original users.

Today, the Web is the commercial part of the Internet. It is usually where companies place their home pages and where much of the commerce of the Internet is conducted. According to Nielsen, there are more than 4 billion Web sites and the number is growing exponentially every day. Whenever you see *http://* in a Universal Resource Locator (URL) address, you know that the address points to a Web page.

The Web is graphically oriented, meaning you can see images and hear sounds on your computer screen instead of viewing simple, boring text. Web resources are linked together, so you can click on highlighted words (hypertext) or pictures and go directly to related Web resources, which makes the Web very user friendly. These hypertext links carry you to computer sites that exist all over the Internet. One minute you may find yourself reading a document that resides on a computer in New York, and the next minute you will click on a word that sends you flying off to Australia. Using distributed hypermedia, the Web moves you effortlessly across the Internet with blinding speed. Think of the World Wide Web as a spider's web with all of the strings interconnected. The spider (you) can get to any location on the web by simply traveling along the strings.

❑ *Browsers*

In order to travel on this Web, you must have a browser, a computer software program that resides on your hard drive and allows you to read special files. Some of the better known browsers include Internet Explorer and Netscape. When you subscribe to a commercial online service, a browser is installed automatically on your hard drive when you install the program. Internet Explorer is preinstalled with the Windows operating system and ready for you to simply dial into an account and register.

All of these programs work in basically the same way. They read the files that come into your computer from other computers via the Internet and translate the HTML codes they see into pictures and words on your computer's monitor.

Most sites on the Web are free, but there are some that either charge an additional fee for their products and services or are closed to the general public. If you access a private, password-protected Web site, you will need to get access from the Webmaster of that site. Most closed Web pages also have a public area where you can find out how to access the private area.

❑ *Bookmarks*

As you visit various Web sites, you might want to bookmark the locations that you find particularly interesting. Thanks to hyperlinks, as you surf the Net, it is easy to lose track of where you are and how you got there. Although you could keep a log and write down all of the URLs (addresses) that you want to remember, most browsers offer a bookmark feature that allows you to save the address of a Web site for use later.

In AOL, for instance, simply click "Favorites" from the menu bar and select "Add to Favorites" (see the screen shot below) or click the little red heart. Most browsers will allow you to organize your bookmarks by category and save them as a file to transfer to another computer. Take time to organize your bookmarks into folders by type, that is, Job Banks, Online Networking, Career Resources, etc. When you want to return to a site, you click "Favorites" again and select the site you wish to revisit. This prevents a lot of writer's cramp and allows you to make more efficient use of your time browsing the Web.

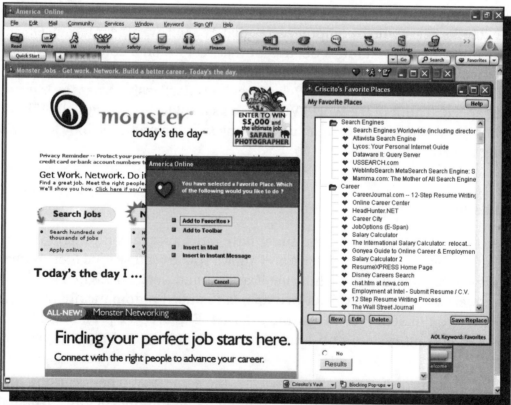

Copyright 2004 America Online. Used by permission.

■ *The How To*

The Internet has revolutionized hiring. In the pre-Internet era, the average job opening took 60 days to fill. Now the average is 30 days or less. In fact, with the introduction of services like Chimes, recruiters sometimes have as little as 30 minutes to find a candidate!

Since the cost of a 60-day job ad at Monster.com is only around $350, companies are choosing to save the $1,000 per column inch it can cost to advertise in major newspapers. Instead, they will search their own internal résumé databases, post jobs on their own Web sites first, and then select either industry-specific niche job banks or one of the larger nonspecialized sites like CareerBuilder.com.

As a job seeker, it pays to use a mixture of larger, more general job banks as well as the smaller, more specialized sites. That means, if you are a Java programmer, you should search JustJavaJobs.com (specialized) in addition to Yahoo! HotJobs. com (one of the bigger, more general career sites).

❑ *Career Hubs/Networks*

Forrester Research predicted the emergence of career networks (or hubs) in 2000. They saw these sites as places that would offer not just classified ads and résumé databases but also pre-screening, assessment, placement, and training services to help companies source, attract, screen, rank, process, check, and place candidates.

"Career networks will serve as the marketplace for human capital in the digital age," said Charlene Li, senior analyst in Media and Entertainment research at Forrester. "These one-stop career management sites will aggregate career services for consumers and recruiters alike and serve them both in an ongoing relationship."

Since the first edition of this book was published in early 1997, there have been three major changes in the Web site that facilitate job searching:

1. Consolidation—The big fish have been swallowing the smaller fish as soon as they make a name for themselves on the Internet.

2. Niche career sites have proliferated at the same time general career sites have been consolidating—specializing in executives, nurses, construction, sales, and the list goes on.

3. And the types of jobs advertised on all sites has expanded beyond technical and management positions and into ads for hourly, skilled, and blue collar workers, among others.

Today, the new "career hub" paradigm is fast becoming the model for both large and niche career sites on the Internet. There are so many résumés available via the Internet that employers can't possibly digest them all using traditional processes. They need faster and better ways to sift through résumés received in response to their job ads.

To remain competitive, career sites are adding tools for selecting and assessing candidates, including technical and aptitude testing and assessment to help companies with their initial screening process. This need is also being filled by e-commerce companies dedicated to human capital management, such as Chimes, Manpower's UltraSource (in collaboration with PeopleSoft), and Yahoo! Resumix's Hiring Gateway.

One of the most tedious employment application processes is for U.S. government jobs through *http://www.usajobs.opm.gov*. Not only do you need a specially formatted résumé (often called a Resumix—see pages 124–130 of Chapter 6) or an OF-612 Optional Application for Federal Employment, but you will also need a separate document detailing your knowledge, skills, and abilities (KSAs), SF-15 Application for Veterans Preference, security clearance forms, and others. One of the links to standard forms at *http://www.usajobs.opm.gov/forms.asp* lists nearly 60 possible forms!

For the job seeker, this means spending more time at Web sites filling out little e-forms, so you really need to pay close attention to the instructions in Chapter 6, which are highlighted below.

❑ *First, Some Basics*

The generic ASCII text file of your résumé that you created in your word processor can be used to cut and paste into various fill-in-the-blank e-forms on the Internet. For instance, when you access a company's home page and search its database of job openings, there will be a hyperlink (highlighted text or picture) that will allow you to send your résumé directly to the company's recruiters or human resource department by e-mail.

You can also use your ASCII text file to post your résumé to career hubs like Monster.com, CareeBuilder.com, Yahoo! HotJobs.com, and NationJob.com where it can be searched by potential employers at any time of the day or night. This 24-hour access to your résumé increases your exposure to potential employers. Think about how many résumés you would mail out in a normal, nonelectronic job search . . . maybe 100 at the most. By posting your résumé at a career hub, you increase your exposure thousands of times over with one simple submission!

One caution here. Don't expect to post your résumé to one database and get hundreds of telephone calls from recruiters. It doesn't happen. Less than four percent of new hires come from online résumé postings to career Web sites. Another 13 percent of total hires come directly through an employer's own Web site. My company posts résumés into online databases and then receives e-mail replies as an answering service for some clients. We get a much better response when we use these career hubs as a resource for classified ads rather than expecting blind calls from recruiters from a posted résumé.

Even though you must post your résumé into a database in order to register for the site's job agent services, you will hear from more companies if you surf the list of jobs available and apply directly to each position that interests you. Many times the career site will direct you to the hiring company's own Web site to apply for the job, bypassing the résumé you posted on the career hub itself.

There is something else you should know. Once you post your résumé online, you lose control over who sees it and where it is copied. With Internet spider technology, anyone who pays to access the résumés in a site's database can copy those résumés and post them to his own site or forward them to a newsgroup. That's why you will receive e-mail from sites you never heard of when you posted your résumé to a handful of résumé databases.

After you've found a new job, you can't call back your résumé from these sites where you didn't personally post it. If your current employer looks for candidates on the Web, then he or she could run across your résumé anywhere. Since it is nearly impossible to guarantee confidentiality of your online résumé (see Chapter 6, page 103), be prepared for questions about why your résumé is on the Internet. One of the best answers is, "My résumé has been online since I was hired here. I'm happy with my job and am not actively looking for a new position. It would have to be an awfully good offer to take me away from here."

Another frequent problem you will encounter after posting your résumé into an online database is junk mail and sometimes—thank goodness infrequently—even fraud. Illegitimate companies will join Monster.com or CareerBuilder or one of the larger career hubs and post jobs that are actually scams. For instance, there was one case where credit card thieves found unwitting money launderers through Monster.com. A European software company posted a job for a telecommuting job that required a worker to process payments using his PayPal account, who would then forward the payment to the company's contacts in the Ukraine via Western Union. The employee kept a 5–20 percent commission, but after a month or so of transactions, PayPal informed him that he had been receiving funds from stolen credit cards and he now owed PayPal $2,000. Yikes!

Fortunately this doesn't happen often. Most of the large career hubs have employed fraud detection teams to identify fraudulent postings, and once discovered, bars the "company" from posting in the future. The key is to use your common sense. If something sounds too good to be true, it usually is.

❏ *Posting Your Résumé*

Now, let's get down to the basics of how to use these Web sites. There are three ways to get your résumé onto these types of databases. The most common is an electronic form that you can complete while you are at the Internet site. With e-form sites like this one at Monster.com, you fill in each box by typing the answers one at a time, often from scratch.

Whenever possible, you want to open your ASCII text résumé in MS Word or the Notepad, copy the text you want to transfer, and paste it into the larger boxes of the e-form (like the one on the next page). That way you can ensure that there are no typographical errors. For more detailed instructions on the copy and paste procedure, see Chapter 6, pages 118–120.

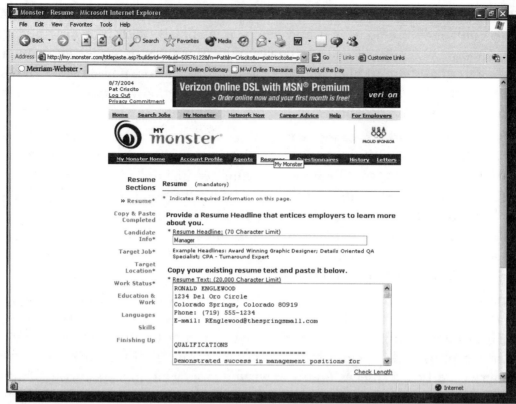

Screen shot used with permission of Monster.com.

The second way to get your résumé into a database is by uploading a copy of your formatted MS Word document, like at NationJob.com (see below).

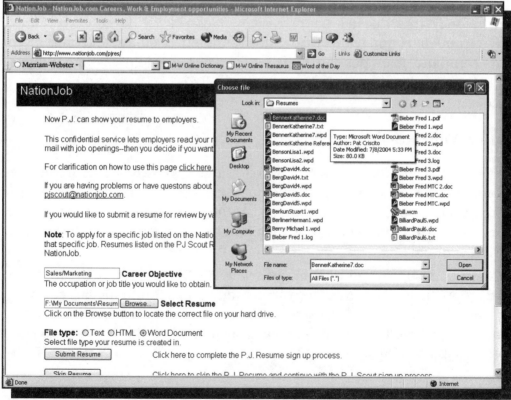

Screen shot of Microsoft Internet Explorer used with permission of Microsoft.

At NationJob.com, you are given the option of uploading your MS Word document, an ASCII text résumé, or an HTML résumé, which you will learn more about in Chapter 11. I generally recommend sending your MS Word document in cases where you are given an option. You will also have to complete an e-form on all of these sites.

The third way to get your résumé into these databases is to send an e-mail message with your résumé as the text of the e-mail message, like in the screen shot below. See Chapter 6 for complete instructions on how to cut and paste.

This option is often provided at CareerBuilder.com where you can choose between e-mailing or faxing a résumé directly to an employer. Sometimes there will even be a link that will take you to an e-form application on the company's Web site. Company sites are more likely to request an e-mailed résumé than one of the large career hubs.

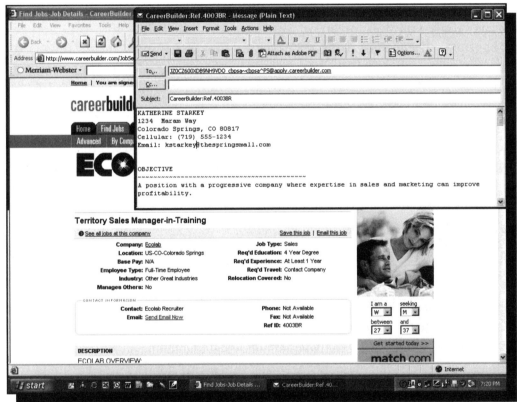

Screen shot used with permission of CareerBuilder.com.

❏ *Posting Your Résumé Directly to a Company's Web Site*

Before you even begin posting your résumé to career hubs and niche career sites, you should first post your résumé directly to the Web sites of the companies for which you would most like to work. If you don't know the URL for a particular company, then use a search engine like Google, Yahoo!, or AltaVista to find their main Web site.

Once there, you will also find current press releases, annual reports, company histories, executive profiles, and an incredible wealth of other information to prepare you for an interview or to help you determine whether or not you would really like to work for this company.

If it is well designed, somewhere on the company's home page you will find a hyperlink to job openings or their résumé database. Keep digging. Sometimes these sections are buried on deeper pages, meaning you have to hyperlink to other sections off the main home page before finding them. Once you discover the pot of gold, search the job openings by keyword and then submit your generic ASCII text file résumé by e-mail or fill out their online application for positions that interest you.

Each company's site will be designed to accept this information in a slightly different way. Some will simply list a hyperlink e-mail address for a recruiter. When you click on the hyperlink, an e-mail box will appear and you will need to cut and paste your résumé into the spaces provided. Don't forget to use the subject line to your full advantage by typing in the title of the job for which you are applying or strategic keywords. Follow the instructions beginning on page 118 for cutting and pasting your information into the e-mail message box.

Occasionally you will see an "attach" box that will allow you to attach your MS Word résumé to the e-mail message. That allows you to use the message box for a short cover letter, followed by the pasted ASCII text version of your résumé. Then attach the file of your MS Word résumé to the e-mail message. Follow the instructions beginning on page 123 for attaching a file to an e-mail message.

Other times, you will be asked to fill in boxes on an electronic form that requests specific information. You can still cut and paste some of the larger blocks of text from your ASCII file (see pages 118–120 for instructions). Avoid retyping information anytime you can, since it introduces the possibility of spelling errors. When you can cut and paste from the file that has already been spell checked by your word processor and, hopefully, proofread several times, your e-mail will be of higher quality, which reflects favorably on you.

When you have completely filled in the e-form (don't leave out any information the form says is mandatory), there will be a button or highlighted text that allows you to submit the information directly to the company's computer. In most of these cases, your résumé is e-mailed to a specific person, usually the recruiter assigned to fill the job opening or sometimes directly to the hiring manager.

One of the pet peeves of corporate recruiters and headhunters alike is receiving résumés for which the applicant isn't qualified. They are innundated with résumés every day and get irritated quickly when they waste time sorting through résumés looking for the most qualified applicants. It's okay to apply for a job where you have most of the qualifications, even if you don't have them all. Just don't randomly apply for a job simply to get your résumé into a company's database when you aren't even remotely qualified for the job. You don't want to develop a "reputation" in a company's HR department.

After the recruiter has finished with your résumé (usually when the job is filled—hopefully by you—or you are eliminated from consideration), the file is then forwarded to the company's main résumé database (applicant tracking system) where your résumé becomes accessible to any recruiter or hiring manager in the company who decides to perform a keyword search to fill a position. Your résumé will continue to float in this cyberspace for a specified period of time (usually six months to a year, although sometimes indefinitely) before being purged.

Set up a system for keeping track of the expiration dates of your résumé. Most résumé databases, job banks, and companies keep your résumé for only a specific length of time. Most will keep your résumé for a year, but there are some that will only store your résumé for 30 to 90 days. Always check each Web site for its individual storage policies.

After posting thousands of résumés for my clients and then watching the responses as they come through our e-mail system, I have discovered that the life expectancy of a hot résumé is less than two weeks. In a search of a résumé database, recruiters are shown résumés that match their keywords in date order. After your résumé has been posted for two weeks or so, recruiters begin to assume that you have been approached by some other company already. That's why you will see a burst of response to your online posting in the first 72 hours. Then it will trickle down to nothing by the end of 30 days.

To keep your résumé "fresh," log on to the job site and edit your résumé often. Some sites allow you to "renew" instead of "edit" your résumé. Every time you access your résumé, it jumps to the top of the search results. Do this every couple of weeks, or more often if your responses begin to slow.

Many companies that use computerized applicant tracking systems generate automatic letters of acknowledgment that will usually tell you how long they will keep your résumé. For instance, in a recent letter mailed to one of my clients by Hewlett-Packard's automated applicant tracking system, she was informed that her résumé would be kept in the computerized database for six months and checked for a possible match with each job opening that became available. At the end of the six-month period, it was possible for her to call the Employment Response Center and request that her résumé be kept on file for another six months, but it was up to her to call. These options for renewing your résumé without resubmitting it will disappear if you are past the deadline. Make a note of the date your résumé will expire on each database. Back up a week or so to give yourself time to renew or resubmit it and write a reminder on your calendar.

Since 81 percent of organizations in North America with between 250 and 5,000 employees have distinct corporate career sites for recruiting, it is impossible to list the Web sites of all companies in this book. Instead, use search engines to find the companies that interest you, or use some of the meta-sites in Chapter 9 that track public and private companies on the Web.

■ *Résumé Databases and Job Banks*

A résumé database is a file of résumés stored electronically on a computer. Employers pay a fee to search the résumé databases on the Internet when they need to fill a particular position. Résumé databases are similar to the ones that are maintained by companies that use applicant tracking systems (scanned résumés, faxed résumés, e-mailed résumés, and e-forms combined into one database). The difference is that

Internet résumé databases are available to any company who will pay the service to access the database, while the other is more proprietary (used only by the one company who owns the database).

Job banks, on the other hand, are like help wanted ads, a place where job openings are posted. They will almost always maintain a résumé database for their employer clients as well. That way you can both search for job openings and post your résumé.

So, what types of companies are posting their job openings in these job banks? About 45 percent of them are in the computer, scientific, or technical industries, which means that the job openings they are posting tend to be more technically oriented. When I wrote the first edition of this book in 1997, almost all job postings online fell into this category. Today, however, job openings are being posted across the board in every industry and level from upper management to laborers.

Not counting corporate Web sites, there are more than 40,000 sites on the Internet where you can either post your résumé or search for job openings. Rather than turn this book into a "link" book that will be out of date the minute it hits bookstores, I have chosen instead to keep the links live on my personal Web site at *www.patcriscito.com.* The links are divided into industries so you don't have to waste time sifting through Web sites that aren't related to your current search.

All of the URLs listed on the Web site are periodically checked to make sure they are still working, and new ones are added every month. However, the Internet is ever changing, so be prepared for a few dead links. Remember that you can try to delete all of the Internet address after the *.com* and attempt to reach the home page. Then you can hyperlink deeper into the site. If that doesn't work, it is also possible to visit the following meta-sites to find lists of career-related Internet addresses:

Craig's List . . . . *http://www.craigslist.com*
HR-Guide.com . . . . *http://hr-guide.com*
Job-Hunt.org . . . . *http://www.job-hunt.org*
JobHuntersBible.com . . . . *http://www.jobhuntersbible.com/jobs/links.shtml*
PatCriscito.com . . . . *http://www.patcriscito.com*
Rensselaer Polytechnic Institute Career Resources *http://www.rpi.edu/dept/cdc/student/careeropps.html*
The Riley Guide: A to Z Index . . . . *http://www.rileyguide.com/atoz.html*
The Riley Guide International Job Opportunities . . . . *http://www.rileyguide.com/intlbus.html*
SAT UK Recruitment Guide . . . . *http://www.recruit-online.co.uk/*
TekBay . . . . *http://www.Tekbay.com*
Work Index.com . . . . *http://www.workindex.com/exthome.asp#HR_Index*
WorkTree.com . . . . *http://www.worktree.com*

❑ *The Big Six Career Hubs*

There are a few sites that deserve a listing here. These sites have either been around for a while or are so large that they are worth checking out first. They tend to have more jobs listed, represent more companies, and have larger résumé databases, which attract even more companies.

As I mentioned earlier, there has been an incredible amount of consolidation of career sites over the past seven years since the first edition of this book was printed.

CareerMosaic merged with Headhunter.net, which was purchased by CareerBuilder. com, and the list goes on.

The benefits to you of this consolidation include more job listings, more résumés to attract more employers, and value-added services like chat rooms, company profiles, networking opportunities, career advice, salary surveys, résumé help, samples, résumé distribution, and access to career experts, to name just a few.

The following sites are a good place to start, but don't neglect posting your résumé to or looking for jobs in the niche sites that you will find on my Web site.

America's Job Bank . . . . *http://www.ajb.dni.us/*

A service of the United States Department of Labor and more than 1,800 state Employment Service offices, America's Job Bank is one of the largest career hubs on the Internet. The site is guided by the U.S. Department of Labor's vision for the American's Labor Market Information System, the CareerOneStop, a collection of electronic tools managed as a federal-state partnership and operated through grants and partnerships with state and private sector organizations. Only a small percent of the jobs listed on the site are in government. The rest are in the private sector. There is no charge to either the employers who list their job vacancies or to job seekers, because each state's Employment Service program is funded through unemployment insurance taxes paid by employers. A companion site called America's Career InfoNet *(www.acinet.org)* offers wage and employment trends, occupational requirements, state-by-state labor market conditions, and an extensive career resource library. The site offers contacts to millions of employers nationwide.

CareerBuilder.com . . . . *http://www.careerbuilder.com*

Founded in 1995 as NetStart, CareerBuilder launched its Internet services in 2000, expanded by purchasing Headhunter.net in 2001, and launched exclusive alliances with AOL in 2004 and MSN in 2004. CareerBuilder has surpassed its competitors in job search traffic and became one of the leaders in the online recruitment industry. It now commands about 45 percent of the market share for job postings, the highest in the industry. CareerBuilder offers job seekers a Career Resource Center, Résumé Distribution, Brainbench Skills Certification, and Personal Salary Reports, among other services. The Personal Search Agent feature allows you to track jobs that match your skills and preferences precisely. You can also have your Personal Search Agents e-mail to you the results of your searches daily or weekly.

Yahoo! HotJobs.com . . . . *http://hotjobs.yahoo.com*

HotJobs was acquired by Yahoo! in early 2002 and has since grown to one of the largest career hubs on the Internet. Job seekers voted HobJobs the "Best General Purpose Job Board for Job Seekers." Yahoo! also purchased the Resumix applicant tracking software and developed the Hiring Gateway to help companies manage their human capital. Users of HotJobs can search for jobs by keyword, job category, location, experience level, or a combination of any of the above. Personal job search agents match a job seeker's criteria with the latest job postings and send e-mail back to the job seeker. If you want to keep your search confidential from your current employer, HotJobs allows you to block some or all of its member companies from viewing your résumé with the "HotBlock" feature. To help you with online networking, HotJobs gives you access to communities varying by industry where you can chat and develop relationships with workers in member companies.

Monster.com . . . . *http://www.monster.com*

Everyone has heard about the "monster"! The flagship brand of TMP Worldwide, Monster.com has 20 sites worldwide and is considered one of the world's leading online career networks. Job seekers can search Monster's database of more than 800,000 job opportunities offered by 130,000+ employers and set up job search agents to search postings by location, keyword, job type, and job category. Results can be delivered via e-mail as often as you choose. You can input your résumé using Monster.com's résumé builder form, cut and paste an ASCII text résumé, or upload an MS Word résumé. You can create and store different versions of your résumé in your My Monster home page to target different types of jobs or specific employers. Monster.com has a three-tiered résumé privacy technology that gives job seekers complete control over who may access their personal information. In addition to the job bank and résumé database, Monster.com has a unique dynamic content delivery that lets you customize your My Monster home page for a more personalized and meaningful online experience. Job seekers can choose topics of interest, and Monster. com will automatically pull articles and advice related to those interests from its thousands of pages of content. The range of topics includes career change, managing your boss, life/work balance, time management, interviewing, work and health, self-assessment, relocation, and much more.

NationJob . . . . *http://www.nationjob.com*

NationJob was initially formed as the National Employment Wire Service Corporations in California in 1988. The original business of the company was to advertise job openings on stand-alone personal computers placed in college career centers. The company's network of sites grew with the purchase of competitors, and the company began offering service via the Internet in January 1995. A November 1993 *Wall Street Journal* article recognized NationJob's privacy policy as one of the best in the industry. In a study conducted by the World Privacy Forum, NationJob was named as one of the top three companies best at protecting private information. NationJob offers P.J. Scout, a personal job search agent that sends job seekers a list of openings that meet their keyword-defined requirements. Even though NationJob was purchased by Resumix, which was subsequently purchased by Yahoo! NationJob has continued to maintain its separate identity.

USAJobs . . . . *http://www.usajobs.opm.gov*

Do you want to work for the U.S. government? Then this is the site for you. USAJobs is the official site of the United States Office of Personnel Management. It is your one-stop source for federal jobs and employment information. Many federal agencies fill their jobs like private industry by allowing applicants to contact the agency directly for job information and application processing. Most federal agencies are responsible for their own hiring actions. While the hiring process is now very similar to that in private industry, there are still significant differences due to the many laws, executive orders, and regulations that govern federal employment. Even the résumé requirements are different (see the Federal résumé at the end of Chapter 6). The USAJobs Web site features an online résumé builder that allows job seekers to create online résumés specifically designed for applying for federal jobs. Read each job's application requirements very closely. There are always additional documents needed besides your résumé.

8 Career Resources on the Web

Expectations of employers have changed drastically since the 1990s. They fully expect you to know who they are, what they do (or sell), and who their competition is long before you arrive for an interview. "When I talk to a candidate, I expect them to be a little more knowledgeable about my business and industry," says David Pritchard, Microsoft's senior director of recruiting. "Our expectations are higher now when we ask candidates what questions they have for us." Candidates who are prepared stand head and shoulders above the competition.

Before an interview, you should know what the company sells, who its customers are, how healthy it is financially, and something about its culture. What if you could quickly discover how many employees the company has, its current press releases, and financial statements? Wouldn't you be better prepared for an interview if you could conduct a bit of competitive intelligence or uncover a need that your particular skills could meet? That's what Internet research can help you do, and this chapter is designed to teach you how to get that information fast.

This chapter will also address the plethora of career resources that has grown exponentially since the first edition of this book was published in 1997. You can now find just about any information on the Internet you can imagine, including salary surveys, personality assessments, résumé help, interview coaching, career counseling, résumé distribution services, newsletters, and the list goes on.

■ *Everything You Always Wanted to Know About a Job Search*

It's out there! No matter what your question, there is an answer on the Web. In fact, nearly every career site on the Internet offers more than just a place to look for jobs or post your résumé. All of the large career hubs offer a wealth of information to help you make career decisions. Some even hire experts to answer your questions personally.

The following lists are the tip of the iceberg when it comes to career resources online. When you use the links mentioned in Chapter 6, keep your eyes open for unique career resources offered as value-added services through each site. Some of the resources are industry specific and others simply link to the sites listed here.

General Career Resources

America's Career InfoNet . . . . *http://www.acinet.org/acinet*
Ask the Headhunter . . . . *http://www.asktheheadhunter.com*
CareerBuilder.com . . . . *http://www.careerbuilder.com/*
Career Journal by The Wall Street Journal . . . . *http://www.careerjournal.com*
Career Resource Center . . . . *http://www.careers.org*
CareerNFOSource . . . . *http://mooni.fccj.org/~gharr*
The Catapult on JobWeb . . . . *http://www.jobweb.org/catapult/catapult.htm*
Excite Careers . . . . *http://www.excite.com/careers*
Experience Advice and Info . . . . *http://www.experience.com/topics*
Hot Jobs . . . . *http://www.hotjobs.com*
Hr-esource . . . . *http://www.hr-esource.com*
JobHuntersBible.com . . . . *http://www.jobhuntersbible.com*
JobSeekerNews.com . . . . *http://www.jobseekernews.com*
Monster.com . . . . *http://www.monster.com*
Nation Job . . . . *http://www.nationjob.com*
Review.com . . . . *http://www.review.com/career*
Quintessential Careers . . . . *http://www.quintcareers.com*
SHRM . . . . *http://www.shrm.org*
Vault.com . . . . *http://www.vault.com*
WetFeet.com . . . . *http://www.wetfeet.com*
Yahoo Careers . . . . *http://dir.yahoo.com/Business_and_Economy/Employment_and_Work*
The Riley Guide . . . . *http://www.rileyguide.com*

Hiring Trends

America's Career InfoNet . . . . *http://www.acinet.org/acinet/default.asp*
America's Labor Market Information System . . . . *http://www.doleta.gov/almis/index.htm*
Bureau of Economic Analysis . . . . *http://www.bea.doc.gov*
Business 2.0 . . . . *http://www.business2.com*
Career Magazine . . . . *http://www.careermag.com*
Exec-U-Net Hiring Trends . . . . *http://www.execunet.com/markettrend.cfm*
Fast Company Magazine . . . . *http://www.fastcompany.com*
GoinGlobal . . . . *http://www.goinglobal.com/*
New Work News . . . . *http://www.newwork.com*
STAT-USA . . . . *http://www.stat-usa.gov*
U.S. Bureau of Labor Statistics . . . . *http://www.bls.gov*
U.S. Census Bureau . . . . *http://www.census.gov*
U.S. Department of Labor . . . . *http://www.dol.gov*
U.S. Department of Labor Employment and Training Administration . . . . *http://www.doleta.gov*
U.S. Workforce . . . . *http://usworkforce.org*
Veterans' Employment and Training Service . . . . *http://www.dol.gov/dol/vets*
Wall Street Journal Careers . . . . *http://www.careerjournal.com*

Occupational/Career Guides

America's Career InfoNet . . . . *http://www.acinet.org/acinet/default.asp*
Career Guide to Industries . . . . *http://www.bls.gov/oco/cg*
Careers Online Virtual Careers Show . . . . *http://www.careersonline.com.au/show/menu.html*
Exploring Occupations from the
    University of Manitoba . . . . *http://www.umanitoba.ca/counselling/careers.html*
JobProfiles.com . . . . *http://www.jobprofiles.org/index.htm*
Occupational Outlook Handbook . . . . *http://www.bls.gov/oco*

Occupational Outlook Quarterly . . . . *http://www.bls.gov/opub/ooq/ooqhome.htm*
Vault.com . . . . *http://www.vault.com*

Career Planning and Assessments

Advisor Team Temperament Sorter . . . . *http://www.advisorteam.com/default.html*
Assessment.com . . . . *http://www.assessment.com*
Career Development Manual, University of Waterloo . . . . *http://www.cdm.uwaterloo.ca/*
Career Center at Berkeley . . . . *http://career.berkeley.edu/*
Career Hub . . . . *http://www.careerhub.org/home.html*
Career Interests Game . . *http://career.missouri.edu/modules.php?name=News&file=article&sid=146*
The Career Key . . . . *http://www.careerkey.org/english/*
Career Manager, U.S. Department of the Interior . . . . *http://www.doi.gov/octc/index.html*
Career OneStop . . . . *http://www.careeronestop.org/TESTING/TestingAssessmentHome.asp*
CareerBuilder . . . . *http://www.careerbuilder.com*
CareerPerfect . . . . *http://careerperfect.com*
Employment Guide . . . . *http://www.employmentguide.com*
Excite Career Planning Services . . . . *http://www.excite.com/*
Fortune . . . . *http://www.fortune.com/fortune/careers*
HotJobs . . . . *http://www.hotjobs.com/htdocs/tools/tests/index.html*
HumanMetrics *http://www.humanmetrics.com/cgi-win/JTypes2.asp*
iVillage Career Quiz . . . . *http://www.ivillage.com/quiz/*
Jobs for America's Graduates . . . . *http://www.jag.org*
Job Profiles.org . . . . *http://www.jobprofiles.org/index.htm*
JobFutures (Canada) . . . . *http://www.jobfutures.ca*
JobHuntersBible.com . . . . *http://www.jobhuntersbible.com*
Keirsey Character and Temperament Sorter . . . . *http://www.keirsey.com*
Mind Tools . . . . *http://www.mindtools.com/index.html*
Motivational Appraisal of Personal Potential . . . . *http://www.assessment.com/*
My Future Career Toolbox . . . . *http://www.myfuture.com/t3_career/t3ct_workquizzes.html*
NextSteps.org, Youth Employment Center . . . . *http://www.nextsteps.org*
Occupational Information Network . . . . *http://www.onetcenter.org/IP.html*
Princeton Review Online . . . . *http://www.review.com/career*
Riso-Hudson Enneagram Type Indicator *http://www.9types.com/rheti/homepage.actual.html*
QueenDom *http://www.queendom.com/index1.html*
Quintessential Careers . . . . *http://www.quintcareers.com*
Self-Directed Search . . . . *http://www.self-directed-search.com/index.html*
TypeFocus on Careers . . . . *http://www.typefocus.com*
U.S. News Self-Evaluation Questionnaire . . . . *http://www.usnews.com/usnews/nycu/work/wocciss.htm*

Employment Law

ACLU . . . . *http://www.aclu.org/issues/worker/hmwr.html*
Employee Rights *http://www.aclu.org/library/pbp12.html*
HR Esquire . . . . *http://www.hresquire.com/*
HR.BLR.com . . . . *http://hr.blr.com*
Immigration-Related Unfair Employment Practices . . . . *http://www.usdoj.gov/crt/osc/index.html*
Legal Database . . . . *http://www.legal-database.com/laborlaw.htm*
Legal Information Institute . . . . . . *http://www.law.cornell.edu/topics/employment_discrimination.html*
U.S. Equal Employment Opportunity Commission . . . . *http://www.legaldirectory.ws/Labor_Law/*
Employment_Law/default.aspx
Workplace Fairness . . . . *http://www.workplacefairness.org/*

Salary Research

Abbott, Langer & Associates . . . . *http://www.abbott-langer.com*
About.com . . . . *http://jobsearch.about.com/library/blsalary.htm*
Monster Career Advice . . . . *http://content.monster.com/*
Aviation Today, Annual Salary Survey *http://www.aviationtoday.com/reports/amsalary99.htm*
Bureau of Labor Statistics . . . . *http://www.bls.gov*
CareerBuilder . . . . *http://www.careerbuilder.com*

CompGeo Online . . . . *http://www.claytonwallis.com/cxgonl.html*
Datamaster Salary Survey . . . . *http://www.datamasters.com/survey.html*
EETimes.com, Electrical Engineering Salary Surveys . . . . *http://www.eet.com/salarysur*
NSPE Engineers . . . . *https://nspe.salaries.com/pls/nspep/survey_frontend.homepage*
Homefair.com Salary Calculator . . . . . . *http://www.homefair.com/homefair/calc/salcalc.html?type=to*
HotJobs . . . . *http://www.hotjobs.salary.com*
iSeek (MN) . . . . *http://www.iseek.org*
JobStar's Salary Surveys . . . . *http://jobstar.org/tools/salary*
kForce Salary Survey *http://www.kforce.com/kforce/2000salary.htm*
Monster.com Salary Center . . . . *http://salarycenter.monster.com*
Nation Job . . . . *http://nationjob.salary.com/*
The Real Rate Salary Survey . . . . *http://www.realrates.com/ssearch.htm*
Romac International, Experience on Demand Salary Survey . . . . *http://www.experienceondemand.com*
Salary Expert . . . . *http://salaryexpert.com/*
Salary Source . . . . *http://www.salarysource.com*
Salary Wizard . . . . *www.salary.aftercollege.com*
Salary.com . . . . *http://www.salary.com*
U.S. Department of Labor, Bureau of Labor Statistics . . . . *http://www.bls.gov*
Vault.com, The Insider Career Network . . . . *http://vault.com*
Wage Web . . . . *http://www.wageweb.com*
Wages.com.au . . . . *http://www.wages.com.au/*

Relocation Guides

AfterCollege . . . . *http://www.aftercollege.com*
CareerBuilder . . . . *http://www.careerbuilder.com*
CNN/Money:Real Estate . . . . *http://money.cnn.com/real_estate/index.html*
Excite . . . . *http://realestate.excite.com/*
Homefair.com . . . . *http://www.homefair.com*
MonsterMoving.com . . . . *http://www.monstermoving.monster.com/*
Nation Job . . . . *http://nationjob_com.vanlines.com/cb/*
Realtor.com . . . . *http://www.realtor.com*

Career Fairs

Career Fairs . . . . *http://www.careerfairs.com*
CareerBuilder . . . . *http://www.careerbuilder.com*
Career Fairs Global. . . . . *http://www.cfg-inc.com*

Interviewing

CareerBuilder . . . . *http://www.careerbuilder.com*
CareerPerfect . . . . *http://careerperfect.com*
Career City Interview Tips . . . . *http://www.careercity.com/content/interview/index.asp*
GoinGlobal . . . . *http://www.goinglobal.com/*
HotJobs . . . . *http://www.hotjobs.com/htdocs/tools/index-us.html*
Interview Network . . . . *http://www.pse-net.com/interview/interview.htm*
Interviewing Tips Links . . . . *http://www.jumpstartyourjobsearch.com*
Job-Interview.net . . . . *http://www.job-interview.net*
Monster.com . . . . *http://content.monster.com*

Reference Checking

Allison & Taylor . . . . *http://www.allisontaylor.com/*
Documented Reference Check . . . . *http://www.badreferences.com*
HotJobs . . . . *http://www.hotjobs.com/htdocs/tools/index-us.html*
References, etc. . . . . *http://www.references-etc.com*

Résumé Distribution

There are services that will "blast" your résumé via the Internet to hundreds or thousands of recruiters and employers at a time. Since they are not sending your résumé in response to an advertised opening, the response will be similar to direct mail campaigns—3 percent to 5 percent at the most. All of these résumé distribution services will charge you a fee.

To increase the effectiveness of this type of campaign, make sure that the service targets companies based on your geographic preferences, industry classification, and/or preferred job title. Peter Weddle (*www.weddles.com*) recommends going to a résumé distribution service's Web site and clicking the "For Recruiters" button and not the "For Applicants" button. If a recruiter is allowed to complete a profile of the kinds of résumés he or she is looking for, then the odds are better that yours will hit the right target. You don't want to use a distribution service that doesn't target your industry, geographical preferences, or areas of specialty.

Here are a few of the more popular services:

CareerPerfect	*http://careerperfect.com*
EmailMyResume	*http://www.emailmyresume.com*
Profile Research	*http://www.profileresearch.com*
Résumé Agent	*http://www.resumeagent.com*
Résumé Broadcaster	*http://www.resumebroadcaster.com*
Résumé Machine	*http://www.resumemachine.com*
Résumé Mailman	*http://resumemailman.com*
Résumé Post Engine	*http://resumepostengine.com*
Résumé Rabbit	*http://www.resumerabbit.com*
Résumé Stork	*http://www.resumestork.com*
Résumé Zapper	*http://www.resumzapper.com*
ResumeSafari.com	*http://resumesafari.com*
ResumExpress	*http://resumexpress.com*
ResumeZapper.com	*http://resumezapper.com*
Target Résumé	*http://www.targetresume.net*
Your Missing Link	*http://www.yourmissinglink.com*

Diversity Resources

Advancing Women	*http://www.advancingwomen.com/awcareer.html*
Asia-Net	*http://www.asia-net.com*
Asian Professional Exchange	*http://www.apex.org*
The Black Collegian Online	*http://www.black-collegian.com*
Diversity/Careers Online	*http://www.diversitycareers.com*
Diversity Employment Solutions	*http://www.my-des.com/*
Hispanic Alliance for Career Enhancement	*http://www.hace-usa.org*
HotJobs	*http://hotjobs.yahoo.com/jobseeker/diversity/*
iHispano	*http://www.iHispano.com*
iVillage (Women)	*http://www.ivillage.com/workingdiva*
Latin America Professional Network	*http://www.latpro.com*
Saludos	*http://www.saludos.com*
WorkplaceDiversity.com	*http://www.workplacediversity.com/*

Executive Research

6FigureJobs.com	*http://www.6figurejobs.com*
American Society of Association Executives	*http://www.asaenet.org*
Exec-U-Net	*http://www.execunet.com*
IMCOR Portable Executives	*http://www.imcor.com*

■ *Researching Potential Employers*

Using the search engines described in Chapter 12, you can find a wealth of information on company Web sites and in online newspapers, magazines, and databases, including annual reports, press releases, company histories, products and/or services, numbers of employees, ownership, and other information that will be invaluable during your interview.

Imagine going to an interview armed with the company's latest sales figures, product development ideas, opportunities, strengths, and weaknesses. What if you knew the latest trends and competitors in your industry? This kind of information would give you a definite competitive advantage during the interview.

How do you access this information? You simply type in the keywords for your search (a company name or topic) and send the search engine to do its job. You may have to narrow your search if you end up with 200,000 hits, but the first few pages of the search results should be sufficient to get you started.

You will be much more successful finding information on public companies than private ones, since publicly held companies must reveal their financial information to stockholders and to the Securities and Exchange Commission. Larger companies make bigger waves, so you will find more information about them in publicly accessible sources, like newspapers and industry journals.

Begin with the company's own Web site, but don't stop with their job listings. Check every section of the company's site for press releases, mission statement, annual report, and awards. Make sure you leave the site with information about the company's personnel, history, products, basic structure, financial health, organizational hierarchy, and reporting structure. Pay close attention to the design of the site, since it will tell you a little something about their culture or philosophy—funky, young, contemporary, cutting edge, traditional, or conservative.

It is very impressive at an interview to know what a company's competitors are doing, so don't limit your search to the company itself. Try searching by product or industry, for example, pharmaceutical, and not just Merck or Eli Lily.

Use the following terms as your search criteria in any search engine, and you will be amazed at the amount of inside information you can find on a company: *blog + company name* (don't forget to use the + sign, and of course, replace the words "company name" with the name of the company).

A number of companies even allow their employees to create Web pages where you can learn a lot about a company's culture. You can send e-mail messages back and forth to these same employees and develop networking contacts within the company.

University archives are another incredibly rich source of information about almost any topic. They can be accessed via the Internet just like the company information above. Simply search by company name or topic, and you will find everything from information databases to student theses on almost any subject imaginable. While searching for information on McCormick seasonings, I recently ran across a term paper in a university archive that covered the company's history in great detail. This kind of information will strengthen your performance during an interview and help you decide whether or not a particular company is your kind of place.

After you have researched what the company wants you to know about itself—which is what you find at its own Web site—do more searching to discover what other people are saying about it as well. The following Web sites will provide you with additional information on individual companies and/or industries.

AnnualReports.com .... http://www.annualreports.com/
Argus Clearinghouse .... http://www.clearinghouse.net
Better Business Bureau .... http://www.bbb.org
Corporate Information .... http://www.corporateinformation.com
CorpTech Database of 50,000 High-Tech Companies .... http://www.corptech.com
Dow Jones .... http://dowjones.com
Dun & Bradstreet .... http://www.dnb.com
Eliyon Technologies .... http://www.eliyon.com
Fortune Magazine .... http://www.fortune.com
Hoover's Online .... http://www.hoovers.com
Intellifact Research .... http://www.intellifact.com
Monster.com's Company Research .... http://company.monster.com
PRNewswire .... http://www.prnewswire.com
The Public Register's Annual Report Service (PRARS) .... http://www.prars.com
RefDesk Facts on the Net .... http://www.refdesk.com
Search Systems .... http://www.searchsystems.net/
FreeEdgar .... http://www.freeedgar.com
Thomas Register of American Manufacturers .... http://www.thomasregister.com
Internet News.Com .... http://www.internetnews.com/bus-news/
Vault.com .... http://www.vault.com
Whois.net .... http://www.whois.net
Yahoo Ticker Symbol Lookup .... http://finance.yahoo.com/l
Yahoo! Finance Company and Fund Index .... http://biz.yahoo.com/i/

Newspapers and other periodicals are a great source of information on companies and industries. For a fee, a Lexis-Nexis search *(http://lexis-nexis.com)* will allow you to access information from more than 36,000 news, legal, business, and government sources. However, you can access many of those same sources over the Internet for free with a simply company name search through a search engine. Don't neglect the local and national newspapers, periodicals, chambers of commerce, and business journals. Here are some excellent news sources:

ABC News .... http://abcnews.go.com
American Journalism Review .... http://www.ajr.org/
BizJournals .... http://www.bizjournals.com
Anchorage Daily News (AK) .... http://www.adn.com
Boston Globe On-line (MA) .... http://www.boston.com
Boston Herald (MA) .... http://www.bostonherald.com
Business Journals .... http://www.bizjournals.com
CBS News .... http://www.cbsnews.com
Chicago Tribune (IL) .... http://chicagotribune.com
CNN .... http://www.cnn.com
Dallas Morning News (TX) .... http://www.dallasnews.com
EntrepreneurMag.com .... http://www.entrepreneurmag.com
Editor and Publisher.com .... http://www.editorandpublisher.com/eandp/index.jsp
Entrepreneur.Com .... http://www.entrepreneurmag.com
Fast Company .... http://www.fastcompany.com/homepage
Fox News .... http://www.foxnews.com
Hampton Roads Career Connection (VA) .... http://www.pilotonline.com
Harvard Business School, Baker Library, Local, and
    Regional Business Publications on the Web .... http://www.library.hbs.edu/
Houston Chronicle (TX) .... http://www.chron.com
Inc. Online .... http://www.inc.com
Industry Week .... http://www.industryweek.com

Los Angeles Times (CA) . . . . *http://www.latimes.com/*
Minneapolis/St. Paul Star Tribune (MN) . . . . *http://www.startribune.com/workavenue*
MSNBC . . . . *http://www.msnbc.com*
New York Times . . . . *http://www.nytimes.com/*
News and Newspapers Online . . . . *http://library.uncg.edu/news*
News Bank . . . . *http://www.newsbank.com*
News Directory . . . . *http://www.newsdirectory.com*
NewsCentral Links to 3,500 Newspapers Online . . . . *http://www.all-links.com/newscentral*
Newslink . . . . *http://newslink.org*
Newspapers.com . . . . *http://www.newspapers.com/*
NewsVoyager.com . . . . *http://www.newsvoyager.com/voyager.cfm*
Time.com . . . . *http://www.time.com/time/*
U.S. News.com . . . . *http://www.usnews.com/usnews/home.htm*
USA Today . . . . *http://www.usatoday.com/*
Wall Street Journal . . . . *http://online.wsj.com/public/us*
Washington Post . . . . *http://www.washingtonpost.com/*
Worcester Telegram (MA) . . . . *http://www.telegram.com/*
ZDNet E-Business . . . . *http://www.zdnet.com/enterprise/e-business*

International News Resources

African Business and Economy . . . . *http://www.afbis.com*
Arab Net (Middle East and North Africa) . . . . *http://www.arab.net*
Asia Source . . . . *http://www.asiasource.org*
Asia-Inc. . . . . *http://www.asia-inc.com*
Asian Development Bank . . . . *http://www.adb.org*
Canada's Business and Consumer Site . . . . *http://strategis.ic.gc.ca/engdoc/main.html*
CNN.com World News . . . . *http://www.cnn.com/WORLD/*
Embassy.org . . . . *http://www.embassy.org*
European Business Directory . . . . *http://www.europages.com*
JobFutures (Canada) . . . . *http://www.jobfutures.ca/en/home.shtml*
GoinGlobal . . . . *http://www.goinglobal.com/*
Hoover's Online United Kingdom . . . . *http://www.hoovers.co.uk*
Import-Export Bank of the United States . . . . *http://www.exim.gov*
Inter-American Development Bank (Latin/South America) . . . . *http://www.iadb.org*
Orientation.com . . . . *http://www.orientation.com*
Rubicon's Digital Passport . . . . *http://www.rubicon.com/passport.html*
U.S. State Department . . . . *http://www.state.gov*
The World Bank Group . . . . *http://www.worldbank.org*

Here is some of the information that you should know about a company before your interview:

- What are its history and basic structure (corporation, LLC, etc.)?
- What are its product or service lines?
- Who are its competitors?
- Is the company ahead of the market or trailing behind?
- How is its financial health?
- What are its latest sales figures?
- What is the state of the industry—is it in a recession or boom?
- What do you know about the CEO and other key leaders?
- What are the company's values and culture—will you fit?
- What are the company's growth trends?
- What are its goals for the future?

- How many locations does the company have?
- Is the company global or domestic?
- How many employees does it have?
- What are the company's threats, opportunities, strengths, and weaknesses?
- What problems has the company overcome?
- What have I done in the past that could help solve these problems?
- What value could I bring to the company that would be worth my cost?
- What product development ideas can I bring to the table?

9 Online Networking

More than 60 percent of all job openings are filled through recommendations from current employees or by word of mouth! That means, as important as the Internet has become to job searching—especially in high-tech companies— you can't neglect your network of contacts during a job search. This hidden job market is made up of positions that aren't even advertised, and many positions are created for the right candidate. This chapter will teach you how to build a virtual network of contacts to facilitate your job search.

According to Richard Bolles, author of *What Color Is Your Parachute?*, "The Internet can make you lazy." Bolles says that Internet job sites "seduce you with the idea that you can just tell them what you're looking for and they'll fetch it while you sleep." According to Boles, 15 percent of your total job-hunting time should be clicking a mouse. The rest of your time should be spent networking, knocking on doors, and pounding the pavement.

Networking must be something you do constantly, not just when you are unemployed. It must become an integral part of your strategy to be in control of your career. As the word *networking* implies, *work* to make new contacts every day and track them in contact management software, a Palm Pilot, a little black book, or a Rolodex.

Your current network is made up of peers, business colleagues, customers, former managers, vendors, suppliers, professional clubs/associations, recruiters, friends, relatives, social contacts, neighbors, fellow volunteers, mentors, college alumni, professors, church members, parents of your children's friends, an exercise partner, your dentist, attorney, accountant, realtor, and anyone else with whom you have already developed a relationship. However, it's not just about who you already know but about who *they* know. Ask your contacts for introductions to their contacts.

Touch base with everyone you know, and the higher up the ladder, the better. Most employers fill jobs by hiring from within their companies. If they can't hire from within, they go to friends or business associates and ask if they know anyone who would be qualified for the positions. Only after that do they advertise a position or hire a recruiter. That's why developing and tapping into relationships with key people is so important in job hunting. The more people who know about your job search, the better your chances of finding a job in today's competitive labor market.

To identify your existing network, first write a list of the names and addresses of at least 100 people you know or use the note card on page 162. Make a note beside each name of how this person can help you get a job. Then send either a letter or an e-mail message to each one, letting them know you are looking for a job. You would be surprised at how many people you know and how many people they know. Add to your list every day by asking your contacts for more contacts, and call everyone at least one time during your job search. Always remember to thank these people for anything they do to help you make contacts.

Networking is a two-way street that involves mutual respect and giving on both sides. It is all about building relationships, being remembered, being referred, and giving back. By supporting and helping those in your network, you will in turn receive information, help, support, and maybe even a job. But don't keep score. Networking isn't bartering. It's about developing relationships based on a sincere desire to see someone else do well and succeed. Get to know people because you respect them, not because they could get you a job someday.

It is perfectly acceptable to ask your contact to critique your résumé (but not at your first meeting), provide advice about the industry, give you inside information on a company, mentor you, or refer you to someone else. There is a big difference between being assertive and being aggressive. Career counselor Carla Owens teaches Kent State University students and alumni the right way to network. The trick, Owens said, is to phrase questions in the third person. For instance, instead of asking a colleague, "Can you get me a job in your company?" you should say, "Do you know if there are any openings at your company?" That way you put your networking contact at ease because he or she won't feel any direct obligation to you.

It isn't okay to ask for a job or push yourself on someone who isn't interested in working with you, and don't make a contact without being prepared—research, research, research! It is also important not to focus entirely on your own needs. Listen and look for opportunities to repay the courtesy of your contact's time. As you build your network, things like unpublished job openings and the inside scoop on the company will come naturally.

■ *What Makes e-Networking Unique*

Now that you know what networking is and why you should use it in your job search, let's talk about what makes e-networking unique. According to Nancy Halpern, career coach, networking expert, and founder of Strategic Positioning for People in Business (*http://www.inter-net-working.com*), e-networking has the following advantages.

- For those people who find it awkward to cold call, the anonymity of online interactions eliminates the fear of the first encounter. When you feel more comfortable networking, you will do more of it.

- E-networking doesn't require an introduction. The person online is the primary contact who can also refer you to others.

- E-networking gets immediate responses since people who use e-mail tend to check it often. No telephone tag!

- Everyone on the Internet is accessible to you.

- Managing your circle of contacts is greatly simplified with electronic address books.

- Many sites dedicated to e-networking host events throughout the country to give colleagues an opportunity to meet in person.

■ *How to Build a Network on the Internet*

There are many way to build a network using the Internet. Here are just a few ways of tapping into the hidden job market:

- E-mail allows you to dialogue with your contacts, but dialogue is a two-way street. Don't overwhelm your contacts by using e-mail to send funny stories every day that don't require a response, although it is perfectly okay to send an occasional interesting article or congratulations on an achievement. In fact, that is exactly how you *should* use e-mail. It is a quick, easy way to maintain your network. For your first contact, make certain you include how you found the person, areas of common interest, some personal information to create a mutual bond and put your recipient at ease, and a request for further information. Follow standard business courtesy and don't use an alias.

- Newsgroups and Mailing Lists—Subscribe to industry- or interest-specific mailing lists and newsgroups. After you have "lurked" for a while, join in the discussions, share your expertise, and make sure you have an appropriate signature line with your e-mail address, Web site URL (if you have one—see Chapter 10), and a line about who you are. You will soon become part of the "community," which will provide you with opportunities for expanding your contacts. See the next two sections of this chapter for the specifics about how to use newsgroups and mailing lists.

- Chat Rooms and Forums—If you belong to a commercial online service like AOL, CompuServe, or MSN, you know all about forums. They allow you to participate in real-time chats on every subject imaginable. Many career Web sites offer the same opportunities. You can learn a great deal about industry trends and developments in these types of chats, and sometimes they will even announce job openings before they are advertised.

- Affiliations—Join professional associations, nonprofit organizations, community service groups, or religious organizations. Read their publications, check their Web sites, participate in their online chats, and attend meetings regularly. Volunteer for activities and mingle with participants, spending no more than 10 minutes with any one person. Take the time to remember each person's name and what he or she does for a living. Ask for business cards and e-mail addresses and then follow up with a quick e-mail that tells your new contact how much you enjoyed meeting them. For valuable contacts, arrange a convenient time to buy lunch so you can strengthen your relationship. Remember that professional affiliations are sometimes used by hiring managers to narrow down a candidate search. They like to see that you are making a difference in your industry.

- College/University Contacts—Alumni of your alma mater are instant contacts. They know the same school songs, cheer for the same sports teams, remember the same professors, and belonged to the same fraternity/sorority. Many colleges and universities maintain lists of alumni who have volunteered to mentor other graduates or just answer questions. These lists can be accessible from the school's career center home page, although you may need a password from the career center first. See the list of meta-sites for career service centers at the end of this chapter.

- Networking Internet Web Sites—E-networking sites are cropping up all over the Internet. At many sites, you can create an individual profile that lists your experience and background and search the site for members who share your interests. Others bring together like-minded strangers in face-to-face gatherings, which is okay as long as you are wary of one-on-one meetings with total strangers you meet on the Internet. You may need to pay a fee to join some of these groups.

Amity Zone . . . . *http://www.amityzone.com/*
Buddy Bridge . . . . *http://www.buddybridge.com/*
CareerJournal.com . . . . *http://www.careerjournal.com/calendar/*
Chia Friend . . . . *http://www.chiafriend.com/*
Christianster . . . . *http://www.christianster.com/*
Community Zero . . . . *http://www.communityzero.com/*
Company Alumni Networks . . . . *http://www.job-hunt.org/employer_alumni_networking.shtml*
Ecademy . . . . *http://www.ecademy.com/*
Eliyon . . . . *http://www.eliyon.com/PublicSite/public/default.asp*
enCentra . . . . *http://www.encentra.com/*
EntreMate . . . . *http://www.entremate.com/*
eSideWALK . . . . *http://www.esidewalk.com/*
EveryonesConnected . . . . *http://www.everyonesconnected.com*
Execunet . . . . *http://www.execunet.com/*
Fast Company Community of Friends . . . . *http://www.fastcompany.com/cof*
Forty Plus *http://www.fortyplus.org/6.5/*
Friendster . . . . *http://www.friendster.com//*
Friendzy . . . . *http://www.friendzy.com*
Globe Alive . . . . *http://www.globealive.com/*
Knowmentum . . . . *http://www.itsnotwhatyouknow.com/*
Linked In . . . . *https://www.linkedin.com/*
Los Comadres . . . . *http://www.lascomadres.org/*

160

Meet Up . . . . *http://www.meetup.com/*
Monster Networking . . . . *http://network.monster.com*
Open Business Club . . . . *http://www.openbc.com/*
Real Contacts . . . . *http://jobs.realcontacts.com/home.asp*
Ryze Business Networking . . . . *http://www.ryze.com/*
Seattle Networking Guide . . . . *http://www.iloveseattle.org/*
Six Degrees . . . . *http://www.sixdegrees.com*
The Square Network for Alumni of Prestigious Universities . . . . *http://www.thesquare.com*
Squiby *http://www.squiby.com/index2.asp*
The Five O'Clock Club . . . . *http://www.fiveoclockclub.com/*
Tribe . . . . *http://www.tribe.net*
WhizSpark . . . . *http://www.whizspark.com/*
Word of Mouth Research . . . . *http://wordofmouthresearch.com*
WorldWIT . . . . *http://www.worldwit.org/*
Yahoo! E-Groups . . . . *http://www.egroups.com*
Zero Degrees . . . . *http://www.zerodegrees.com/*

■ Ask the Experts—Independent contractors and other freelancers offer their services through Web sites dedicated to independent professionals. They generally provide complete contact information in their profiles so companies can find them, which also makes them available to you. Because they are exposed to a wide range of companies, independent workers are great sources of information regarding industry trends in their geographic region. They also tend to know which companies are growing and hiring. Here are some favorites:

allExperts.com . . . . *http://www.allexperts.com*
eLance.com . . . . *http://www.elance.com*
FreeAgent.com . . . . *http://www.freeagent.com*
Free Agent Nation . . . . *http://www.freeagentnation.com*
Guru.com . . . . *http://www.guru.com*
Working Solo . . . . *http://www.workingsolo.com*

■ Create an action plan and set goals for yourself. Cold calling is hard, and networking doesn't come naturally to most of us, especially if we are introverts. Force yourself to set goals for the number of people you will contact every day. Keep track of each contact on a 4" × 6" index card like the one on the next page, or transfer the same information to a single sheet of paper per contact in a three-ring notebook. Always send thank you notes either by e-mail or snail-mail as part of your action plan/follow-up.

NAME:	
COMPANY:	
JOB TITLE:	
ADDRESS:	
E-MAIL ADDRESS:	
WORK PHONE:	HOME PHONE:
CELL PHONE:	RÉSUMÉ SENT: ☐ Yes ☐ No
REFERRED BY or MET AT:	

CONTACT TRACKING		
Date	Information Gained	Action Plan or Follow-up

■ *How to Use Newsgroups (Usenet)*

Usenet stands for Users Network, which consists of thousands of computers that are organized under a set of groupings known as newsgroups. Each newsgroup is devoted to a particular subject, such as jobs or chemistry or dance. These newsgroups can be serious, fun, work related, or even obscene. There is no regulation of the Internet, so be forewarned.

Kevin Savetz, an Internet consultant with America Online, describes newsgroups as follows: "Usenet is simply the largest, most active, and most varied discussion forum in the world. Imagine a bulletin board on a wall. Imagine that as people pass it, they glance at what's there, and if they have something to add, they stick their note up, too. Now imagine that there are thousands of bulletin boards in this building, and that there are actually tens of thousands of such buildings throughout the world, each with its own identical copy of the bulletin boards. Got it? That's Usenet."

Newsgroups are the Internet equivalent of the live chat rooms and forums of commercial online services. They offer you the opportunity to broadcast articles (i.e., messages) back and forth on a topic thread among a large number of computers. When you reply to an article, you can continue the thread or start a new thread. There are millions of people actively using thousands of newsgroups around the world, and it is estimated that the number of newsgroups is growing by 20 to 30 every week.

Some newsgroups are moderated, meaning that your article (message) is sent to a moderator who first reviews it before making it available to the public. This keeps the discussion focused on a given subject and limits the number of inappropriate or irrelevant messages. In unmoderated newsgroups, you simply post an article and it is broadcast to everyone in the newsgroup. Alternative newsgroups tend to be unmoderated and much less structured than traditional newsgroups.

Each newsgroup contains messages from the people who participate in them. At the top of each message is the author's name, subject, date and time, the name of the originating computer system, and the body of the message itself. Some of the messages will be new and others will be responses to previous messages. Because newsgroups generate responses from countries around the world, you will be exposed to an incredibly diverse audience.

To access a newsgroup from your computer, log on to your Internet service provider or commercial online service account and click on the newsgroup (or Usenet) icon under the Internet options. Type in the URL for the site, press the Enter key, and you are there. You can read to your heart's content or add to the message thread with options provided by your news reader software. For technical instructions on using newsgroups and lists of Usenet groups, go to the Usenet Info Center Launch Pad at *http://metalab.unc.edu/usenet-i/*.

❑ *Domains*

Newsgroups are organized into a very structured format with periods separating the various topic levels. The first part of a newsgroup name is its general topic. The following are the major Usenet domains:

alt	Alternative topics (this is where you must be your own censor)
bionet	Topics of interest to biologists
bit	A collection of newsgroups that are redistributions of the more popular BitNet LISTSERV mailing lists
biz	Business topics, especially computer products and services
clari	Newsgroups gatewayed from commercial news services and other official sources
comp	Computer subjects (hardware, software, programming languages, systems, etc.)
humanities	General topics in the arts and humanities
k12	Conferences devoted to K–12 educational curriculum, language exchanges with native speakers, and classroom projects designed by teachers
misc	Subjects that are difficult to classify under other categories
news	Newsgroup, network, and administration topics
rec	Arts, hobbies, and recreational activities
sci	Scientific topics (both physical and social sciences)
soc	Social, socializing, and cultural issues
talk	Controversial issues (these groups are more debate oriented)

There are other, more local top-level newsgroup domains (actually hundreds of them) that generally refer to a specific school, city, state, country, or area of interest.

att	AT&T
byu	Brigham Young University
eye	*EYE* magazine, based in Toronto, Canada
gnu	A set of newsgroups from the Internet mailing lists of the GNU project of the Free Software Foundation
hepnet	High-energy and nuclear physics research sites
ieee	Institute of Electrical and Electronics Engineers
info	A collection of mailing lists gatewayed into news at the University of Illinois
relcom	Russian-language newsgroups
uk	United Kingdom
vmsnet	Topics of interest to VAX/VMS users
wpi	Worcester Polytechnic Institute

For a complete description of these first-level newsgroups, check the gigantic NIC master list at *http://metalab.unc.edu/usenet-i/hier-s/0top-1.html.* This allows local groups in, say, New York *(ny.jobs)* to discuss things of interest to them that would not be of interest to someone in San Jose *(ca.san-jose).* You may not be able to access corporate or school newsgroups without permission, but it never hurts to try. You can find out a lot about a company's culture in its newsgroup.

These general areas are then subdivided into other newsgroups that deal with more specific topics within the subject area. For example, the *sci.bio* newsgroup is designed for the discussion of biology. The sub-newsgroups of *sci.bio.microbiology* and *sci.bio.technology* focus on more specific topics within the biology discipline.

❏ *Networking with Newsgroups*

As part of a newsgroup, you can join conversations about issues and trends in your industry and make great networking contacts. Then you can use e-mail to nurture those relationships that might lead to a job. It is usually a good idea to sit back and lurk for a week or two in a newsgroup before you speak. As you get a feel for the topics that are appropriate for discussion in a particular newsgroup, you can ask for feedback on your résumé or talk about the culture or job opportunities within certain companies.

Not all newsgroups appreciate résumé postings, so watch and learn, and then ask before posting. Posting a résumé inappropriately or making rude comments is considered bad manners, which can be disastrous to your job search. You don't want to leave a bad impression on even one potential contact, let alone thousands of people in a newsgroup!

❏ Netiquette

The unwritten rules of the Internet are called netiquette. These rules include being honest, polite, and legal when dealing with others in the virtual community of the Internet. Lurking is considered good manners in newsgroups. Before posting anything, including your résumé, you should lurk for a while until you understand the focus of the newsgroup.

Some newsgroups are primarily for announcements or questions and not for discussions. Each newsgroup has its own unique culture. Some are virtual free-for-alls (like "misc," "talk," and "alt"), while others are more civilized. As a general rule, the "sci," "comp," and "news" newsgroups focus on facts and not opinions. "Soc" and "rec" newsgroups are a little more opinionated and are open to new member opinions. Check the following sites for more information about etiquette on the Internet:

E-mail Netiquette . . . . *http://www.linfield.edu/policy/netiquette.html*
Internet Guidelines and Culture . . . . *http://www.fau.edu/netiquette/net/culture.html*

❏ FAQs

Most newsgroups have a list of frequently asked questions (FAQs) that you should always read before posting an article. You will generally find the list of FAQs when you access the Usenet site, but there is a meta-site on the Internet that is a compilation of all the Usenet FAQs. It can be found at *http://www.faqs.org*. Also read the articles at *news.announce.newusers* and *news.answers* before joining in the discussion on a newsgroup. These sources will help you understand the purpose of the newsgroup and keep you out of hot water—or better yet, keep you from getting flamed (the Internet equivalent to hate mail).

Some other tips for posting articles in newsgroups include:

1. Avoid needless messages (like thank you or other things not of general interest). Send these messages via e-mail instead. Your message could be read by millions of people, so make your words count. Your message reflects on you. You want to make a good impression on possible networking contacts, and you never know who might be reading your message.

2. It is okay to include additional information about yourself at the end of your article, but avoid a long signature (no more than four lines). Avoid those cutesy pictures created from text characters.

3. Don't advertise on general-purpose newsgroups. There are newsgroups that allow commercial postings ("comp" and "biz"), but always check the FAQs for each newsgroup first.

4. Make the subject line of your message clear and informative. It is here that people will decide whether to read the rest of your message.

5. Format your article clearly so it is easy to read and uses 60-character lines. Remember that it must be sent as an ASCII text message.

6. If you get an e-mail message with only RTFAQ in it, you know you are in trouble. RTFAQ stands for Read the Frequently Asked Questions. Newsgroup readers get tired of answering the same questions again and again, so they create FAQs. If you are new to newsgroups, read the FAQs before asking questions.

7. Don't send a "This is just a test" message to any newsgroup or you will get some pretty nasty e-mail messages in return. If you must try a test, there is a newsgroup just for that purpose. It is *misc.test.*

8. Avoid submitting your article to multiple newsgroups (spamming). It may be okay to cross-post to a few appropriate newsgroups, but don't do so randomly without some specific purpose.

9. Don't send your article to the same newsgroup twice. It takes a while for your file to end up in the newsgroup, so don't assume it isn't there because you can't find it immediately. Give it some time before reposting your article.

There are dozens of newsgroups devoted to jobs and job hunting, but not all of the messages in them are directly related to employment. Some are solicitations, get-rich-quick schemes, questions about interviewing techniques or how to write a résumé. Despite this, however, newsgroups can yield connections to jobs.

Executive recruiters post most of the real jobs found in newsgroups, and recruiters are valuable contacts for any job hunter. Use these newsgroup job postings to get a feel for a particular recruiter's specialty, and then contact the recruiter whose job postings match your experience. If you network within more industry-specific newsgroups, you will find fewer get-rich-quick schemes but fewer jobs. These groups are better for building professional contacts and learning more about an industry.

There are some newsgroups that encourage you to post your résumé, including *atl.resumes, ba.jobs, israel.jobs, misc.jobs.* Many industry-oriented newsgroups include subtopics that are related to job hunting, so don't search simply for "jobs" or "résumés" (remember not to use the accent marks over the e).

One thing to keep in mind when writing a résumé for a newsgroup is that you are generally limited to 20,000 characters. Longer newsgroup messages may be split into two or more parts, and employers won't bother to look for the pieces or to glue them together again. The subject field that is a part of every newsgroup message is a great place to grab an employer's attention. Be specific. Instead of saying, "A career position with a dynamic company," it is better to say, "Sports marketing professional, proven track record, willing to relocate." Never leave a subject line blank.

❏ *Job-related Newsgroups*

Industry Specific

bionet.jobs	Biotechnology
bionet.jobs.offered	Biotechnology
bionet.jobs.wanted	Biotechnology

alt.building.jobs	Building
alt.jobs.as400	AS 400 Computers
alt.medical.sales.jobs.resumes	Medical Sales
dod.jobs	Department of Defense
misc.jobs.resumes	General
pdaxs.jobs.clerical	Clerical
pdaxs.jobs.computers	Computers
pdaxs.jobs.construction	Construction
pdaxs.jobs.delivery	Delivery
pdaxs.jobs.domestic	Domestic
pdaxs.jobs.engineering	Engineering
pdaxs.jobs.management	Management
pdaxs.jobs.restaurants	Restaurants
pdaxs.jobs.retail	Retail
pdaxs.jobs.sales	Sales
pdaxs.jobs.secretary	Secretary
pdaxs.jobs.temporary	Temporary
pdaxs.jobs.volunteers	Volunteers
sci.research.careers	Science Research
sci.research.postdoc	Science Research Post Doctoral

Alabama

alabama.jobs	Statewide
hsv.jobs	Huntsville

Arizona

az.jobs	Statewide

Arkansas

alt.jobs.nw-arkansas	Statewide
uark.jobs	University of Arkansas

California

ba.jobs	San Francisco Area
ba.jobs.agency	San Francisco Area
ba.jobs.contract	San Francisco Area
ba.jobs.contract.agency	San Francisco Area
ba.jobs.contract.direct	San Francisco Area
ba.jobs.direct	San Francisco Area
ba.jobs.discussion	San Francisco Area
ba.jobs.misc	San Francisco Area
ba.jobs.resumes	San Francisco Area

```
ca.jobs . . . . . . . . . . . . . . . . . . . . . . . . . . . . . . . . . . . . . . . Statewide
la.jobs . . . . . . . . . . . . . . . . . . . . . . . . . . . . . . . . . . . . . Los Angeles
oc.jobs . . . . . . . . . . . . . . . . . . . . . . . . . . . . . . . . . . . . . . . Statewide
sac.jobs . . . . . . . . . . . . . . . . . . . . . . . . . . . . . . . . . . . . Sacramento
sdnet.jobs . . . . . . . . . . . . . . . . . . . . . . . . . . . . . . . . . . . San Diego
sdnet.jobs.discuss . . . . . . . . . . . . . . . . . . . . . . . . . . . . . San Diego
sdnet.jobs.offered . . . . . . . . . . . . . . . . . . . . . . . . . . . . . San Diego
sdnet.jobs.services . . . . . . . . . . . . . . . . . . . . . . . . . . . . San Diego
sdnet.jobs.wanted . . . . . . . . . . . . . . . . . . . . . . . . . . . . . San Diego
slac.jobs . . . . . . . . . . . . . . . . . . . Stanford Linear Academic Center
su.jobs . . . . . . . . . . . . . . . . . . . . . . . . . . . Stanford University
ucb.jobs . . . . . . . . . . . . . . . . . University of California at Berkeley
ucd.cs.jobs . . . . . . . . . . . . . . . . . . . University of California at Davis
ucd.kiosk.jobs . . . . . . . . . . . . . . . . . . University of California at Davis
```

Colorado

```
co.jobs . . . . . . . . . . . . . . . . . . . . . . . . . . . . . . . . . . . . . . Statewide
```

Connecticut

```
ct.jobs . . . . . . . . . . . . . . . . . . . . . . . . . . . . . . . . . . . . . . Statewide
ne.jobs . . . . . . . . . . . . . . . . . . . . . . . . . . . . . . . . . . . . . . Statewide
ne.jobs.contract . . . . . . . . . . . . . . . . . . . . . . . . . . . . . . . Statewide
```

District of Columbia

```
dc.jobs . . . . . . . . . . . . . . . . . . . . . . . . . . . . . Washington, D.C.
balt.jobs . . . . . . . . . . . . . . . . . . . . Washington, D.C., and Maryland
```

Florida

```
fl.jobs . . . . . . . . . . . . . . . . . . . . . . . . . . . . . . . . . . . . . . . Statewide
fl.jobs.resumes . . . . . . . . . . . . . . . . . . . . . . . . . . . . . . . . Statewide
```

Georgia

```
atl.jobs . . . . . . . . . . . . . . . . . . . . . . . . . . . . . . . . . . . . . . Atlanta
atl.resumes . . . . . . . . . . . . . . . . . . . . . . . . . . . . . . . . . . . Atlanta
git.ohr.jobs.digest . . . . . . . . . . . . . . . . . . . Georgia Institute of Technology
```

Illinois

```
chi.jobs . . . . . . . . . . . . . . . . . . . . . . . . . . . . . . . . . . . . . . Chicago
il.jobs.offered . . . . . . . . . . . . . . . . . . . . . . . . . . . . . . . . . Statewide
il.jobs.resumes . . . . . . . . . . . . . . . . . . . . . . . . . . . . . . . . Statewide
uiuc.cs.job . . . . . . . . . . . . . . . . . . . . . . . . . . . University of Illinois
```

Indiana

in.jobs . . . . Statewide

Kansas

kc.jobs . . . . Kansas City

Louisiana

lou.lft.jobs . . . . Statewide

Maine

ne.jobs . . . . Statewide
ne.jobs.contract . . . . Statewide

Maryland

balt.jobs . . . . Baltimore

Massachusetts

ne.jobs . . . . Statewide
ne.jobs.contract . . . . Statewide

Michigan

mi.jobs . . . . Statewide
umich.jobs . . . . University of Michigan

Minnesota

umn.cs.jobs . . . . University of Minnesota
umn.general.jobs . . . . University of Minnesota

Missouri

kc.jobs . . . . Kansas City
stl.jobs . . . . St. Louis
stl.jobs.offered . . . . St. Louis
stl.jobs.resumes . . . . St. Louis

Nebraska

nebr.jobs . . . . Statewide

Nevada

nv.jobs . . . . Statewide
vegas.jobs . . . . Las Vegas

New Hampshire

ne.jobs . . . . Statewide
ne.jobs.contract . . . . Statewide
nh.jobs . . . . Statewide

New Jersey

nj.jobs . . . . Statewide

New Mexico

nm.jobs . . . . Statewide

New York

ithaca.jobs . . . . Ithaca
li.jobs . . . . Long Island
niagara.jobs . . . . Niagara
ny.jobs . . . . Statewide
nyc.jobs . . . . New York City
nyc.jobs.contract . . . . New York City
nyc.jobs.offered . . . . New York City
nyc.jobs.misc . . . . New York City
nyc.jobs.wanted . . . . New York City

North Carolina

triangle.jobs . . . . Statewide

Ohio

akr.jobs . . . . Akron
cinci.jobs . . . . Cincinnati
cle.jobs . . . . Cleveland
cmh.jobs . . . . Columbus
oh.jobs . . . . Statewide
osu.jobs . . . . Ohio State University

Oregon

pdaxs.jobs.misc . . . . Statewide

pdaxs.jobs.resumes . . . . Statewide
pdaxs.jobs.wanted . . . . Statewide

Pennsylvania

pa.jobs.offered . . . . Statewide
pa.jobs.wanted . . . . Statewide
pgh.jobs.offered . . . . Pittsburgh
pgh.jobs.wanted . . . . Pittsburgh
phil.jobs.wanted . . . . Philadelphia
phil.jobs.offered . . . . Philadelphia

Rhode Island

ne.jobs . . . . Statewide
ne.jobs.contract . . . . Statewide

Tennessee

memphis.employment . . . . Memphis

Texas

austin.jobs . . . . Austin
dfw.jobs . . . . Dallas/Ft. Worth
houston.jobs . . . . Houston
houston.jobs.offered . . . . Houston
houston.jobs.wanted . . . . Houston
sat.jobs . . . . San Antonio
tx.jobs . . . . Statewide
tx-bcs.jobs . . . . Statewide
utexas.jobs . . . . University of Texas

Utah

ut.jobs . . . . Statewide
utah.jobs . . . . Statewide
utah.valley.jobs . . . . Salt Lake City

Vermont

ne.jobs . . . . Statewide
ne.jobs.contract . . . . Statewide

Virginia

va.jobs . . . . Virginia

Washington

seattle.jobs.offered . . . . Seattle
seattle.jobs.wanted . . . . Seattle

Wisconsin

milw.jobs . . . . Milwaukee

United States

alt.job . . . . All
alt.jobs . . . . All
alt.jobs.offered . . . . All
biz.jobs . . . . All
us.jobs . . . . All
us.jobs.offered . . . . All
us.jobs.offered.contract . . . . All
us.jobs.resumes . . . . All

International

ab.jobs . . . . Alberta, Canada
alt.jobs.overseas . . . . All
aus.jobs . . . . Australia
aus.ads.jobs . . . . Australia
aus.ads.jobs.moderated . . . . Australia
aus.ads.jobs.resumes . . . . Australia
bc.jobs . . . . British Columbia, Canada
bermuda.jobs.offered . . . . Bermuda
can.jobs . . . . Canada
can.jobs.gov . . . . Canada
euro.jobs . . . . Europe
israel.jobs.offered . . . . Israel
israel.jobs.misc . . . . Israel
israel.jobs.resumes . . . . Israel
ont.jobs . . . . Ontario, Canada
ott.jobs . . . . Ottawa, Canada
qc.jobs . . . . Quebec, Canada
tor.jobs . . . . Toronto, Canada
uk.jobs . . . . United Kingdom
uk.jobs.contract . . . . United Kingdom
uk.jobs.d . . . . United Kingdom
uk.jobs.fortyplus . . . . United Kingdom
uk.jobs.offered . . . . United Kingdom
uk.jobs.wanted . . . . United Kingdom
za.ads.jobs . . . . South Africa
z-netz.fundgrube.job-boerse . . . . Germany

There are several resources for finding newsgroups on the Internet. One of the best search engines dedicated to Usenet newsgroups is Deja News, which was purchased by Google and is now called Google Groups. Since its inception in May of 1995, it has had the largest collection of Usenet news available anywhere. Several of the other major search engines—AltaVista, Excite, and Yahoo!—also index newsgroups.

To find newsgroups that relate to your industry or to your job search, you can use the following resources to look for messages about particular topics or companies discussed in both newsgroups and mailing lists.

AltaVista . . . . *http://www.altavista.com*
Excite . . . . *http://www.excite.com*
Google Groups . . . . *http://groups.google.com/*
Tile.net Newsgroups . . . . *http://tile.net/news/*
Topica . . . . *http://lists.topica.com/*

■ *Using e-Lists to Make Contacts*

A mailing list (or e-list) is an organized form of e-mail. You subscribe to a mailing list that interests you and mail comes to you automatically. You can also send e-mail to many people at the same time using a mailing list. These lists are wonderful sources of information about your chosen profession. You can also enhance your general knowledge base, which will make you more employable, or learn something that will make you appear more knowledgeable in an interview. There are some general rules, or netiquette, however, that you should know before participating in mailing lists.

First, as a general rule, mailing lists are noncommercial and participants dislike receiving commercial ads and solicitations. Doing business on the Internet is acceptable; it's just a matter of how it is conducted. Mailing lists are generally not the place to conduct business unless you belong to a mailing list exclusively set up for that purpose. Second, don't waste people's time by sending junk e-mail messages of little value ("spamming").

Now, let's get down to the business of subscribing to a mailing list. There are many kinds of mailing lists (electronic magazines and newsletters, personal information distribution lists, small clubs where people of like mind share information, public debate and discussion lists, and news and information dissemination lists, among others)—an estimated 381,855 of them exist on the Internet as of this writing. Some e-lists are moderated (meaning each message is filtered by a human reader before being posted) and others are not. In moderated e-lists, not all messages are sent on to subscribers, especially if they are inappropriate or do not meet the rules of the list.

All mailing lists fall into either the interactive or reactive categories. Interactive lists encourage the participation of list members in exchanging ideas and information, either in unrestricted or restricted ways. Reactive lists are more for news/information distribution. Reactive lists will accept submissions of articles or digests from members but rarely encourage member-to-member discussion. In either type, members are expected to relate their information to the topics normally discussed in that particular mailing list.

Before you subscribe to a mailing list, you should do a little research to make sure the list will meet your needs. Commercial online services often have mailing list databases where you can read comprehensive information on any given list. If you are using an ISP to access the Internet, these resources will not be available to you and your best option is to check with the list owner via e-mail for more information and answers to frequently asked questions. Avoid joining a mailing list and then quickly leaving it, since doing so is considered rude.

❏ *To Subscribe*

Once you have determined that a particular mailing list is relevant, you must send an e-mail message to the list owner asking to subscribe or subscribe through the list's Web site. When subscribing by e-mail, the exact wording of the message differs with each mailing list, but generally a simple command like the following, typed in your e-mail message screen, is all that is needed:

Sometimes, a mailing list will require that you list the reasons why the list owner should admit you to the list. In some cases, you may even need to send a second piece of e-mail to confirm your desire to be added to the list. The Web site for the mailing list will show you the exact messages you need to send in order to subscribe.

Once you subscribe to a mailing list, the actual day-to-day participation is easy.

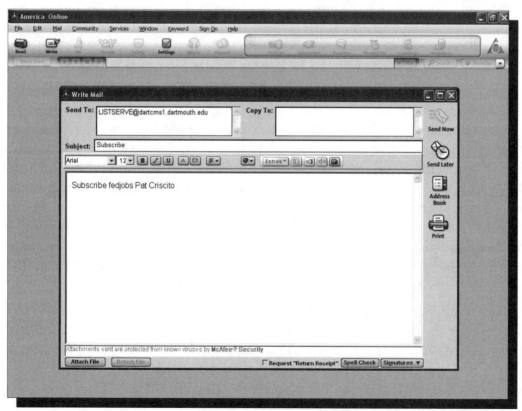

Copyright 2004, America Online. Used by permission.

You simply read your e-mail every day. If you don't, your mailbox can quickly overfill, depending on how many pieces of e-mail your service allows you to have at any one time. You may also exchange e-mail with other list members and sometimes even participate in real-time chats. Look before you leap, however. It is always a good idea to read a list for several weeks before attempting to post.

❏ *To Unsubscribe*

If you are going to be away from your computer for some time, either unsubscribe from the list or use the NOMAIL or POSTPONE features to temporarily suspend your subscription (not all mailing lists support these features). When you are ready to discontinue your subscription, you simply send a one-word e-mail message to the list owner that says:

UNSUBSCRIBE [type the list name here]

Mail from the list may continue to be delivered for several days after you have actually left the list, but it should stop within a few days. If not, then check the FAQs you read before subscribing to make sure there wasn't some other procedure you needed to follow to unsubscribe. Contact the list owner if the problem continues.

Many mailing lists are echoed at Usenet sites, which means that you can fully participate in the mailing list without having to worry about reading your e-mail everyday. You simply go to the Usenet site and read or download the information you want. This is like driving to the corner store and buying a newspaper instead of reading whatever mail is delivered to your mailbox.

Many e-lists also allow you to receive a digest version of the day's posts in a single e-mail instead of receiving each message separately.

❏ *Catalogs of Mailing Lists*

There are sites on the Internet that catalog mailing lists, although they are not specifically job related, so you will need to sift through them for clues as to their subject.

Catalist: The Catalog of LISTSERV lists . . . . *http://www.lsoft.com/lists/listref.html*
Tile.net Lists . . . . *http://tile.net/lists/*
Topica: The Mailing List Directory . . . . *http://lists.topica.com/dir/?cid=0*
Yahoo! Groups . . . . *http://groups.yahoo.com/*

■ *Professional Associations and Your Network*

Many professional associations offer résumé databases and job banks as membership benefits, either through a presence on the Internet or in newsgroups. Check your association's newsletter or other correspondence to get their URL. Even if an association doesn't list jobs, it is a valuable resource for industry information and contacts for your network.

On this book's companion Web site *(www.patcriscito.com)* you will find a list of associations with a presence on the Internet, divided into industry classifications. For more associations, use the search engines discussed in Chapter 12 or check the following meta-sites:

Canadian Society of Association Executives . . . . *http://www.csae.com/*
Career Resources . . . . *http://www.careerresource.net*
Chamber of Commerce Community Resources . . . . *http://www.chamberofcommerce.com/*
Guidestar Database of Nonprofit Organizations . . . . *http://www.guidestar.org/*
Idealist Action without Borders . . . . *http://www.idealist.org/*
International Public Library . . . . *http://www.ipl.org/ref/AON*
Job-hunt.org's Associations and Societies . . . . http://www.job-hunt.org/associations.shtml
Medical Academies and Professional Associations *http://www.pohly.com/assoc2.html*
Union of International Associations . . . . *http://www.uia.org*
The Scholarly Societies Project of the
    University of Waterloo, Canada . . . . *http://www.lib.uwaterloo.ca/society/overview.html*
Yahoo! Professional Organizations Listing . . . *http://dir.yahoo.com/economy/organizations/professional*

■ *Colleges and Your Electronic Job Search*

If you are presently a student at a college or university, your career service center is the first place to start your electronic job search. They have wonderful resources for helping you write and design your electronic résumé. They also have reference books that can guide you in all aspects of your job search, not just the electronic kind.

Many of these schools maintain a résumé database of all their students that can be accessed by companies worldwide. Career service centers are connected with many employers who list entry-level job openings and internships available to students of that particular school in job banks. Take advantage of those internships and other work experiences long before your graduation. Join student chapters of professional associations, like the American Marketing Association, American Geological Association, and so on. They will produce marketable keywords that will help your electronic résumé pop to the top in a keyword search.

Many larger companies have special sites on their Internet home pages just for students. For instance, Microsoft has a hyperlink under "Employment Opportunities" at *http://www.microsoft.com* where students can peruse full-time and internship opportunities developed specifically for college students.

Sometimes colleges offer reciprocal services to students of other schools, but the only way to find out is to make a telephone call to the career center of the school nearest you.

Alumni associations are another good place to start. There is an Internet site at *http://www.careerresource.net/carserv/* that is an excellent source for hyperlinks to hundreds of college alumni services. Check these Web sites first to see what type of support your alma mater provides. Colleges and universities often offer their alumni the same services as current students, while others limit free services to a year after graduation. Again, check your school just to make sure.

The career center may have a home page or a hyperlink from the university's main home page where you can find lists of the career resources available from your particular school. In addition, most major universities and colleges post their own job openings on the school's Web site.

To find your college's Web site, simply type the name of the school in a good search engine (see Chapter 12) and link to the career center.

To locate online information about universities and colleges in general, including the addresses for their home pages, check the following resources:

American Universities . . . . *http://www.clas.ufl.edu/CLAS/american-universities.html*
Career Resource . . . . *http://www.careerresource.net*
CollegeNET . . . . *http://www.collegenet.com*
MonsterTrak . . . . *http://www.monstertrak.monster.com/*
Peterson's Education Center . . . . *http://www.petersons.com*
Scholarstuff.com . . . . *http://www.scholarstuff.com/colleges/colleges.htm*
U.S. Universities and Community Colleges . . . . *http://www.utexas.edu/world/univ/*

10 Creating a Web Résumé or e-Folio

Imagine a musician playing her latest composition from the Internet or a teacher incorporating a video of his teaching style or a poet reading clips from her poetry on the screen or an entertainer demonstrating his latest dance steps. The creative juices are flowing! Web-based HTML résumés and portfolios (or e-folios) are the perfect place to showcase skills that are better seen (or heard) in all their glory.

As discussed in Chapter 1, if you are a computer programmer, Web site developer, graphic designer, artist, sculptor, actor, model, animator, cartoonist, poet, writer, or anyone who would benefit by the photographs, graphics, animation, sound, color, or movement inherent in a Web résumé or e-folio, then you should definitely read this chapter. If you don't fall into one of these categories, read this chapter anyway, because you will be surprised how a portfolio can enhance your job search and help you manage your career even while you are currently employed.

■ *A Web Résumé or an e-Folio?*

A Web résumé is simply your paper résumé converted to a Web site using HTML code (see the next chapter). It is rather basic without a lot of extra information.

Rather than having a single page on your Web site, however, a Web résumé is usually divided into sections that are accessed through hyperlinks from an introductory page—Career Objective, Summary, Skills, Experience, Education, Affiliations, etc. You can add information that you couldn't include in your paper résumé, but the more information you add, the more like a portfolio your Web résumé will become.

If you have more information about your career than you can practically include in a résumé, then a Web portfolio is a great option for making this additional information available to a potential employer. An e-folio provides visible evidence of your knowledge, skills, abilities, and core competencies.

For years, in my own practice, I've been advising my clients to keep an "I Love Me" file with performance evaluations, job descriptions, letters of recommendation, thank you notes from customers, vendors, or supervisors, sales statistics, growth charts, writing samples, awards, honors, scanned product images, photographs, or even three-dimensional items that expand on or support the outline that is inherent in their résumés. If you have collected that information during your entire career, then you have the foundation for an e-folio that will help you sell your special abilities and manage your entire career. If you haven't, then create an e-folio with whatever you do have or can get yours hands on now. It's never too late to start collecting for your "I Love Me" file.

A Web résumé or e-folio is just another type of e-résumé, but it cannot take the place of your paper résumé, ASCII text e-mailable résumé, and MS Word file. In today's busy world, most recruiters and hiring managers have so little time to read résumés that they are turning to e-mailed and scanned résumés and applicant tracking systems to lighten their load. Unless they are highly motivated, they won't take the time to search for and then spend 15 minutes clicking their way through a multimedia presentation of someone's qualifications, either online at your Web-based portfolio or on a CD-ROM you might mail to them with your e-folio.

But, it never hurts to add this networking tool to your job search. You can always direct your reader to your e-folio by listing the URL on your résumé, letterhead, and personal business card. That way, your reader has the option of going there for more information. Just don't expect to get a job offer by simply creating a Web résumé or e-folio and waiting for a recruiter to find you.

The real purpose of an e-folio is to provide extra information for when a potential employer is trying to narrow down his or her applicant pool. You can even direct the hiring manager to your Web site during an interview. Your e-folio may just tip the scales when a hiring manager is trying to choose between you and someone else.

You never know when someone will "Google" you before an interview. All a hiring manager needs to do nowadays is to enter your name in any major search engine and see what pops up . . . or doesn't! Hopefully what he or she finds is good. If you want to control what that hiring manager sees, a well-designed and promoted e-folio is your answer. It allows you to control your online image.

An e-folio is also a great career management tool that you don't have to save just for your job search. Imagine preparing for your annual performance evaluation with your current employer by reviewing the accomplishments you have collected in your "I Love Me" file and putting together either a paper-based or Web-based portfolio. When it is time to sit down with your supervisor and talk about what you have achieved this year, you can take control of the discussion by making a "sales presentation" of your accomplishments and tangible examples of work samples. What an impression you will make! You've got a raise!

But don't wait for your annual evaluation to think about using this tool. Many companies have implemented performance assessment programs that are ongoing with periodic meetings throughout the year to assess goals, milestones, and incremental achievements toward objectives.

If your company isn't that progressive and barely uses annual performance evaluations, let alone performance goal setting, then make yourself stand out in the crowd of other employees by being proactive. Develop your e-folio or paper portfolio and set the meeting with your supervisor yourself. Take charge of your career path and show your entrepreneurial spirit. Remember that entrepreneurship is all about "ownership," and you can own your career whether or not you own the business for which you work. This kind of independent thinking is often rewarded with promotions and/or pay increases that reflect your value to the company. It also makes your job more secure, since you have proven value to your employer. With downsizing the norm in today's workforce, the more valuable you are, the less likely you will to be laid off. Businesses are in the business of making money. If you make your employer more money than you cost to keep around, it just makes business sense that you will be retained.

■ *Advantages of an e-Folio*

You've heard the old saying, "A picture is worth a thousand words." That is the primary advantage of an e-folio. You can talk about what you've accomplished in words (either on paper or verbally) from now until doomsday, but nothing makes an impression like tangible, visual backup, especially today when so many recruiters and hiring managers are skeptical of claims made on résumés (see page 24).

Most of us think of artists, models, actors, and photographers when we think of a portfolio, but that's not the case today. Everyone should maintain a portfolio. More and more employers are asking to see concrete evidence of the experience, skills, education, and accomplishments shown on your résumé, especially during the interview. I've even had employers ask recent MBA graduates for copies of their school term papers or other special projects and writing samples.

Besides keeping your résumé in front of recruiters by being on the Internet all of the time, a well-planned e-folio is great for formal employment interviews, networking, informational interviews, performance assessments and evaluations on your current job, and admission to colleges and universities, among other functions. It is a professional self-marketing tool that can help you manage your entire career.

An e-folio is especially useful for entrepreneurs and consultants, since it can serve as a marketing tool for whatever products or services they sell. If you think about it, though, we should all be treating our careers as "entrepreneurial" ventures. When you take control of your career as a business owner controls his or her company, you make conscious choices about how to market your product—in the case of your career, that's *you*. Your résumé becomes your print advertising and your e-folio is your online brochure that convinces a "buyer" to call you instead of the "competition."

Another advantage of an e-folio is the first impression it makes. Dr. John Sullivan, Head Professor of Human Resource Management in the College of Business at San Francisco State University, says that "because portfolios take some effort, they demonstrate a degree of commitment on the part of the candidate that is not required in a résumé . . . so it improves the quality of new hires."

Making a presentation with a portfolio gives you a leg up on your competition and makes it more likely that you will be noticed. Have you ever been asked in an interview, "Can you tell me a little something about yourself?" Even if you have rehearsed your answer a million times, you probably floundered a bit, right? We have been taught all our lives not to brag, so blowing our own horn makes most people very uncomfortable.

Now, picture entering the interviewer's office with a neat leatherette binder or CD-ROM in your briefcase. You shake hands and have a seat. The dreaded question is asked, "Why don't you tell me about yourself?" You answer, "I would like to show you instead." You open your briefcase, remove the binder or CD-ROM, stand up, and walk around to the interviewer's side of the desk. "As you noticed in my résumé, I have . . ." and you launch into your work history and accomplishments, turning the pages in the binder or clicking through the CD-ROM of your e-folio on your own laptop computer, pointing to key items to reinforce what you are saying. Now, you are in control of the interview. By the way, if the interviewer has Internet access and your e-folio is online, you don't even need the CD-ROM, although I always recommend having a backup of your e-folio with you in either paper or digital format in case the interviewer's Internet connection is down.

Using a portfolio like this during an interview makes it easier to highlight your planning, problem solving, critical thinking, and verbal communication skills, and it serves as a catalyst for discussion. This discussion provides you with the opportunity to demonstrate just what you can do for the company if you are hired and how quickly the company can generate a return on their investment in you.

The key to an effective portfolio is to research the company you will be interviewing with first. Determine what their needs might be and then select key items for your portfolio that you think would be of special interest to that employer. The portfolio you take to the next interview might be totally different, although it doesn't necessarily have to be different if you are applying for the same types of jobs in the same or similar industries. However, you must be able to tell a coherent story with the information. Make sure there is a connecting thread so you can easily transition from one item to the next. Practice before the interview!

■ *Portfolio Ideas by Job Type*

Everybody's portfolio will be different, especially across industries and job titles. Even when two people share the same position in the same company, they shouldn't expect the contents of their portfolios to be the same. We each have our own unique backgrounds, qualifications, and accomplishments. However, there are some basic items that will appear in all portfolios:

1. *A résumé*—Your résumé (or bio in some cases) generally serves as the foundation of your e-folio. If it is well written, your résumé determines the basic outline for your Web site and helps you decide what sections to include. Don't simply rehash your résumé verbatim in your e-folio, however, or there is no point to your Web site. Summarize and expand on your résumé with job descriptions, employer reviews, work samples, problem-solving examples, leadership examples, organizational charts, customer survey results, proposals, business plans, and so on.

2. *Proof of achievements*—This can be charts or graphs if your accomplishments are quantifiable (like in sales and positions with P&L responsibility, i.e., bottom line), copies of publicity, articles you have written, photographs, videos, company newsletters, white papers, special projects, newspaper or magazine articles, thank you letters from supervisors/customers/vendors, performance evaluations with key accomplishments highlighted, honors, awards, and so on. If any of the information you want to use is copyrighted by someone else, you will need to get written permission to use it on your Web site first.

3. *Credentials*—This is where you back up your education, special training, licenses, certifications, and other credentials with scanned images of your diplomas, certificates, transcripts (for some positions), and other proof documents. Lists of major course work and select projects might be included if you are a recent graduate with little experience.

4. *Recommendations*—Scan your letters of reference from past employers, current supervisors, key customers or vendors, and other people who know your work well. Highlight key phrases or simply type a list of quotes with the person's name, job title, and company. These third-party recommendations validate what you say about yourself in your own documentation.

It is easy to overdo both a hard-copy portfolio and an e-folio. It is sometimes hard to narrow down the items you want to include, so people have a tendency to make their portfolios much too long. Dr. Sullivan feels that a world-class portfolio has the following five characteristics:

1. It must be scannable in 15 minutes or less.
2. It sells you with your work and your ideas.
3. It is customized for each job and each company.
4. It includes and highlights your WOWs.
5. It excites the viewer.

Once your e-folio has the four basics, you can add other things to make it unique. Rather than repeat the items above for every industry, the lists below are in addition to your résumé, credentials, recommendations, and proof of accomplishments (although some items fall into this category just to give you more ideas). Use your imagination. These lists are just jumping off points for your own creativity, which is really what you are trying to display in your portfolio anyway.

Administrative Assistant
- Lists of technical competencies
- Examples of various document preparation skills—correspondence, spreadsheets, PowerPoint presentations, forms, organizational chart, etc.
- Photos, agendas, budgets of events planned
- Letters of appreciation
- Certificates from classes, workshops, seminars, conferences

Antique & Art Dealer
- Areas of expertise
- Select finds and sources
- Valuation/appraisal experience
- Restoration experience with photos
- International travel
- Import/export
- Apprenticeships and other hands-on experience
- Education and credentials
- Letters or comments from clients

Apartment Manager
- Photos of properties
- Size and types of units (luxury, family, senior citizen)
- Amenities
- Construction or renovation
- Occupancy rates
- Special promotions, events, and open houses
- Activities for residents
- Graphics representing impact on the bottom line

Architect
- Drawings, photographs, blueprints
- Styles
- Honors and awards
- Media coverage
- Professional affiliations
- Presentations
- Letters from satisfied customers and builders
- Acknowledgments from peers
- Parade of Homes participation

Artist
- Includes painters, sculptors, illustrators, designers, cartoonists, or anyone producing a visual art
- Mediums
- Education and special training
- Photographs of art work

- Published works
- Reviews in magazines, newspapers, and other publications
- Lists and photographs of exhibitions
- Representations
- Museum collections
- Descriptions of style and artist philosophy
- Hyperlinks to online displays of art work

Athlete
- Sports
- Media coverage
- Records and times
- Competitions
- Honors, awards
- Coaches, trainers

Attorney
- Areas of specialty
- Credentials—diplomas, licenses, etc.
- Track record of success
- Client testimonials
- Lists of significant cases
- Bar and court admissions
- Presentations
- Professional affiliations
- Volunteer work

Chef
- Menus
- Photographs of plated dinners and banquet presentations
- Thank you notes from customers
- Certificates of completion from special training programs
- Participation in stages and international programs
- Reviews in magazines, newspapers, and other publications
- Honors, awards, contests, chef's tables

Computer Professional
- Photographs of software packages or manuals
- Examples of unique or difficult code and its result
- Screen shots of GUI interfaces
- Charts and graphs that show increases in productivity or profitability as a result of the finished product
- Technical skills divided into types
- Special projects
- Technical documents produced

Construction
- Areas of specialty
- Photos of completed projects
- Honors, awards, parade of homes, etc.
- Proof of licenses and bonding

- Letters from satisfied customers
- Community participation
- Professional affiliations

Customer Service Representative
- Letters from satisfied customers
- Awards for exceeding quotas
- Customer service scores
- Personality tests (like Myers-Briggs) that show an aptitude for working with people

Diplomat
- Negotiations, conflict resolutions, treaties
- Languages, cultures
- Special events
- Media coverage
- White papers, publications
- Pictures with famous people
- Noteworthy speeches and other presentations

Economist
- Credentials are very important in this industry—education, degrees, training
- Areas of expertise—energy, inflation, imports, employment, monetary policy, consumer theory, markets, profits, costs, public policy
- Examples of research and analysis
- Expertise with statistical analysis software
- Sample spreadsheets, graphs, charts
- Publications
- Presentations
- Publicity

Editor
- Education and special training
- Writing samples
- List of own published works
- Types of editing—fiction, creative nonfiction, trade, nonfiction
- Editing samples—both hard copy and digital
- Titles of books edited

Engineer
- Drawings
- Schematics
- White papers
- Research
- Education and credentials
- Media attention
- Honors and awards

Event Planner	■ List of functions ■ Venues ■ Entertainment ■ Menus ■ Photos of decorations ■ Thank you letters and other kudos ■ Print promotions, invitations, newspaper coverage ■ Video clips
Executive	■ Executive summary ■ Management philosophy ■ Charts and graphs reflecting impact on the bottom line and performance improvement data ■ List of business competencies showing levels of expertise ■ Description of a major problem, your solution, and the result ■ Leadership examples ■ Organizational charts showing subordinate personnel and areas of responsibility ■ Affiliations and professional memberships with any leadership positions
Firefighter	■ Certifications ■ Areas of expertise ■ Education and training ■ Professional development ■ Community involvement ■ Special projects ■ Professional affiliations ■ Promotion record
Flight Attendant	■ Photographs—head shot and full-body shot ■ Special training ■ Letters of appreciation from customers ■ Recognition from supervisors ■ Routes—domestic or international ■ Languages and cross-cultural experience
Florist	■ Lots of photographs that show quality of work ■ Examples of different styles and types of arrangements ■ Artistic designs using other media besides flowers ■ Comments from satisfied customers
Groomer	■ Photographs, photographs, photographs! ■ Show dogs and champions ■ Styles ■ Humane treatment philosophy

Hospitality	■ Lists or photos of hotels or restaurants managed
	■ Growth charts showing proof of impact on the bottom line
	■ Occupancy rates
	■ Letters of appreciation from satisfied guests
	■ Property improvements / construction / renovation
	■ Operating improvements
	■ News coverage
	■ Grand openings

Human Resources
- Employee benefits packages
- Interview worksheets
- Motivational and training programs
- Union negotiations
- Documentation of faster hiring or better retention
- Proof of lower costs for the hiring process
- Industry association participation
- Implementation of new technologies to manage the hiring process

Inventor or R&D
- Areas of expertise
- Patents
- Photographs of inventions
- Professional associations
- Presentations and academic assignments
- Publications and white papers
- Media coverage

Jeweler
- Photos! Photos! Photos!
- Design specialties—rings, necklaces, bracelets
- Materials expertise—gold, silver, platinum, precious stones, stone cutting, jewelry repair
- Testimonials from customers

Manufacturing
- Proof of product development
- Charts and graphs showing process improvements
- Implementation of new technologies and processes
- Safety improvement
- Quality control
- Volume increases
- Schematics, blueprints, designs, technical drawings

Marketing
- Marketing plans
- Advertising programs (video, print, voice)
- New media productions (Web sites, CD-ROMs)
- Focus group design and results
- Proposals

- Photographs
- Results, results, results!

Mechanic
- Areas of specialty
- Photos of body work or design
- Certifications
- Testimonials from satisfied customers
- Location of shop with map

Minister
- Religious philosophies
- Family photos
- Personal information about children and spouse
- Sermon outlines
- List of topics
- Letters and comments from church members and leaders
- Presentations and special teaching assignments
- Media coverage
- Video clips or radio broadcasts

Model
- Photos, photos, photos!
- Copies of magazines or newspaper coverage
- Fashion show advertisements and runway shots
- Specialty areas
- Languages, singing, acting, musical instruments, sports, etc.
- Video tapes of commercial spots, movie appearances, etc.

Museum Curator
- Special events with invitations, photos, media coverage
- Lists and photos of special exhibits
- Fund-raising results
- Speakers acquired
- Permanent exhibits and acquisitions
- Capital improvements
- Advertising and promotions, including brochures, museum literature, television, radio, and print campaigns

Musician
- Recordings of performances and/or compositions made into sound files for the e-folio and CD-ROM
- Reviews in magazines, newspapers, and other publications
- Conservatory and special training programs
- Performances
- Honors, awards, contests

Nonprofit Sector
- Fund raising
- Event planning
- Capital campaigns
- Volunteer management

	■ Areas of specialty
	■ Low turnover of employees and volunteers
	■ Publicity, media coverage
Photographer	■ Photos! Photos! Photos!
	■ Genre specialties
	■ Recognitions, honors, awards
	■ Exhibits (both solo and group)
	■ Purchases—museum, gallery, business, individual
	■ Media reports and reviews
Physician, Nurse, or Other Healthcare Practitioner	■ Licenses and other credentials
	■ Degrees
	■ Research projects
	■ Grants, awards, and honors
	■ Patient testimonials
	■ Philosophies
	■ Academic appointments and teaching assignments
	■ Publications
	■ Presentations
	■ Professional affiliations
	■ Community service
Police Officer	■ Special projects and committees
	■ Community involvement
	■ Areas of expertise
	■ Education and special training
	■ Awards and honors
Professor	■ Education and credentials are very important
	■ Courses developed and taught
	■ Research and development
	■ Professional presentations
	■ Publications—books, journals, and other periodicals
	■ Special committees and projects
	■ Student evaluations
	■ Administrative responsibilities
	■ Awards, honors, and other recognition
	■ Community involvement
Project Manager	■ Lists of projects
	■ Outcomes
	■ Processes—needs analysis, resource allocation, project scheduling, product development, budgets, implementation
	■ Letters from satisfied customers (internal and external)

Radio Broadcaster	■ Audio clips of shows, promos, jingles, etc.
	■ Expertise with digital editing equipment and other technology
	■ Examples of original scripts, journalism, and other writing
	■ Community outreach
	■ Promotions

Real Estate Agent	■ Sales achievements—graphs, awards, honors
	■ Areas of specialty
	■ Success stories with photographs
	■ Client comments

Recent Graduate	■ Diplomas
	■ Scholarships, grants, awards, honors
	■ Samples of class papers, projects, reports, videos
	■ Transcripts or lists of relevant courses
	■ Course descriptions to add keywords and depth
	■ Teacher evaluations
	■ Community service projects
	■ Clubs, honor societies, fraternities, and leadership positions

Sales	■ Types of products sold, customers, and territories
	■ Documented achievements—increased revenue or profits
	■ Charts and graphs
	■ Significant account acquisition
	■ Number of leads generated and converted
	■ Closing ratio
	■ Letters from customers
	■ Sale team-building exercises
	■ Training and motivation programs developed and presented
	■ Results, results, results!

Scientist	■ Areas of specialty
	■ Special projects
	■ Inventions
	■ Patents
	■ Professional affiliations
	■ Honors, awards, or other special recognition
	■ News reports
	■ White papers
	■ Research
	■ Grants
	■ Presentations

Social Services	■ Areas of specialty
	■ Credentials, licenses, diplomas
	■ Testimonials from clients helped

| | ▪ Professional affiliations |
| | ▪ Volunteer work |

Speaker
- Video of key presentations
- Areas of expertise
- Topics, prices, and schedules
- Honors, awards, accolades
- Future speaking engagements
- Past audiences
- Invitations to share your expertise
- Thank you letters
- Membership in speaker organizations
- Photographs of you in action
- Brochures from events

Teacher
- Teaching philosophy statement
- Lesson plans, syllabi, curricula
- Photographs of bulletin boards and learning aids
- Staff development projects
- Examples of special challenges and how you overcame them
- Credentials are really important in this industry—degrees, transcripts, continuing education
- Examples of community partnerships, legislative or volunteer work, and special committees
- Student portfolios or other proofs of your legacy
- Affiliations and professional memberships

Television Newscaster
- Lists of major stories covered
- Writing examples
- Video clips
- Areas of specialty—hard news, breaking news, feature stories
- Professional head shots
- Promotional materials created by the station

Translator
- Writing examples
- Lists of special projects
- Areas of specialty
- Languages and levels of proficiency
- Teaching or tutoring programs developed and presented
- Letters of appreciation

Web Designer
- Web sites, Web sites, Web sites!
- Show off your designs
- What makes them unique?
- Java scripts, flash graphics, e-commerce features
- Letters from satisfied clients

- List of technical competencies
- List of projects and clients with hyperlinks to their sites

Writer
- Poems
- Excerpts from published works
- Media coverage
- Reviews
- Copies of articles in newspapers and magazines or hyperlinks to the online version of the article

■ *Portfolio Sample*

I was recently referred to Brandego™ LLC (*http://www.brandego.com*) as a source for unique, executive-level portfolio services. After reviewing the portfolio samples on their Web site, I called Kirsten Dixson to obtain their permission to use screen shots of one of their portfolios in this book.

We had a fascinating discussion about branding and using e-folios for career management. Kirsten agrees that "an e-folio is much more effective when it does more than just reiterate a person's paper résumé." She is also adamant about making sure that the design of the Web site doesn't detract from its message. Kirsten says, "Brandego™ provides a comprehensive career-management solution that combines the best of personal branding, career portfolios, Web design, and direct marketing."

With Brandego's™ permission, here is an excellent example of a sophisticated e-folio throughout its various levels. For more samples, check their Web site at *http://www.brandego.com.*

❏ *A Web Site Outline*

When you develop a Web site for the first time, deciding what message you are going to convey and then laying out the flow of the site to facilitate delivery of that message is the key to an effective finished product. Patricia Moriarty (the sample e-folio that follows) is a specialist in education and technology curriculum integration, so her Web site focuses on her knowledge, skills, and abilities in this arena. Her site is laid out using the following outline.

1. INTRODUCTION

- A summary paragraph of her history and qualifications
- A list of her areas of expertise
- A keyword list of her personal attributes or strengths

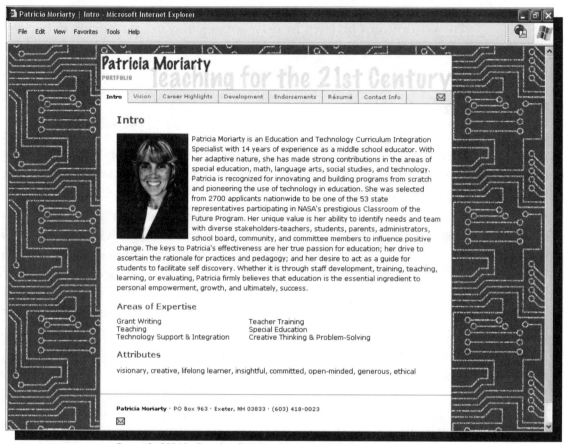

2. *VISION*

- A statement of her personal philosophies about her work
- Notice that every page of her Web site contains:
  - Full links to every other page of her site
  - Full contact information at the bottom of the page to make it easier for a potential employer to call her
  - A little envelope that jumps directly to a contact form that the viewer can use to send an e-mail to Patricia immediately
- The point is to make the site easy to navigate

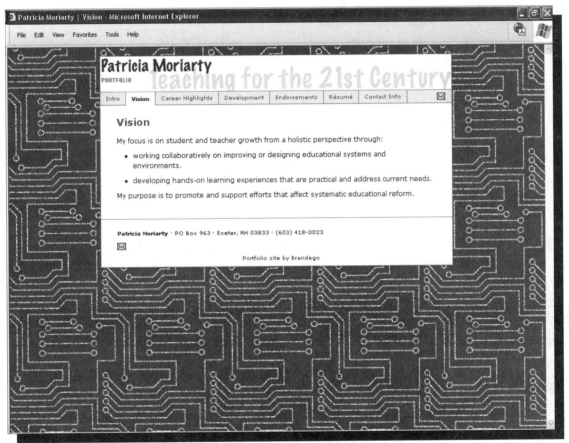

Copyright 2004 by Brandego™ LLC and Patricia Moriarty. Used by permission.

3. *CAREER HIGHLIGHTS*

- This section is not just a reiteration of her résumé
- I especially like that fact that you don't have to use the "Back" button to return from the scanned images to the main page
- Details of the NASA Classroom of the Future Program
  - Challenge, Action, Results (CAR) statements
  - Scanned image of the citation
  - Scanned image of a newspaper article
- Details of the Technology Literacy Program
  - CAR statements
  - Scanned image of a Compaq training certificate
  - Scanned image of a newspaper article
- Details of a New Hampshire Special Education Grant
  - CAR statements
  - Quote from the parent of a former student
- Details of a State Work-to-School Grant
  - CAR statements
  - Scanned image of a newspaper article
- Details of her study abroad
  - CAR statements

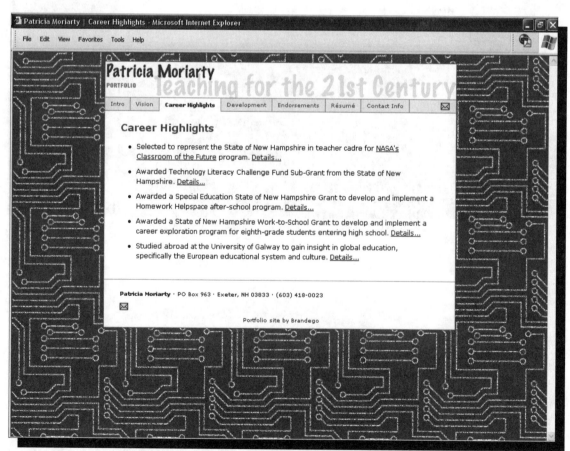

Copyright 2004 by Brandego™ LLC and Patricia Moriarty. Used by permission.

4. DEVELOPMENT

- Formal Education
  - Scanned images from her Master's degree
  - Scanned images from her Bachelor's degrees
- Ongoing Professional Development
  - Scanned images of various certificates

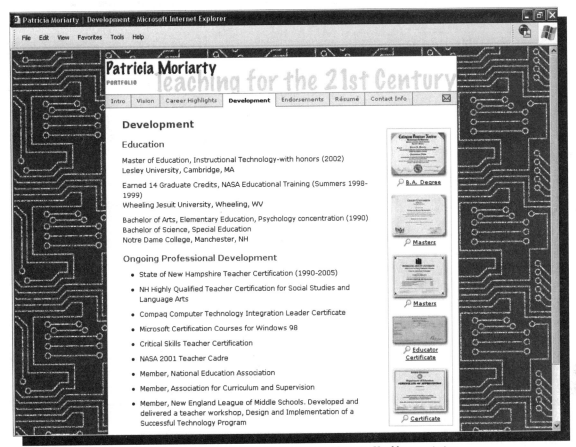

5. ENDORSEMENTS

- Quotes from former students
- Quote from a parent of a former student
- Quotes from colleagues
- Quotes from an administrator

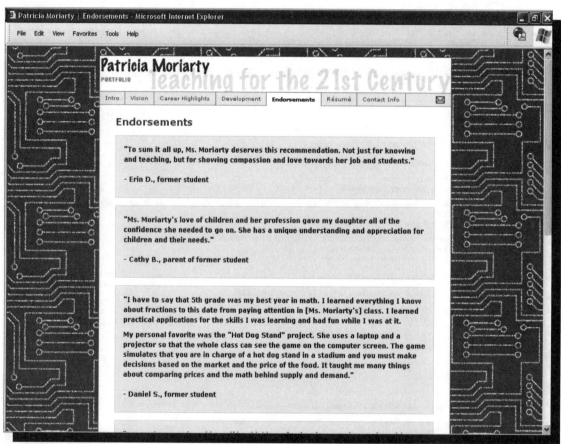

Copyright 2004 by Brandego™ LLC and Patricia Moriarty. Used by permission.

6. *RÉSUMÉ*

- The complete paper résumé is re-entered here using HTML formatting
- The reader can choose to download either a PDF, ASCII text, or MS Word version of the résumé
- The ASCII text file can be downloaded by the viewer for input into computerized applicant tracking systems
- The MS Word file is for recruiters who like to customize résumés before submitting them to their clients

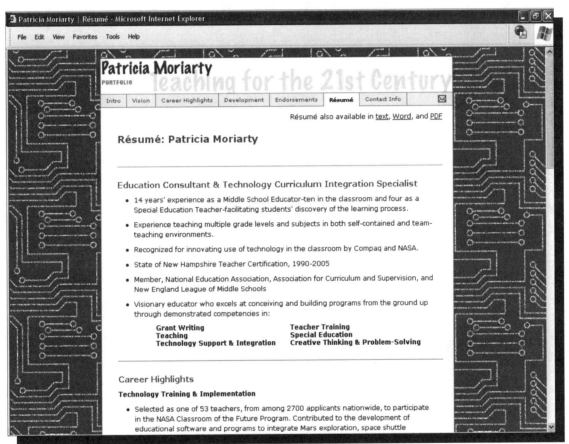

7. CONTACT INFO

- In addition to the full mailing address and telephone numbers at the bottom of the page, this page provides a form that the viewer can complete and e-mail directly to Patricia

- If you have only a cellular number, always identify it as a cell phone so the viewer knows they can try to reach you during business hours

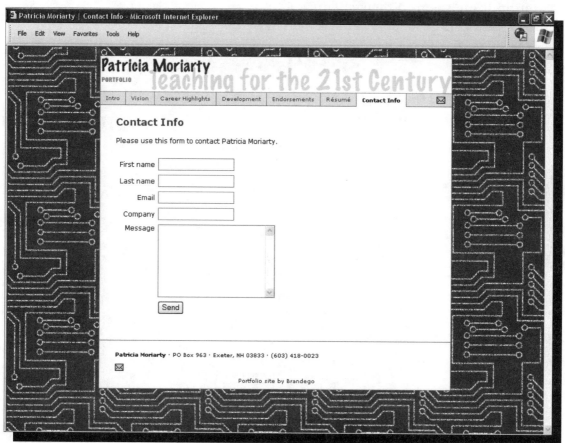

Copyright 2004 by Brandego™ LLC and Patricia Moriarty. Used by permission.

11 How to Create a Home Page for Your e-Résumé

For those do-it-yourselfers who choose not to use a professional Web designer, there are simple ways to create a home page, but first you need to understand a little about Hypertext Markup Language. HTML is an uncomplicated computer programming language used to format documents for display on the World Wide Web. When displayed using a WWW browser, documents created with HTML look like they were typeset. In other words, they look pretty.

HTML is built from tags that tell a computer the text size, font, style, graphics placement, links to other Web pages, and so on. As an example, if you want to make a headline large, you would put a tag at the beginning of the line of text that reads <h1> and a tag at the end of the line to turn it off, </h1>. The slash turns off the code. Your actual line would look something like this:

```
<h1>This Is My First Headline</h1>
```

<h1> produces the biggest headlines, <h2> makes a slightly smaller one, and so on through <h6>. Once you turn on any style using a tag, you must remember to turn it off with a slash in order to return to normal text. As you can see, you are working in plain vanilla ASCII text, but your Web browser sees the codes and turns the text, graphics, and sounds into something beautiful on your computer monitor.

One of the easiest ways to create your home page is to use an HTML editor that automatically converts your formatting codes into HTML tags. Many of the editors are free through commercial online services. For instance, America Online provides you with its Personal Publisher program, which guides you step-by-step through the creation of a home page. Even Microsoft Word and Corel WordPerfect can convert your word processing files into Web pages through a simple "Save As" process, complete with HTML codes and ready to be uploaded to your Web site.

It would take an entire book to list all of the tags possible in HTML, which is outside the scope of this text. It is much better to direct you to several excellent resources that are available on the Internet free of charge. You simply need to navigate to the site and print the documents that interest you.

- W3C's style guide to online hypertext
  http://www.w3.org/Provider/Style/Overview.html

- Web Page Design for Designers
  http://www.wpdfd.com/

- Official HTML specifications
  http://www.w3.org/MarkUp/

- Dos and don'ts of web design
  http://millkern.com/do-dont.html

- Web Design Group
  http://www.htmlhelp.com/

- Web Style Guide
  http://www.webstyleguide.com/index.html?/contents.html

- Web development resources
  http://www.eborcom.com/webmaker/

- Web design resource
  http://www.pageresource.com/

- Java scripts for perking up your Web site
  http://java.sun.com/

- Interactive HTML tutorial for beginners
  http://www.davesite.com/webstation/html

- Webmonkey
  http://webmonkey.wired.com/webmonkey/

The key to creating a successful Web site is consistency and relevancy. Plan your site long before you begin designing it. Know what you want to say and what your audience will want to read. Use a logical system of links that takes the reader to more and more information, but avoid overwhelming your reader with too much information. Make sure your most valuable information isn't layers deep into your site.

For a Web résumé or e-folio, you must keep in mind the same rules you followed for your paper résumé. Avoid photographs unless your appearance is a bona fide occupational qualification in your industry (model, newscaster, actor, etc.). You don't want to set yourself up for discrimination based on sex, race, age, or even something as silly as your hair color or the length of your nose. If there is something about your appearance that would make it hard for an HR professional not to discriminate, then don't include your photograph on your Web site.

Don't list personal information—especially anything that would set you up for age, racial, gender, ethnic, or religious discrimination but also your hobbies, interests, children, spouse, or your favorite dog. A recent article in *The Wall Street*

Journal reported that "interviewers are often turned off by being told more about the applicant's personal life on their Web sites than they care to learn."

With those limitations in mind, you can make your Web résumé a true e-folio of your accomplishments. The latest trend in hiring is to bring a portfolio to the interview. With a Web-based e-folio, you can direct the hiring manager to your Web site long before the interview, and you can put your best foot forward in a planned environment that you control.

As discussed in Chapter 10, your e-folio contains your résumé, work samples, concrete proof of your accomplishments (charts, graphs, news clippings, etc.), products you have designed, testimonials, letters of recommendation, proof of credentials (licenses, certifications, diplomas), and the list goes on.

Following are some design tips for making your Web résumé or e-folio stand out in a crowd:

1. Remember when desktop publishing first surfaced and people loaded up their documents with 20 different fonts just because they could? That is called "design bloat," and the opportunity to repeat those excesses and even magnify them lies wide open before you as you embark on your first attempts at a World Wide Web home page. Of course, the best way to get an idea of what you want to do with your personal digital space is to first visit a lot of other people's Web homes. Spend some time visiting the pages of your friends, business associates, and the bigger commercial sites.

2. When using headlines, stick to the smaller sizes. The three largest headline sizes display a lot larger on some browsers.

3. Don't use italics too often. They can be *very hard to read* when used in regular text, and nearly impossible to decipher at smaller font sizes. ***Boldfacing italicized type,*** or simply **boldfacing** instead, will help legibility.

4. Use centering liberally. You don't have many formatting tools available to you on the Web, and this is a good one.

5. Replace the standard gray background to give your page a more contemporary look. White is a safe choice, although that color will give horizontal rules on the page a "tail" on the left side. Other background colors can be more difficult to work with since they have a noticeable impact on other page elements or make the text difficult to read.

6. Don't use textured backgrounds that are too busy. Like italics, most make the text harder to read.

7. Changing link colors? If you're bothering to alter the colors of visited and unvisited links, at least sync them up with colors occurring in images you've used on the page. And keep link colors consistent across multiple pages.

8. Web surfers really appreciate knowing whether the information they are perusing is fresh stuff or moldy bread. Somewhere on your home page, let users know when the page was last updated.

9. Your opening graphic should display fully on the user's screen without scrolling. That means nothing larger than 640 × 480 pixels. Always assume that a user's browser will be on its default settings at its smallest size vertically.

10. Always ALT! Some browsers display small windows where yet-to-be-downloaded images will be laid out on the page. ALT information, which is easily entered using Web site design software, describes the image's contents and gives Web surfers something to look at while your pictures trickle down the pipe.

11. Keep graphics as simple and small as possible. Remember that computer screens are low in resolution compared to the quality of a print magazine, so things that might work in that medium won't translate to the Web where 256 colors are the standard. Most monitors today can actually display millions of colors, but their users often don't run them at higher resolutions. After you have uploaded your page, log on with a browser and time how long it takes for an opening graphic or the entire page to load. If it's too long, make adjustments to get the size of your graphics (or the number of graphics on the page) down. Design for slower Internet connections. You might have a fast broadband connection, but someone else may be logging on at 56 kbps or slower. If you have something that might take several minutes to transfer, it had better be worth the time the user spends waiting to see it.

12. Make hot buttons look hot. If you are using images as hotlinks and are removing the colored border that identifies them as links (using the HTML image command BORDER=0), do something to distinguish them from images on the page that aren't clickable links. The user shouldn't have to try to figure out what's hot and what's not.

13. Be cognizant of color. If you are scanning personal images for use on your page, plan to spend a lot of time fine-tuning them. Make sure all images on the same page share a common palette. If you use a custom palette, it should include the 16 colors that Windows uses. If the image isn't transparent, putting some type of border around it will usually give the page it is on a more finished look.

14. Lower the resolution on scanned graphics, too. Microsoft Windows machines can't display anything higher than 96 dpi (dots per inch), so saving graphics at 150 or 300 dpi is overkill and will make them too large to download anyway.

15. Wrap text around images that are less than half as wide as the display area. The text may not wrap in all browsers, but at least you have added the feature for those who can take advantage of it.

16. Crop! Nothing is worse than a 200K graphic that contains 25K of information. Use a graphic-manipulation program not only to improve color and contrast, but also to edit out parts of a picture that don't relate anything useful.

17. GIF versus JPEG? Save your images as JPEGs when they are continuous tone (i.e., photographs). JPEG files will compress to a smaller size and generally look better than GIFs of the same image. GIF should be used only for line-art images such as screen shots and logos created in a paint program.

18. Don't use "under construction" graphics. Just go with what you have. Web pages, if you haven't noticed, are *always* under construction.

19. No moving experiences, please. Scrolling text, marquees, and some animated GIFs chew up just enough processor time to make interacting with a page annoying. And blinking text is widely regarded on the Net as "just plain evil."

20. If your site is composed of multiple pages (HTML documents), include links on every page that return users to the master page with its table of contents. Such "orphan" pages can be confusing if a Web surfer bypasses your home page and hits one of your secondary pages directly.

21. Break it up. As you might guess, a very small percentage of people ever bother to scroll an unfamiliar page to see what's further down, unless it contains information they really need. Put all of your navigation functions and gee-whiz information on the top part of the page, and move long passages of text across multiple pages so readers feel as though they are getting somewhere.

22. It's the browser! Whether your page is viewed in Netscape or Internet Explorer ultimately determines what it will look like. Try viewing your page in various browsers to get a feel for what happens, and then adjust your design to achieve the best compromise. If you use a 17-inch or larger monitor, also test your design on a computer with a 14-inch screen just to be certain you like how your site looks when viewed in a smaller box.

23. And, last but not least, fine-tune the thing to death. A word or two more or less in a key location will change the way the copy lays out on the screen, and a little more or less height (maybe 2 or 3 pixels) on a graphic image can frequently clean things up considerably. It's the little things that count.

The last thing you will want to consider is adding a counter to your home page. A counter will allow you to keep track of how many people are passing through your site. Granted, it doesn't tell you who was there, but it is nice to know that someone has seen your home page besides you and your mom.

Hit counters are not written in HTML. They are a CGI script that is dependent on your Internet service provider's computer, so you will need to contact your ISP in order to get directions for adding a counter to your home page. To make one a part of your site, you use a tag similar to an image tag that directs the browser to go to the counter every time someone hits your page. The counter itself is a GIF image that is updated every time the page is chosen. The code in America Online looks something like this:

```
<img src="/cgi-bin/counter?criscito">
```

Some Web site hosting services (generally not the free ones) offer traffic counters and site statistics automatically. If yours does not, then you should also download or purchase a tracking service to monitor the origin of your traffic. That way you can fine-tune the design and placement of your site. For a list of counters and trackers, visit *http://www.adbility.com?SPAG/* or check eXTReMe Tracking's Web site at *http://www.extreme-dm.com/tracking/*.

■ *Adding Multimedia to Your e-Folio*

Adding a PDF file, photograph, or other graphic image to your home page is a simple matter of typing in an HTML tag that sends the browser in search of either a PDF, GIF, or JPEG image file. You can create these graphic files in a couple of ways, but first you need to understand what these files are. GIF (Graphics Interchange Format) files and JPEG (Joint Photographics Experts Group) are both common image file formats used in Web pages. They are just different ways of storing graphics information on a computer.

A Portable Document File (PDF) is created using Adobe Acrobat or your word processor if you are using one of the latest versions of MS Word or Corel WordPerfect. It is more like a photograph of your résumé than the original word processed file. A PDF files allows you to have total control over the appearance of your résumé once it is downloaded.

A PDF file is great to use on your Web site, but don't attach a PDF file to an e-mail when you send your résumé to a company's recruiter. Right now, most applicant tracking software can't process PDF files. That is changing, but you need to accommodate the lowest common denominator, so don't take a chance. Send your MS Word file attached to an e-mail message instead.

JPEG images are generally better suited for photographic images since they can support millions of colors. If you scan a photograph of, say, one of your paintings if you are an artist, it will look better and take up less disk space in JPEG format than in GIF format. GIF images are best used for line art, like logos, and are limited to 256 colors. Both types of files are relatively small in size and won't take long to download when someone views your home page. All Web browsers can display both GIF and JPEG images.

To create these graphic files, you must first have a scanner that will save your files in either format or you must use a drawing program to create the graphic images you want to place on your home page and then save them in the appropriate format or you can have your film developed by a service that offers digital files. If you need help, turn to your phone directory's Yellow Pages and find a graphic artist or graphics service bureau that can create these files for you. Just make sure they know you need GIF or JPEG files on disk in addition to a hard copy printout of the scanned image or other graphics.

If you are the do-it-yourself type, your local Kinko's photocopy and printing store *(http://www.fedexkinkos.com/)* will usually have a computer hooked to a scanner that you can use for a fee, and they may even show you how to use it!

If you have a roll of film with your photograph (or any other picture) on it, there is another way to get a JPEG file. Most film developers today will process your film and place the picture on a disk for you. The disk includes a Windows-based software program that allows you to view, edit, and print the images. Of course, if you are using a digital camera, the files are already saved in JPEG format.

There are also resources on the Internet that are loaded with free graphics and sound files that you may use on your home page:

100% All Free Clipart	*http://free-clipart.com*
1001 Free Fonts	*http://www.1001freefonts.com*
123 ClipArt	*http://www.123clipart.com*
3DExpo	*http://www.3dexpo.com*
A-1 Icon Archive Free Web Graphics	*http://www.free-graphics.com*
Absolute Web Graphic Archive	*http://grsites.com/webgraphics*
All Clipart site	*http://www.allclipartsite.com*
Art a al Carte Free Stuff	*http://www.artcarte.com/free.html*
Barry's Clip Art Server	*http://www.barrysclipart.com*
Best Clip Art	*http://www.bestclipart.com*
Boogie Jack's Graphics Plus	*http://www.boogiejack.com*
Clip Art Center	*http://clip-art.easy-interactive.com/*
Clip Art Connection	*http://www.clipartconnection.com*
Clip Art Review	*http://www.webplaces.com/html/clipart.htm*
The Clip Art Universe	*http://nzwwa.com/mirror/clipart/*
Clip Art Warehouse	*http://www.clipart.co.uk/*
ClipArt Searcher	*http://www.webplaces.com/search/*
Clipart.com	*http://www.clipart.com*
Clipartsite.com	*http://www.clipartsite.com*
Free Clip Art	*http://www.free-clip-art.to/*
Free Clip Art.net	*http://www.free-clip-art.net/index2.shtml*
Free Clip Art Junction	*http://www.cksinfo.com/scripts/index.html*
FreeGraphics	*http://www.freegraphics.com*
Fresher Image	*http://www.free-clip-images.com*
Graphic World	*http://graphic-world.com/*
Instant Free Icons	*http://www.stormloader.com/spdypdy/icons/icon.html*
Media Links Free Graphics	*http://my.erinet.com/~cunning1/tiles.html*
Realm Graphics	*http://www.ender-design.com/rg/*
Stuff Web Site Tools	*http://www.stuff.uk.com/index.shtml*
Top 20 Free	*http://www.top20free.com/*
Web Wasteland	*http://www.aceent.com/w2/*

Don't forget the huge stock of graphics and sound clips that are stored in the libraries and forums of your commercial online service. CompuServe has an entire forum devoted just to graphics (GO GRAPHICS), and almost every forum library has a stash of graphics files.

Once you have the files on disk, the HTML tags that you would place in your document in order to call down a graphic image (say your photograph is centered on the page) would look something like this:

```
<CENTER><IMG SRC="photo.jpg"></CENTER>
```

Adding sound files, animation, and movies to your Web page gets a little more complicated. The resources mentioned above should give you some guidance, but keep in mind that audio and video take up a lot of disk space and there may be only a limited amount of free server space available through your ISP or commercial online service. For some premade animated GIF files and sound files, check out these sites:

Animation Factory	*http://www.animationfactory.com/*
Animation Library	*http://www.animationlibrary.com*
Audio Browser Sound Files	*http://www.webplaces.com/html/sounds.htm*
Stanford Archive of Recorded Sound	*http://www-sul.stanford.edu/depts/ars/ars.html*

■ *Where and How to Upload Your Home Page*

Once you have created your home page, you can view it with your browser to make sure it looks good without being connected to the Internet. After you have saved your HTML documents to your hard disk (usually in a separate directory where you can find them easily), load your Web browser. You don't have to be logged on to do this. Select "Open File" or "Open Local" from the "File" menu of the Web browser and open the HTML file that you saved earlier. Your Web page will appear, complete with graphics and formatting. If you don't like what you see, you can switch back and forth between your browser and your HTML editor as you make changes, save them, and reload the image until you are satisfied with the results.

When your page is perfect, you can log on to your commercial online service or your Internet service provider and upload your home page. That means copying your files to your provider's computer. You can't just leave the files on your computer, since your computer is probably not connected to the Internet 24 hours a day to allow access by anyone wishing to see your home page. If your provider doesn't offer free space for a home page, then there are services that do. The only "price" you pay is allowing the service to place advertisements on your page. Here are a few of the free hosting services and meta-lists of hosts:

Angelfire	*http://www.angelfire.com*
Compare Web Hosts	*http://www.comparewebhosts.com*
Find Your Hosting	*http://www.findyourhosting.com/*
Findahost.com	*http://findahost.smesource.com/Hosting/*
Freeservers.com	*http://www.freeservers.com*
Freewebspace.net	*http://www.freewebspace.net*
GeoCities	*http://geocities.yahoo.com/*
Homestead	*http://www.homestead.com/*
Hostglobal.com	*http://www.hostglobal.com*
Register.com	*http://www.register.com/*
The Directory	*http://www.thedirectory.org/*
The List	*http://www.thelist.com*
Tophosts.com	*http://www.tophosts.com*
Tripod	*http://www.tripod.lycos.com/*
Web Host Directory	*http://www.webhostdir.com*
Web Host Magazine	*http://www.webhostmagazine.com*
Webhostseek.com	*http://www.webhostseek.com*
Webhosters.com	*http://www.webhosters.com*

Since I have access to America Online, I will talk you through uploading your home page on that service. Not all ISPs offer free space and every service will have a different process for uploading a home page, so you will need to check the frequently asked questions document, which most services post online, in order to get full instructions for uploading your home page.

Uploading your Web site to AOL is a simple matter of copying your files from your computer into AOL Hometown. If this is your first time to use your ftp space, you should go to HOMETOWN and read the frequently asked questions under ABOUT FTP.

After you have read the FAQs, navigate to MY FTP SPACE. See the screen shots on the next three pages for an example of the process.

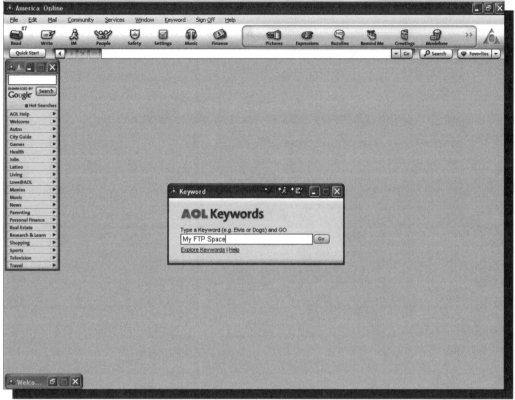

At the ftp space, select UPLOAD to transfer the files from your computer to AOL's computers.

Select ASCII (text mode) for your HTML files and BINARY mode for any graphic image files. When you type in the file names, make sure you use the same case you used in your HTML document. In other words, if you typed in all capital letters in your HTML document, the file name you type in AOL must also be in all capital letters. Be sure that your HTML files all end with the file extension .html or .htm (index.html or index.htm) and that all of your graphic images end with the appropriate file extensions (.gif or .jpg).

When you are finished, you can close all of the ftp windows and run your Web browser to check your home page. Your URL would look something like this:

http://hometown.aol.com/criscito/index.htm

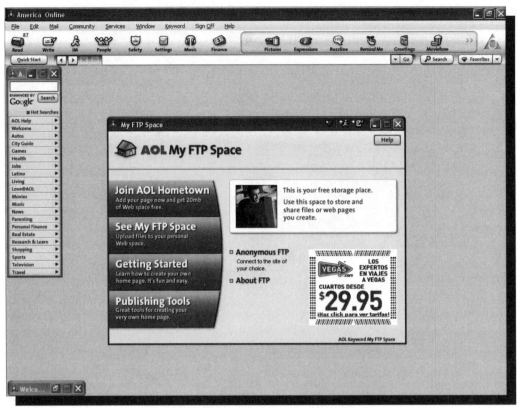

Copyright 2004 by America Online. Used by permission.

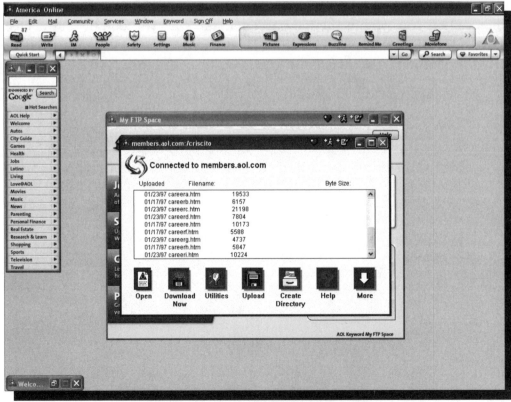

Copyright 2004 by America Online. Used by permission.

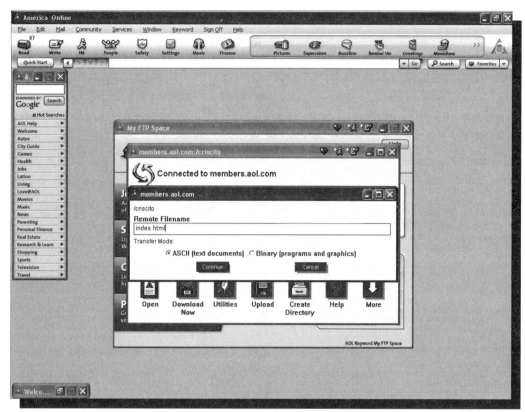

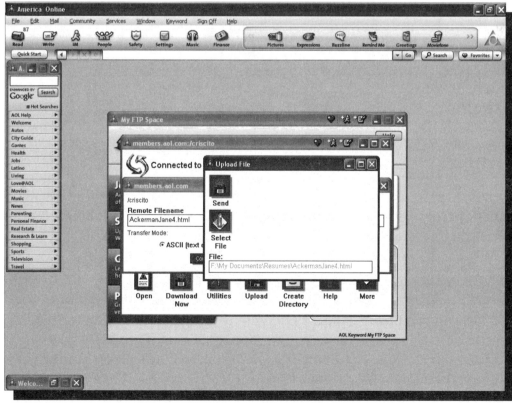

■ *Getting the Word Out*

Now that you have a home page for your résumé on the Internet, you have to get the word out to potential employers and networking contacts. Besides putting the address of the home page (its URL) on your business cards and every piece of correspondence and paper résumé you send out, you need to tell the search engines on the Internet where you are located.

You can accomplish that in three ways.

1. You can wait until the search engines find your site, which isn't a good idea. It can take a year of more for a search engine's "spider" or human review process to find your Web site on its own.

2. You can go to each search engine separately and type in some basic information about your home page. I recommend that you first choose the top ten search engines and directories listed in Chapter 12. Some search engines will index your URL within a couple of days of your submission, while others may take a few weeks.

3. Or you can use a Web announcement service that allows you to fill in the information once and submit it to a variety of search engines and directories. If you type "Web Announcement" at Yahoo! or any other search engine, you will get a long list of Web announcement services, but here are a couple of the better known sites that can help you list your Web address on search engines:

   - *http://www.submit-it.com*
   - *http://www.worldsubmit.com*

One of the ways search engines decide how to rank your Web site in a keyword search is by analyzing its link popularity. If other people include links to your site on their own Web pages, search engines consider your site worth recommending and your home page automatically ranks higher in search finds. Don't hesitate to ask other people to link to your site, but always offer to include a reciprocal link to their Web site.

❏ *Meta Tags*

Search engines send out "spiders" that gather data on Web pages automatically. When these spiders reach your home page for the first time, they read the first few lines of text in the document and use those words to index your page. To better control how these spiders index your page, use a META tag in your HTML coding.

A META tag contains descriptive information about your page but the information doesn't show up on the Web page itself when human beings view it. The tag is only visible to search-engine spiders and should contain the keywords that describe the purpose of your page, separated by commas. (Check Dr. Clue's guide to META tags at *http://www.drclue.net/F1.cgi/HTML/META/META.html* for a more in-depth discussion of the subject.) If you viewed your HTML document in an HTML editor or in the Notepad of Windows, the first few lines would look something like this:

```
<HTML> <HEAD>
<TITLE>Patricia K. Criscito, CPRW</TITLE>
<META NAME="keywords" CONTENT="resume writer, author, entrepre-
neur, senior management, national speaker">
    <META NAME="description" CONTENT="Author of Barron's <i>e-
Résumés, How to Write Better Résumés and Cover Letters,</i> and
<i>Designing the Perfect Resume,</i> President of ProType, Ltd.,
Colorado Springs, Resume Writer, National Speaker.">
```

Notice that HTML doesn't use foreign accents, so *résumé* is written *resume* in META tags. Once the search engine's spider has accessed this home page and captured the lines, someone searching for a résumé writer would see the following search results:

Patricia K. Criscito, CPRW

Author of Barron's *e-Résumés, How to Write Better Résumés and Cover Letters,* and *Designing the Perfect Resume,* President of ProType, Ltd., Colorado Springs, Resume Writer, National Speaker. *http://www.patcriscito. com/index .html*

Another way to get the word out is to add a link to your online résumé at *http://www.galaxy.com/galaxy/Community/Workplace.html.*

As discussed in Chapter 9, newsgroups are a great way to network and sometimes post your résumé. Once you have a home page for your résumé on the Internet, you can add its URL to your signature line every time you upload an article to a newsgroup. It is a discreet way of advertising to everyone who reads your comments that you have a home page. Don't forget to include your e-mail address so people can contact you.

■ *Getting Professional Help*

If you have just finished this chapter and feel like this is all just too complicated, then you can turn to professional Web developer or online portfolio development services for help. Be prepared to spend some serious money, however, for some of these services, but they can create a slick presentation of your qualifications. The higher your annual salary, the more I recommend this kind of service. You need to make a very professional impression, and that can't be done with a do-it-yourself, first-generation Web site.

If you put the words *web page designer* into any search engine, you will end up with thousands of Internet addresses for design professionals. Some will be better than others, but I have seen the work of the designers at *www.brandego.com.* The portfolio examples in Chapter 10 came from Brandego™. I especially recommend this type of sophistication for executive and entrepreneur career management.

There are lower-end options available as well that use design templates and are basically Web résumés and not portfolios. You write your own résumé, or take one written for you by a professional résumé writer, and then cut and paste it into their designs. Such sites include:

- *http://www.careerfolios.com*
- *http://www.eresumeiq.com*
- *http://www.PortfolioVault.com*
- *http://www.allwebcodesign.com*

12 | Into the Future

The electronic revolution isn't over yet! The Internet of today is simply the beginning. It is changing so rapidly that tomorrow's Internet will be like the difference between black and white televisions of the 1960s and the surround sound, big-picture sets of today, only it won't take 30 years to get there.

The Internet reached as many Americans in its first six years as the telephone did in its first 40 years. In 1990, only a small group of researchers knew about the Internet. Fourteen years later, the Internet has connected more people around the globe than any other communication medium except the telephone. Every day, thousands more people go online for the first time to explore the Internet, changing forever the way we communicate, educate, and do business.

The future of the Internet includes faster computers, more digital phone lines and cable modems, broadband access, lightning-quick data transfer rates, wallet-sized PCs, a video camera on every PC, more use of sound and video, the ability to share applications in real time, and the list goes on. The Internet has become a necessity in many of our lives.

■ How to Keep Up with the Times

Using the Internet in your job search is not just for active job seekers. Today's new reality is that jobs are not forever. The U.S. Bureau of Labor Statistics has determined that you can count on changing jobs from 4 to 20 times during your career! The more high tech your industry, the more times you will change jobs.

The half-life of your college degree is three to five years, which means you must be committed to lifelong learning to move ahead in your career.

The only constant in today's job market is change. You need to be prepared. The Internet is the perfect place to research current job trends, continue your education via distance learning, and prepare for an interview . . . and all from the comfort of your home, school, library, cybercafe, or friend's computer.

Keep your electronic résumé posted even when you are working at a job you love. You never know when the company you work for will fall on hard times or decide to restructure like so many companies are doing today.

■ *Strategies for Finding New Online Resources*

Search engines are your key to finding new career resources on the Internet. The Web is a huge, messy, disorganized place. There are more than three billion unique, publicly available pages floating around in cyberspace, and the number is growing every day. You need search engines to find information in this vast maze of data just like you need a map to find your way in an unfamiliar city.

There is a difference between a search engine and a directory. Search engines (sometimes called "spiders" or "crawlers") constantly visit Web sites on the Internet in order to create searchable catalogs of Web pages. A directory, on the other hand, is created by human beings. Sites are submitted and then assigned to a category by reviewers. Some search engine sites also have directories.

There are thousands of these search engines and directories available on the Web, but you only need a few. Therefore, only the most popular ones are listed in this chapter. To find more search engines on the Internet, check out the meta-sites at:

AllSearchEngines.com . . . . *http://allsearchengines.com*
Beaucoup! . . . . *http://www.beaucoup.com*
Direct Search . . . . *http://www.freepint.com/gary/direct.htm*
DMOZ Open Directory Project . . . . *http://dmoz.org/Computers/Internet/Searching/Search_Engines/*
OmniCrawler . . . . *http://www.maximumedge.com/search/*
SearchAbility . . . . *http://www.searchability.com*
Search Engine Watch . . . . *http://www.searchenginewatch.com*
Search-It-All . . . . *http://www.search-it-all.com*
SiteOwner.com . . . . *http://www.siteowner.com/dgdefault.cfm*
Supercrawler . . . . *http://www.supercrawler.com/*

To reach a search engine, type its address in the space provided by your browser for URLs and press enter. When you reach the site, it is a simple matter to type in the words for which you would like to search. If you are looking for a general topic, like "resume," you type that word in the search box (without the accent marks) and ask the search engine to find pages with that word. Be prepared for 18,600,000+ hits, which is what turned up in Google in August of 2004 (see next page)!

To narrow your search, you might type in two words, like "résumé AND engineer." The search engine will find pages with both of those words, but not necessarily in that order. The AND is Boolean logic. You can also use the word OR to find pages with either word, which actually widens your search instead of narrowing it.

Use NOT to eliminate items you don't want included in a search. Words can be nested in brackets to create phrases. For instance, "[software OR industrial] AND engineer" will retrieve records that contain the word *software* or *industrial*

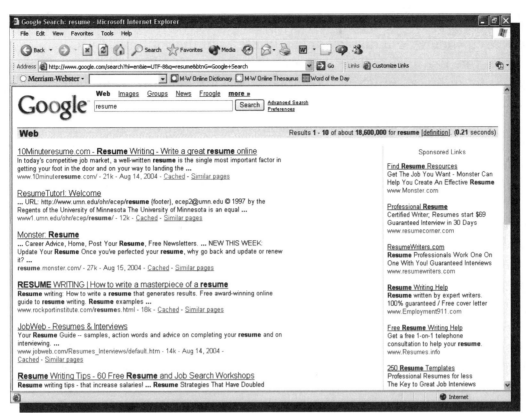

Screen shot of Internet Explorer used with permission of Microsoft.

somewhere in the record but also contain the word *engineer*. Adding a WITH operator instead of AND will ensure that the word *engineer* is always preceded immediately by either *software* or *industrial*, that is, software engineer or industrial engineer.

Boolean terms must be in ALL CAPITAL LETTERS. Not all search engines use Boolean logic, which tends to be for power searching. Ninety percent of us can get by with a few mathematical symbols instead. For instance, use the + sign to join words so that you find pages that reference both words (job + marketing). Only pages that contain both words will appear in your results. Use the – symbol when you want to find pages that have one word on them but not another (clinton – lewinsky). Use quotation marks when you want words to appear exactly in the order you indicate ("senior project manager"). Use the wildcard symbol * if you want to search for variations of a word. For example, *engineer** finds *engineering, engineer, engineers,* and *engineered.* Even search engines that support Boolean logic also support this mathematical approach.

Once you have the search results in front of you, what do you do with them? By clicking on the hypertext (highlighted words or pictures) that you think relate to your subject, the search engine will take you directly to the home page of that site. If you discover that the site isn't what you thought it would be, then click the "Back" button on your browser to return to the search results and try another until you have found what you are seeking.

Search engines use a very sophisticated logic and something called relevance numbers to determine which pages are the most relevant to your query. Therefore, the pages that appear at the top of the list are the most likely to meet your needs. Some search engines will display only a limited number of hits at a time in order to save time, but that can still be 100 or more pages of URLs. It is much better to narrow your query as much as possible with your keyword search than to scroll through page after page of irrelevant search results.

It is always a good idea to try your search in a couple of search engines or to use a metacrawler, which searches multiple search engines and/or directories at the same time, since each engine uses different logic and indexes different Web sites. It is impossible for any single search engine to index *every* site on the Internet, although some claim to do so. With millions of Web pages being added every year, the job of cataloging them is becoming a major problem for search engines. In fact, the most comprehensive searches cover only about 20 percent of the Web, so don't expect your results to be all-inclusive.

Not all of the services listed here are "true" search engines that crawl the Web. For instance, Yahoo! and the Open Directory are "directories" that depend on humans to compile their listings. Subject directories, like Yahoo!, are hierarchically organized indices of subject categories that allow you to browse through hyperlinks by subject. A subject directory displays general subject headings and progresses downward to increasingly more specific subheadings. Directories are often smaller than keyword indexes, but they return fewer irrelevant sites in a search. They also tend to link only to a Web site's home page because they don't typically index every page of a site.

Keyword indices (like Google and Altavista), on the other hand, use massive computing horsepower to "crawl" around the Internet and store entire Web pages into their databases. They then analyze the retrieved documents with indexing software and categorize each site. When you enter your search criteria, the index retrieves Web pages from its database that match the keywords you enter.

The following search engines are some of the best on the Internet, as selected and described by Search Engine Watch *(http://searchenginewatch. com)*. These sites were chosen because they were either the best, the most well-known, or the most popular with users. They are shown here as ranked in order of importance by Search Engine Watch.

Google . . . . *http://www.google.com*

Google was originally a Stanford University project by students Larry Page and Sergey Brin called BackRub. By 1998, the name had been changed to Google and the company went private. Voted four times as the Most Outstanding Search Engine by Search Engine Watch readers, Google has a well-deserved reputation as the top choice for those searching the Web. This crawler-based service provides both comprehensive coverage of the Web along with great relevancy. It's highly recommended as a first stop in your hunt for whatever you are seeking. Google has the option of searching out more than just Web pages. You can also search for images, Usenet newsgroups, news information, product information, or human-compiled information from the Open Directory, catalogs, and other services.

Yahoo! . . . . *http://www.yahoo.com*

Launched in 1994, Yahoo is the Web's oldest "directory," a place where human editors organize Web sites into categories, although in 2002, Yahoo! shifted to crawler-based listings for its main results. Narrower searches use the directory feature, and you can choose the "category" below some of the sites listed in response to a keyword search. When offered, these will take you to a list of Web sites that have been reviewed and approved by a human editor. If you want to bypass the crawler-based listings and go directly to the directory, then navigate to *www.dir.yahoo.com* instead. Yahoo! also owns Overture (formerly called GoTo), AllTheWeb, AltaVista, and Inktomi.

Ask Jeeves . . . . *http://www.askjeeves.com*

Ask Jeeves is a plain-speech search service that tries to direct you to the exact page that answers your question. If it fails to find a match within its own database, it will provide matches from other search engines. Ask Jeeves uses crawler-based technology to provide results, which come from the Teoma search engine, which it owns. Ask Jeeves is doing innovative things with invisible tabs and with what it calls SmartSearch. This technology could be a much smarter approach to delivering more than just Web page results. Ask Jeeves also owns the Direct Hit service.

AllTheWeb.com . . . . *http://www.alltheweb.com*

Powered by Yahoo!, AllTheWeb is a lighter, more customizable and pleasant "pure search" experience than you get at Yahoo! itself. The focus is on Web search, but news, pictures, video, MP3, and FTP searches are also offered. AllTheWeb.com was previously owned by a company called FAST, which is why you sometimes hear this site referred to as FAST or FAST Search. However, the search engine was purchased by Overture in 2003, which was then became the property of Yahoo! It no longer has a connection with FAST.

AOL Search . . . . *http://search.aol.com*

AOL Search allows its members to search both its own content and the Web at the same time. If you access the site as a non-AOL member, you will not see a list of AOL content. AOL Search uses Google's crawler-based index, so if you are a non-AOL user, you are better off using Google directly. For AOL members, however, there is a distinct advantage to using AOL Search.

HotBot . . . . *http://www.hotbot.com*

Launched in May 1996 by Wired Digital, HotBot was purchased by Lycos in 1998. HotBot provides easy access to the Web's three major crawler-based search engines—Yahoo!, Google, and Teoma. Unlike a metasearch engine, it cannot blend together the results from all of these crawlers. Nevertheless, it's a fast, easy way to get different Web search opinions in one place. In 1998, Lycos purchased HotBot, which suffered until 2001 when Lycos refocused its energies on improving HotBot.

Teoma . . . . *http://www.teoma.com*

Teoma is a crawler-based search engine owned by Ask Jeeves. It has a smaller index of the Web than Google or Yahoo!. However, being large doesn't make much of a difference when it comes to popular queries, and Teoma has won praise for its relevancy since it first appeared in 2000. Some people also like its "Refine" feature, which offers suggested topics to explore after you do a search. The "Resources" section of results is also unique, pointing users to pages that specifically serve as link resources about various topics. Teoma was purchased by Ask Jeeves in 2001 and also provides some results to that Web site.

There are thousands of search engines on the Internet, some of which are still considered "major" in the sense that they either still receive significant amounts of traffic or they've earned a reputation in the past that still causes some people to consider them important. For various reasons, they are not among Search Engine Watch's top search choices, but you can feel free to try them when the major search engines and directories don't provide you with the options you are seeking. Here are some of those sites:

AltaVista . . . . *http://altavista.com*
Excite . . . . *http://www.excite.com*
Gigablast . . . . *http://www.gigablast.com*
LookSmart . . . . *http://www.looksmart.com*
Lycos . . . . *http://www.lycos.com*
MSN Search . . . . *http://search.msn.com*
Netscape Search . . . . *http://search.netscape.com*
Open Directory . . . . *http://dmoz.org/*
Web Crawler . . . . *http://www.webcrawler.com*

❑ *Metacrawlers and Metasearch Engines*

Unlike search engines, metacrawlers don't search the Web themselves to build listings. Instead, they search several search engines and/or directories at once and then mix the results together onto a single results page. Following are some of the most popular sites.

The Big Hub . . . . *http://www.thebighub.com*
CurryGuide . . . . *http://www.curryguide.com/*
Dogpile . . . . *http://www.dogpile.com*
Excite . . . . *http://www.excite.com*
Family Friendly Search . . . . *http://www.familyfriendlysearch.com*
Frazzle . . . . *http://frazzle.com*
Gimenei . . . . *http://gimenei.com/*
HotBot . . . . *http://www.hotbot.com*
InfoGrid . . . . *http://www.infogrid.com*
Infonetware RealTerm Search . . . . *http://infonetware.com*
Ithaki . . . . *http://www.ithaki.net/*
Ixquick . . . . *http://www.ixquick.com/*
Kartoo . . . . *http://www.kartoo.com*
Mamma . . . . *http://www.mamma.com*
Meceoo . . . . *http://www.meceoo.com/*
MetaCrawler . . . . *http://www.metacrawler.com*
MetaEureka . . . . *http://www.metaeureka.com*
One Blink / 1Blink *http://www.1blink.com*
One Page . . . . *http://www.bjorgul.com/*
ProFusion . . . . *http://www.profusion.com*

Job hunting with search engines is a little like going to the library to find a specific book and then getting lost in the attic among the stacks. You set out with a goal in mind but stumble across dozens of other avenues to explore. Many of these destinations offer more information than you expected and lead to even other avenues until you finally find yourself far away from where you started but richer in possible sites on which to post your résumé or look for jobs.

For more information about Web search engines and how to use them, check out these sites:

- *http://sunsite.berkeley.edu/Help/searchdetails.html*
- *http://searchenginewatch.com/*

Appendix: Résumé Worksheets

I developed worksheets for my Barron's book, *How to Write Better Résumés and Cover Letters,* that have received rave reviews. Since they follow the twelve-step résumé writing process in Chapter 2 of this book, they can be useful for your résumé development. You can download free MS Word, PDF, or WordPerfect files of the questionnaires at *www.patcriscito.com* by selecting the "Pat's Books" link.

If you need more detail on how to use the worksheets than you find in Chapter 2, you might want to pick up a copy of *How to Write Better Résumés and Cover Letters* at your local library or bookstore.

COLLEGE EDUCATION

Use this form to collect information on your formal college education. Write down everything you can think of, regardless of whether you use it on the final résumé. You will narrow the list later. There is a separate page included in this section for each degree.

DEGREE _____

SCHOOL _____

CITY AND STATE _____

YEARS ATTENDED _____

YEAR GRADUATED _____ GPA _____

MAJOR _____

MINOR _____

THESIS/DISSERTATION _____

_____

~ ~

SIGNIFICANT PROJECTS _____

_____

_____

_____

HONORS, AWARDS, SCHOLARSHIPS, ETC. _____

_____

_____

_____

ACTIVITIES (volunteer, leadership, sports, social groups, etc.) _____

_____

_____

_____

STUDY ABROAD (program, school, country, special areas of study) _____

_____

_____

COLLEGE EDUCATION

Use this form to collect information on your formal college education. Write down everything you can think of, regardless of whether you use it on the final résumé. You will narrow the list later. There is a separate page included in this section for each degree.

DEGREE _____

SCHOOL _____

CITY AND STATE _____

YEARS ATTENDED _____

YEAR GRADUATED _____ GPA _____

MAJOR _____

MINOR _____

THESIS/DISSERTATION _____

_____

~ ~

SIGNIFICANT PROJECTS _____

_____

_____

_____

HONORS, AWARDS, SCHOLARSHIPS, ETC. _____

_____

_____

_____

ACTIVITIES (volunteer, leadership, sports, social groups, etc.) _____

_____

_____

_____

STUDY ABROAD (program, school, country, special areas of study) _____

_____

_____

COLLEGE EDUCATION

Use this form to collect information on your formal college education. Write down everything you can think of, regardless of whether you use it on the final résumé. You will narrow the list later. There is a separate page included in this section for each degree.

DEGREE _____

SCHOOL _____

CITY AND STATE _____

YEARS ATTENDED _____

YEAR GRADUATED _____ GPA _____

MAJOR _____

MINOR _____

THESIS/DISSERTATION _____

_____

~ ~

SIGNIFICANT PROJECTS _____

_____

_____

_____

HONORS, AWARDS, SCHOLARSHIPS, ETC. _____

_____

_____

_____

ACTIVITIES (volunteer, leadership, sports, social groups, etc.) _____

_____

_____

_____

STUDY ABROAD (program, school, country, special areas of study) _____

_____

_____

COLLEGE EDUCATION

Use this form to collect information on your formal college education. Write down everything you can think of, regardless of whether you use it on the final résumé. You will narrow the list later. There is a separate page included in this section for each degree.

DEGREE _____

SCHOOL _____

CITY AND STATE _____

YEARS ATTENDED _____

YEAR GRADUATED _____ GPA _____

MAJOR _____

MINOR _____

THESIS/DISSERTATION _____

_____

~ ~

SIGNIFICANT PROJECTS _____

_____

_____

_____

HONORS, AWARDS, SCHOLARSHIPS, ETC. _____

_____

_____

_____

ACTIVITIES (volunteer, leadership, sports, social groups, etc.) _____

_____

_____

_____

STUDY ABROAD (program, school, country, special areas of study) _____

_____

_____

COLLEGE EDUCATION

Use this form to collect information on your formal college education. Write down everything you can think of, regardless of whether you use it on the final résumé. You will narrow the list later. There is a separate page included in this section for each degree.

DEGREE _____

SCHOOL _____

CITY AND STATE _____

YEARS ATTENDED _____

YEAR GRADUATED _____ GPA _____

MAJOR _____

MINOR _____

THESIS/DISSERTATION _____

_____

~ ~

SIGNIFICANT PROJECTS _____

_____

_____

_____

HONORS, AWARDS, SCHOLARSHIPS, ETC. _____

_____

_____

_____

ACTIVITIES (volunteer, leadership, sports, social groups, etc.) _____

_____

_____

_____

STUDY ABROAD (program, school, country, special areas of study) _____

_____

_____

VOCATIONAL/TECHNICAL TRAINING

Use this form to collect information on your vocational, technical, occupational, and military training. Write down everything you can think of, regardless of whether it relates to your job goal. You will narrow the list later.

NAME OF COURSE _____

PRESENTED BY (company, school, etc.) _____

RESULT (certification, diploma, etc.) _____

DATES ATTENDED _____

~ ~

NAME OF COURSE _____

PRESENTED BY (company, school, etc.) _____

RESULT (certification, diploma, etc.) _____

DATES ATTENDED _____

~ ~

NAME OF COURSE _____

PRESENTED BY (company, school, etc.) _____

RESULT (certification, diploma, etc.) _____

DATES ATTENDED _____

~ ~

NAME OF COURSE _____

PRESENTED BY (company, school, etc.) _____

RESULT (certification, diploma, etc.) _____

DATES ATTENDED _____

~ ~

NAME OF COURSE _____

PRESENTED BY (company, school, etc.) _____

RESULT (certification, diploma, etc.) _____

DATES ATTENDED _____

~ ~

VOCATIONAL/TECHNICAL TRAINING

Use this form to collect information on your vocational, technical, and occupational training. Write down everything you can think of, regardless of whether it relates to your job goal. You will narrow the list later.

NAME OF COURSE _____

PRESENTED BY (company, school, etc.) _____

RESULT (certification, diploma, etc.) _____

DATES ATTENDED _____

~ ~

NAME OF COURSE _____

PRESENTED BY (company, school, etc.) _____

RESULT (certification, diploma, etc.) _____

DATES ATTENDED _____

~ ~

NAME OF COURSE _____

PRESENTED BY (company, school, etc.) _____

RESULT (certification, diploma, etc.) _____

DATES ATTENDED _____

~ ~

NAME OF COURSE _____

PRESENTED BY (company, school, etc.) _____

RESULT (certification, diploma, etc.) _____

DATES ATTENDED _____

~ ~

NAME OF COURSE _____

PRESENTED BY (company, school, etc.) _____

RESULT (certification, diploma, etc.) _____

DATES ATTENDED _____

~ ~

PROFESSIONAL DEVELOPMENT

Use this form to collect information on your professional development and continuing education, including in-services, workshops, seminars, corporate training programs, conferences, conventions, etc. Write down everything you can think of, regardless of whether it relates to your job goal. You will narrow the list later.

NAME OF COURSE _____

PRESENTED BY (company, school, etc.) _____

DATES ATTENDED _____

~ ~

NAME OF COURSE _____

PRESENTED BY (company, school, etc.) _____

DATES ATTENDED _____

~ ~

NAME OF COURSE _____

PRESENTED BY (company, school, etc.) _____

DATES ATTENDED _____

~ ~

NAME OF COURSE _____

PRESENTED BY (company, school, etc.) _____

DATES ATTENDED _____

~ ~

NAME OF COURSE _____

PRESENTED BY (company, school, etc.) _____

DATES ATTENDED _____

~ ~

NAME OF COURSE _____

PRESENTED BY (company, school, etc.) _____

DATES ATTENDED _____

~ ~

NAME OF COURSE _____

PRESENTED BY (company, school, etc.) _____

DATES ATTENDED _____

~ ~

PROFESSIONAL DEVELOPMENT

Use this form to collect information on your professional development and continuing education, including in-services, workshops, seminars, corporate training programs, conferences, conventions, etc. Write down everything you can think of, regardless of whether it relates to your job goal. You will narrow the list later.

NAME OF COURSE _____

PRESENTED BY (company, school, etc.) _____

DATES ATTENDED _____

~ ~

NAME OF COURSE _____

PRESENTED BY (company, school, etc.) _____

DATES ATTENDED _____

~ ~

NAME OF COURSE _____

PRESENTED BY (company, school, etc.) _____

DATES ATTENDED _____

~ ~

NAME OF COURSE _____

PRESENTED BY (company, school, etc.) _____

DATES ATTENDED _____

~ ~

NAME OF COURSE _____

PRESENTED BY (company, school, etc.) _____

DATES ATTENDED _____

~ ~

NAME OF COURSE _____

PRESENTED BY (company, school, etc.) _____

DATES ATTENDED _____

~ ~

NAME OF COURSE _____

PRESENTED BY (company, school, etc.) _____

DATES ATTENDED _____

~ ~

KEYWORDS

❑ Keyword:_____
   ❑ Synonym:_____
   ❑ Synonym:_____

❑ Keyword:_____
   ❑ Synonym:_____
   ❑ Synonym:_____

❑ Keyword:_____
   ❑ Synonym:_____
   ❑ Synonym:_____

❑ Keyword:_____
   ❑ Synonym:_____
   ❑ Synonym:_____

❑ Keyword:_____
   ❑ Synonym:_____
   ❑ Synonym:_____

❑ Keyword:_____
   ❑ Synonym:_____
   ❑ Synonym:_____

❑ Keyword:_____
   ❑ Synonym:_____
   ❑ Synonym:_____

❑ Keyword:_____
   ❑ Synonym:_____
   ❑ Synonym:_____

❑ Keyword:_____
   ❑ Synonym:_____
   ❑ Synonym:_____

❑ Keyword:_____
   ❑ Synonym:_____
   ❑ Synonym:_____

❑ Keyword:_____
   ❑ Synonym:_____
   ❑ Synonym:_____

❑ Keyword:_____
   ❑ Synonym:_____
   ❑ Synonym:_____

❑ Keyword:_____
   ❑ Synonym:_____
   ❑ Synonym:_____

❑ Keyword:_____
   ❑ Synonym:_____
   ❑ Synonym:_____

❑ Keyword:_____
   ❑ Synonym:_____
   ❑ Synonym:_____

❑ Keyword:_____
   ❑ Synonym:_____
   ❑ Synonym:_____

❑ Keyword:_____
   ❑ Synonym:_____
   ❑ Synonym:_____

❑ Keyword:_____
   ❑ Synonym:_____
   ❑ Synonym:_____

❑ Keyword:_____
   ❑ Synonym:_____
   ❑ Synonym:_____

❑ Keyword:_____
   ❑ Synonym:_____
   ❑ Synonym:_____

❑ Keyword:_____
   ❑ Synonym:_____
   ❑ Synonym:_____

❑ Keyword:_____
   ❑ Synonym:_____
   ❑ Synonym:_____

❑ Keyword:_____
   ❑ Synonym:_____
   ❑ Synonym:_____

❑ Keyword:_____
   ❑ Synonym:_____
   ❑ Synonym:_____

KEYWORDS

❏ Keyword:_____
   ❏ Synonym:_____
   ❏ Synonym:_____

❏ Keyword:_____
   ❏ Synonym:_____
   ❏ Synonym:_____

❏ Keyword:_____
   ❏ Synonym:_____
   ❏ Synonym:_____

❏ Keyword:_____
   ❏ Synonym:_____
   ❏ Synonym:_____

❏ Keyword:_____
   ❏ Synonym:_____
   ❏ Synonym:_____

❏ Keyword:_____
   ❏ Synonym:_____
   ❏ Synonym:_____

❏ Keyword:_____
   ❏ Synonym:_____
   ❏ Synonym:_____

❏ Keyword:_____
   ❏ Synonym:_____
   ❏ Synonym:_____

❏ Keyword:_____
   ❏ Synonym:_____
   ❏ Synonym:_____

❏ Keyword:_____
   ❏ Synonym:_____
   ❏ Synonym:_____

❏ Keyword:_____
   ❏ Synonym:_____
   ❏ Synonym:_____

❏ Keyword:_____
   ❏ Synonym:_____
   ❏ Synonym:_____

❏ Keyword:_____
   ❏ Synonym:_____
   ❏ Synonym:_____

❏ Keyword:_____
   ❏ Synonym:_____
   ❏ Synonym:_____

❏ Keyword:_____
   ❏ Synonym:_____
   ❏ Synonym:_____

❏ Keyword:_____
   ❏ Synonym:_____
   ❏ Synonym:_____

❏ Keyword:_____
   ❏ Synonym:_____
   ❏ Synonym:_____

❏ Keyword:_____
   ❏ Synonym:_____
   ❏ Synonym:_____

❏ Keyword:_____
   ❏ Synonym:_____
   ❏ Synonym:_____

❏ Keyword:_____
   ❏ Synonym:_____
   ❏ Synonym:_____

❏ Keyword:_____
   ❏ Synonym:_____
   ❏ Synonym:_____

❏ Keyword:_____
   ❏ Synonym:_____
   ❏ Synonym:_____

❏ Keyword:_____
   ❏ Synonym:_____
   ❏ Synonym:_____

❏ Keyword:_____
   ❏ Synonym:_____
   ❏ Synonym:_____

KEYWORDS

❏ Keyword:_____
   ❏ Synonym:_____
   ❏ Synonym:_____

❏ Keyword:_____
   ❏ Synonym:_____
   ❏ Synonym:_____

❏ Keyword:_____
   ❏ Synonym:_____
   ❏ Synonym:_____

❏ Keyword:_____
   ❏ Synonym:_____
   ❏ Synonym:_____

❏ Keyword:_____
   ❏ Synonym:_____
   ❏ Synonym:_____

❏ Keyword:_____
   ❏ Synonym:_____
   ❏ Synonym:_____

❏ Keyword:_____
   ❏ Synonym:_____
   ❏ Synonym:_____

❏ Keyword:_____
   ❏ Synonym:_____
   ❏ Synonym:_____

❏ Keyword:_____
   ❏ Synonym:_____
   ❏ Synonym:_____

❏ Keyword:_____
   ❏ Synonym:_____
   ❏ Synonym:_____

❏ Keyword:_____
   ❏ Synonym:_____
   ❏ Synonym:_____

❏ Keyword:_____
   ❏ Synonym:_____
   ❏ Synonym:_____

❏ Keyword:_____
   ❏ Synonym:_____
   ❏ Synonym:_____

❏ Keyword:_____
   ❏ Synonym:_____
   ❏ Synonym:_____

❏ Keyword:_____
   ❏ Synonym:_____
   ❏ Synonym:_____

❏ Keyword:_____
   ❏ Synonym:_____
   ❏ Synonym:_____

❏ Keyword:_____
   ❏ Synonym:_____
   ❏ Synonym:_____

❏ Keyword:_____
   ❏ Synonym:_____
   ❏ Synonym:_____

❏ Keyword:_____
   ❏ Synonym:_____
   ❏ Synonym:_____

❏ Keyword:_____
   ❏ Synonym:_____
   ❏ Synonym:_____

❏ Keyword:_____
   ❏ Synonym:_____
   ❏ Synonym:_____

❏ Keyword:_____
   ❏ Synonym:_____
   ❏ Synonym:_____

❏ Keyword:_____
   ❏ Synonym:_____
   ❏ Synonym:_____

❏ Keyword:_____
   ❏ Synonym:_____
   ❏ Synonym:_____

KEYWORDS

❏ Keyword:_____
   ❏ Synonym:_____
   ❏ Synonym:_____

❏ Keyword:_____
   ❏ Synonym:_____
   ❏ Synonym:_____

❏ Keyword:_____
   ❏ Synonym:_____
   ❏ Synonym:_____

❏ Keyword:_____
   ❏ Synonym:_____
   ❏ Synonym:_____

❏ Keyword:_____
   ❏ Synonym:_____
   ❏ Synonym:_____

❏ Keyword:_____
   ❏ Synonym:_____
   ❏ Synonym:_____

❏ Keyword:_____
   ❏ Synonym:_____
   ❏ Synonym:_____

❏ Keyword:_____
   ❏ Synonym:_____
   ❏ Synonym:_____

❏ Keyword:_____
   ❏ Synonym:_____
   ❏ Synonym:_____

❏ Keyword:_____
   ❏ Synonym:_____
   ❏ Synonym:_____

❏ Keyword:_____
   ❏ Synonym:_____
   ❏ Synonym:_____

❏ Keyword:_____
   ❏ Synonym:_____
   ❏ Synonym:_____

❏ Keyword:_____
   ❏ Synonym:_____
   ❏ Synonym:_____

❏ Keyword:_____
   ❏ Synonym:_____
   ❏ Synonym:_____

❏ Keyword:_____
   ❏ Synonym:_____
   ❏ Synonym:_____

❏ Keyword:_____
   ❏ Synonym:_____
   ❏ Synonym:_____

❏ Keyword:_____
   ❏ Synonym:_____
   ❏ Synonym:_____

❏ Keyword:_____
   ❏ Synonym:_____
   ❏ Synonym:_____

❏ Keyword:_____
   ❏ Synonym:_____
   ❏ Synonym:_____

❏ Keyword:_____
   ❏ Synonym:_____
   ❏ Synonym:_____

❏ Keyword:_____
   ❏ Synonym:_____
   ❏ Synonym:_____

❏ Keyword:_____
   ❏ Synonym:_____
   ❏ Synonym:_____

❏ Keyword:_____
   ❏ Synonym:_____
   ❏ Synonym:_____

❏ Keyword:_____
   ❏ Synonym:_____
   ❏ Synonym:_____

KEYWORDS

❑ Keyword:_____
    ❑ Synonym:_____
    ❑ Synonym:_____

❑ Keyword:_____
    ❑ Synonym:_____
    ❑ Synonym:_____

❑ Keyword:_____
    ❑ Synonym:_____
    ❑ Synonym:_____

❑ Keyword:_____
    ❑ Synonym:_____
    ❑ Synonym:_____

❑ Keyword:_____
    ❑ Synonym:_____
    ❑ Synonym:_____

❑ Keyword:_____
    ❑ Synonym:_____
    ❑ Synonym:_____

❑ Keyword:_____
    ❑ Synonym:_____
    ❑ Synonym:_____

❑ Keyword:_____
    ❑ Synonym:_____
    ❑ Synonym:_____

❑ Keyword:_____
    ❑ Synonym:_____
    ❑ Synonym:_____

❑ Keyword:_____
    ❑ Synonym:_____
    ❑ Synonym:_____

❑ Keyword:_____
    ❑ Synonym:_____
    ❑ Synonym:_____

❑ Keyword:_____
    ❑ Synonym:_____
    ❑ Synonym:_____

❑ Keyword:_____
    ❑ Synonym:_____
    ❑ Synonym:_____

❑ Keyword:_____
    ❑ Synonym:_____
    ❑ Synonym:_____

❑ Keyword:_____
    ❑ Synonym:_____
    ❑ Synonym:_____

❑ Keyword:_____
    ❑ Synonym:_____
    ❑ Synonym:_____

❑ Keyword:_____
    ❑ Synonym:_____
    ❑ Synonym:_____

❑ Keyword:_____
    ❑ Synonym:_____
    ❑ Synonym:_____

❑ Keyword:_____
    ❑ Synonym:_____
    ❑ Synonym:_____

❑ Keyword:_____
    ❑ Synonym:_____
    ❑ Synonym:_____

❑ Keyword:_____
    ❑ Synonym:_____
    ❑ Synonym:_____

❑ Keyword:_____
    ❑ Synonym:_____
    ❑ Synonym:_____

❑ Keyword:_____
    ❑ Synonym:_____
    ❑ Synonym:_____

❑ Keyword:_____
    ❑ Synonym:_____
    ❑ Synonym:_____

EXPERIENCE—JOB NO. 1

JOB TITLE _____

NAME OF EMPLOYER _____

CITY AND STATE _____

DATE STARTED _____ DATE ENDED _____

SUMMARY SENTENCE (The overall scope of your responsibility, overview of your essential role in the company, kind of products or services for which you were responsible) _____

_____

_____

_____

NUMBER OF PEOPLE SUPERVISED AND THEIR TITLES OR FUNCTIONS _____

_____

_____

_____

DESCRIPTION OF RESPONSIBILITIES (Don't forget budget, hiring, training, operations, strategic planning, new business development, production, customer service, sales, marketing, advertising, etc.) _____

_____

_____

_____

_____

_____

_____

_____

_____

_____

_____

_____

_____

ACCOMPLISHMENTS (Leave this section blank until Step 6 in Chapter 7) _____

_____

_____

_____

_____

_____

_____

_____

_____

_____

_____

_____

EXPERIENCE—JOB NO. 2

JOB TITLE _____

NAME OF EMPLOYER _____

CITY AND STATE _____

DATE STARTED _____ DATE ENDED _____

SUMMARY SENTENCE (The overall scope of your responsibility, overview of your essential role in the company, kind of products or services for which you were responsible) _____
_____
_____
_____
_____

NUMBER OF PEOPLE SUPERVISED AND THEIR TITLES OR FUNCTIONS _____
_____
_____
_____
_____

DESCRIPTION OF RESPONSIBILITIES (Don't forget budget, hiring, training, operations, strategic planning, new business development, production, customer service, sales, marketing, advertising, etc.) _____
_____
_____
_____
_____
_____
_____
_____
_____
_____
_____
_____
_____
_____
_____
_____

ACCOMPLISHMENTS (Leave this section blank until Step 6 in Chapter 7) _____
_____
_____
_____
_____
_____
_____
_____
_____
_____
_____
_____
_____

EXPERIENCE—JOB NO. 3

JOB TITLE _____

NAME OF EMPLOYER _____

CITY AND STATE _____

DATE STARTED _____ DATE ENDED _____

SUMMARY SENTENCE (The overall scope of your responsibility, overview of your essential role in the company, kind of products or services for which you were responsible) _____

_____

_____

_____

_____

NUMBER OF PEOPLE SUPERVISED AND THEIR TITLES OR FUNCTIONS _____

_____

_____

_____

_____

DESCRIPTION OF RESPONSIBILITIES (Don't forget budget, hiring, training, operations, strategic planning, new business development, production, customer service, sales, marketing, advertising, etc.) _____

_____

_____

_____

_____

_____

_____

_____

_____

_____

_____

_____

_____

_____

ACCOMPLISHMENTS (Leave this section blank until Step 6 in Chapter 7) _____

_____

_____

_____

_____

_____

_____

_____

_____

_____

_____

_____

_____

EXPERIENCE—JOB NO. 4

JOB TITLE _____

NAME OF EMPLOYER _____

CITY AND STATE _____

DATE STARTED _____ DATE ENDED _____

SUMMARY SENTENCE (The overall scope of your responsibility, overview of your essential role in the company, kind of products or services for which you were responsible) _____
_____
_____
_____
_____

NUMBER OF PEOPLE SUPERVISED AND THEIR TITLES OR FUNCTIONS _____
_____
_____
_____
_____

DESCRIPTION OF RESPONSIBILITIES (Don't forget budget, hiring, training, operations, strategic planning, new business development, production, customer service, sales, marketing, advertising, etc.) _____
_____
_____
_____
_____
_____
_____
_____
_____
_____
_____
_____
_____
_____
_____

ACCOMPLISHMENTS (Leave this section blank until Step 6 in Chapter 7) _____
_____
_____
_____
_____
_____
_____
_____
_____
_____
_____
_____
_____
_____

EXPERIENCE—JOB NO. 5

JOB TITLE _____

NAME OF EMPLOYER _____

CITY AND STATE _____

DATE STARTED _____ DATE ENDED _____

SUMMARY SENTENCE (The overall scope of your responsibility, overview of your essential role in the company, kind of products or services for which you were responsible) _____

_____

_____

_____

_____

NUMBER OF PEOPLE SUPERVISED AND THEIR TITLES OR FUNCTIONS _____

_____

_____

_____

_____

DESCRIPTION OF RESPONSIBILITIES (Don't forget budget, hiring, training, operations, strategic planning, new business development, production, customer service, sales, marketing, advertising, etc.) _____

_____

_____

_____

_____

_____

_____

_____

_____

_____

_____

_____

_____

_____

ACCOMPLISHMENTS (Leave this section blank until Step 6 in Chapter 7) _____

_____

_____

_____

_____

_____

_____

_____

_____

_____

_____

_____

EXPERIENCE—JOB NO. 6

JOB TITLE _____

NAME OF EMPLOYER _____

CITY AND STATE _____

DATE STARTED _____ DATE ENDED _____

SUMMARY SENTENCE (The overall scope of your responsibility, overview of your essential role in the company, kind of products or services for which you were responsible) _____

_____

_____

_____

_____

NUMBER OF PEOPLE SUPERVISED AND THEIR TITLES OR FUNCTIONS _____

_____

_____

_____

_____

DESCRIPTION OF RESPONSIBILITIES (Don't forget budget, hiring, training, operations, strategic planning, new business development, production, customer service, sales, marketing, advertising, etc.) _____

_____

_____

_____

_____

_____

_____

_____

_____

_____

_____

_____

_____

_____

_____

ACCOMPLISHMENTS (Leave this section blank until Step 6 in Chapter 7) _____

_____

_____

_____

_____

_____

_____

_____

_____

_____

_____

_____

EXPERIENCE—JOB NO. 7

JOB TITLE _____

NAME OF EMPLOYER _____

CITY AND STATE _____

DATE STARTED _____ DATE ENDED _____

SUMMARY SENTENCE (The overall scope of your responsibility, overview of your essential role in the company, kind of products or services for which you were responsible) _____
_____
_____
_____
_____

NUMBER OF PEOPLE SUPERVISED AND THEIR TITLES OR FUNCTIONS _____
_____
_____
_____
_____

DESCRIPTION OF RESPONSIBILITIES (Don't forget budget, hiring, training, operations, strategic planning, new business development, production, customer service, sales, marketing, advertising, etc.) _____
_____
_____
_____
_____
_____
_____
_____
_____
_____
_____
_____
_____
_____
_____

ACCOMPLISHMENTS (Leave this section blank until Step 6 in Chapter 7) _____
_____
_____
_____
_____
_____
_____
_____
_____
_____
_____
_____
_____

EXPERIENCE—JOB NO. 8

JOB TITLE _____

NAME OF EMPLOYER _____

CITY AND STATE _____

DATE STARTED _____ DATE ENDED _____

SUMMARY SENTENCE (The overall scope of your responsibility, overview of your essential role in the company, kind of products or services for which you were responsible) _____
_____
_____
_____
_____

NUMBER OF PEOPLE SUPERVISED AND THEIR TITLES OR FUNCTIONS _____
_____
_____
_____
_____

DESCRIPTION OF RESPONSIBILITIES (Don't forget budget, hiring, training, operations, strategic planning, new business development, production, customer service, sales, marketing, advertising, etc.) _____
_____
_____
_____
_____
_____
_____
_____
_____
_____
_____
_____
_____
_____
_____

ACCOMPLISHMENTS (Leave this section blank until Step 6 in Chapter 7) _____
_____
_____
_____
_____
_____
_____
_____
_____
_____
_____
_____
_____

EXPERIENCE—JOB NO. 9

JOB TITLE _____

NAME OF EMPLOYER _____

CITY AND STATE _____

DATE STARTED _____ DATE ENDED _____

SUMMARY SENTENCE (The overall scope of your responsibility, overview of your essential role in the company, kind of products or services for which you were responsible) _____

_____

_____

_____

_____

NUMBER OF PEOPLE SUPERVISED AND THEIR TITLES OR FUNCTIONS _____

_____

_____

_____

_____

DESCRIPTION OF RESPONSIBILITIES (Don't forget budget, hiring, training, operations, strategic planning, new business development, production, customer service, sales, marketing, advertising, etc.) _____

_____

_____

_____

_____

_____

_____

_____

_____

_____

_____

_____

_____

_____

_____

_____

ACCOMPLISHMENTS (Leave this section blank until Step 6 in Chapter 7) _____

_____

_____

_____

_____

_____

_____

_____

_____

_____

_____

_____

_____

EXPERIENCE—JOB NO. 10

JOB TITLE _____

NAME OF EMPLOYER _____

CITY AND STATE _____

DATE STARTED _____ DATE ENDED _____

SUMMARY SENTENCE (The overall scope of your responsibility, overview of your essential role in the company, kind of products or services for which you were responsible) _____

_____

_____

_____

_____

NUMBER OF PEOPLE SUPERVISED AND THEIR TITLES OR FUNCTIONS _____

_____

_____

_____

_____

DESCRIPTION OF RESPONSIBILITIES (Don't forget budget, hiring, training, operations, strategic planning, new business development, production, customer service, sales, marketing, advertising, etc.) _____

_____

_____

_____

_____

_____

_____

_____

_____

_____

_____

_____

_____

_____

_____

_____

_____

_____

ACCOMPLISHMENTS (Leave this section blank until Step 6 in Chapter 7) _____

_____

_____

_____

_____

_____

_____

_____

_____

_____

_____

_____

_____

RELATED QUALIFICATIONS

AFFILIATIONS (professional associations, chambers of commerce, Toastmasters, etc.) _____

_____

_____

_____

_____

_____

LANGUAGES (with levels of proficiency*) _____

_____

_____

_____

*Fluent (absolute ability, native), Highly Proficient (3 to 5 years of usage in the country), Proficient (able to understand the subtleties of the language), Working Knowledge (can conduct everyday business), Knowledge (exposure to the language, courtesy phrases)

LICENSES _____

_____

_____

_____

CERTIFICATIONS _____

_____

_____

_____

CREDENTIALS _____

_____

_____

_____

PRESENTATIONS/SPEECHES (title, meeting, sponsoring organization, city, state, date) _____

_____

_____

_____

EXHIBITS _____

_____

_____

_____

PUBLICATIONS (authors, article title, publication title, volume, issue, page numbers, date) _____

_____

_____

_____

GRANTS _____

_____

_____

_____

RELATED QUALIFICATIONS

SPECIAL PROJECTS _____
_____
_____
_____

RESEARCH _____
_____
_____
_____

UNIQUE SKILLS _____
_____
_____
_____

VOLUNTEER ACTIVITIES, CIVIC CONTRIBUTIONS _____
_____
_____
_____
_____
_____

HONORS, AWARD, DISTINCTIONS, PROFESSIONAL RECOGNITION _____
_____
_____
_____

COMPUTERS _____
_____
Applications (MS Word, Excel, PowerPoint, etc.) _____
Operating Systems (Windows, Macintosh, UNIX, etc.) _____
Databases (Access, Oracle, etc.) _____
Programming Languages _____
Networking _____
Communications _____
Hardware _____

OTHER RELEVANT SKILLS _____
_____
Actors (singing, musical instruments, martial arts, etc.) _____
Secretaries (typing speed, shorthand, etc.) _____
Welders (TIG, MIG, ARC, etc.) _____

INTERNATIONAL (travel, living, cross-cultural skills, etc.) _____
_____
_____
_____

OTHER RELATED QUALIFICATIONS

QUALIFICATIONS PROFILE

Keep the qualifications profile short, sweet, and to the point. I tend to limit them to five or six bullets, although there are exceptions to this rule when creating a curriculum vita or other types of professional résumés. I'll give you a few extra places to list that information if you need a longer profile, but try to use no more than six of the blanks.

You can title this section with any of the following headlines: Profile, Qualifications, Highlights of Qualifications, Expertise, Strengths, Summary, Synopsis, Background, Professional Background, Executive Summary, Highlights, Overview, Professional Overview, Capsule, or Keyword Profile.

OBJECTIVE/FOCUS (this can become the first sentence of your profile or stand alone) _____
_____
_____
_____

SECOND SENTENCE (areas of expertise) _____
_____
_____
_____

STRENGTHS _____
_____
_____
_____

STRENGTHS _____
_____
_____
_____

STRENGTHS _____
_____
_____
_____

STRENGTHS _____
_____
_____
_____

STRENGTHS _____
_____
_____
_____

STRENGTHS _____
_____
_____
_____

REFERENCES

Unless an advertisement specifically requests references, don't send them with your résumé. Type a nice list of three to six references on the same letterhead as your résumé to take with you to the interview. Use this form to collect the information for your reference list. Choose people who know how you work and are not just personal friends or family members.

NAME _____
RELATIONSHIP TO YOU _____
COMPANY _____
MAILING ADDRESS _____
CITY, STATE, ZIP _____
WORK PHONE _____ CELL PHONE _____
HOME PHONE _____ E-MAIL _____

NAME _____
RELATIONSHIP TO YOU _____
COMPANY _____
MAILING ADDRESS _____
CITY, STATE, ZIP _____
WORK PHONE _____ CELL PHONE _____
HOME PHONE _____ E-MAIL _____

NAME _____
RELATIONSHIP TO YOU _____
COMPANY _____
MAILING ADDRESS _____
CITY, STATE, ZIP _____
WORK PHONE _____ CELL PHONE _____
HOME PHONE _____ E-MAIL _____

NAME _____
RELATIONSHIP TO YOU _____
COMPANY _____
MAILING ADDRESS _____
CITY, STATE, ZIP _____
WORK PHONE _____ CELL PHONE _____
HOME PHONE _____ E-MAIL _____

NAME _____
RELATIONSHIP TO YOU _____
COMPANY _____
MAILING ADDRESS _____
CITY, STATE, ZIP _____
WORK PHONE _____ CELL PHONE _____
HOME PHONE _____ E-MAIL _____

NAME _____
RELATIONSHIP TO YOU _____
COMPANY _____
MAILING ADDRESS _____
CITY, STATE, ZIP _____
WORK PHONE _____ CELL PHONE _____
HOME PHONE _____ E-MAIL _____

CONTACT INFORMATION

This final stage of information gathering will provide you with all the information you need to begin your résumé. For the contact information, you can use your full name, first and last name only, or shortened names (Pat Criscito instead of Patricia K. Criscito).

Do not use work telephone numbers or a work e-mail address on your résumé. Potential employers tend to consider that an abuse of company resources, which implies you might do the same if you are working for them. Listing a cellular telephone number on your résumé gives a hiring manager a way to reach you during working hours.

Avoid the use of "cutesy" e-mail addresses on a résumé. If you use *babycakes@aol.com* for your personal e-mail, create a second e-mail address under your account that will be more professional. If your only access to the Internet is at work, then create a free-mail account at *hotmail.com, juno.com, usa.net, yahoo.com, mail.com, excite.com, e-mail.com,* or *altavista.com.* Check *www.refdesk.com/freemail.html* for a list of even more free e-mail services.

NAME _____

ADDRESS _____

CITY/STATE/ZIP _____

COUNTRY (if applying outside the country where you live) _____

HOME PHONE _____   CELL PHONE _____

E-MAIL _____

WEB SITE _____

Glossary: The Terms You Need to Know

For more definitions of terms not listed here, check:

- PC Webopedia
  http://www.pcwebopedia.com
- Bob Jensen's Technology Glossary
  http://www.trinity.edu/~rjensen/245glosf.htm#pointer
- The Acronym Finder
  http://www.acronymfinder.com/

Antivirus: A computer software program that detects viruses and destroys them (see *virus*).

Applicant tracking system: A means of storing, finding, and retrieving information about a candidate in a computer database.

ARPAnet: A network created by the Advanced Research Projects Agency to study how to make computer networks secure in the event of nuclear war.

Article: An electronic message sent to a newsgroup or mailing list for distribution to all list members.

ASCII: American Standard Code for Information Interchange—a plain text file, stripped of all formatting codes. This generic file format is created when you save a file in a word processing or text editing program with special "Save As" commands. The Notepad program in Microsoft Windows saves all of its files as ASCII text by default. ASCII (or text) files can be read by any word processor or text editing program.

Baud: The measure of how fast a computer modem can transfer data via a telephone line, measured in bits of information transmitted per second. Speeds range from 2400 baud (slow) to 768,000 (fast and getting faster).

Boolean logic: A form of algebra fundamental to computer operations developed in the mid-1800s by English mathematician George Boole and having to do with logical, true/false values. Boolean operators (AND, NOT, OR) are often used as qualifiers in database searches.

Browser: A computer program used to find, retrieve, display, and move information on the Internet. Netscape, Microsoft Internet Explorer, Netcruiser, and Mosaic are some examples.

Byte: The amount of space required to store a single character on a disk.

Cable Modem: Just like the cable television signals delivered to your home by cable companies, cable modems are always "on" and offer speeds similar to DSL service. (1 million bits per second in each direction). Unlike telephone lines, however, cable services are typically shared with neighbors, which means performance can be affected as more users sign up and transmit data. Your data is also not as secure on a shared line.

CD-ROM: Similar to a music compact disc, CD-ROMs can store large volumes of data for access by computers. They are read only, meaning you cannot save information onto a CD-ROM but can run programs or read information directly from the disk. There are WORM (write once, read many) drives that allow your computer to write to a CD-ROM, but they tend to be costly and offer slower access speeds.

Client: A program that requests services from another computer, called the server.

Commercial online service: A company that allows you to dial in via modem to access its computer servers. Examples are CompuServe, America Online, Prodigy, MSN, Earthlink, Juno, etc.

Cookie: Not to be confused with the food! A cookie, in Internet terminology, is a message given to a Web browser by a Web server that is stored on your hard drive. Cookies identify you and even customize a Web page for you when you return to the Internet site. For example, when you return to a site, you might see a welcome page with your name on it instead of a generic page.

Cyberspace: A term that refers to a place where people can communicate through the use of computers and computer network services. A term coined by William Gibson in his novel, *Necromancer*.

Database: A collection of electronically stored information structured in such a way that it can be sorted by fields, either alphabetically or numerically. In this book, it refers to a collection of résumés or jobs that can be searched by keywords.

Digest: A collection of mailing list articles.

Domain name: A multi-part name that identifies an Internet computer. Each component of the name refers to a computer, network, or organization.

DOS: Disk Operating System—a program that runs a PC. The original version is from Microsoft, hence the name MS-DOS.

Download: The process of transferring information from another computer to your computer. If you want to retrieve a file from the Internet, BBS, or a commercial online service, you download the file from the remote computer to your own computer.

DSL: Digital Subscriber Line—a telephone service that offers very high-performance digital connections with speeds of up to 768k. DSL options include HDSL, ADSL, and ISDN/DSL. These services are more expensive than analog phone service.

Electronic résumé: A résumé that is in an electronic format ready for transfer in cyberspace, via the Internet or e-mail. The computer file is in a generic ASCII text format, either created by you or generated by a scanner from your paper résumé.

E-folio: An electronic portfolio of information that helps to manage your career. It contains your résumé plus other information to justify the claims you make in your résumé.

E-mail: Electronic mail—an electronic message sent from one computer to another via the Internet or a commercial online service.

Encryption: The encoding of information to prevent someone from reading the information.

FAQ: Frequently Asked Questions—a document that covers basic information from a Usenet newsgroup, mailing list, or Internet site.

Forum: A chat room on a commercial online service where you can carry on live conversations with people of similar interests.

ftp: File Transfer Protocol—a means of sending computer files from one computer to another. The file does not have to be an ASCII text file. Entering "anonymous" as your log-on and your e-mail address as your password allows you to use resources that the site has made accessible to the public.

Gateway: A computer that handles moving data from one network to another. Normally used to refer to communications between two different kinds of networks.

GIF: Graphic Interchange Format—the most common format for graphics on the Web.

Google: Besides the name of a popular search engine, the word *Google* has evolved into a verb to describe the process of using any search engine to research information on a person, company, or thing.

Home page: The first page of an Internet site.

HTML: Hypertext Markup Language—a simple programming language used to format documents for display on the World Wide Web. It is this language that makes a home page appear "pretty" when your browser views it on your computer screen.

http: Hypertext transfer protocol—one of the behind-the-scenes protocols that computers on the Internet use to exchange information. When you see an URL that begins with http://, you know that the address points to a Web page.

Hyperlink: The part of the Web page that links you to another file. It is either images or words in a different color from the other items on the page.

Hypermedia: The ability to display a range of different media, accessible through hyperlinks. A Web page, for example, may contain photographs or drawings, formatted text, and links to audio and video sources. Distributed hypermedia simply means that these resources are distributed all over the world.

Hypertext: Highlighted text or picture on a Web page that provides a link between pages or sites, allowing you to move through information at random.

Information superhighway: An electronic communications network that will link homes, businesses, computers, televisions, and telephones into an integrated information network. The Internet is the beginning of the information superhighway, and interactive television and cable modems are the next step toward combining the various mediums.

Internet: The world's largest network of connected computers, linking government, military, businesses, organizations, educational institutions, and private individuals.

ISDN: Integrated Services Digital Network—a digital telephone service that allows dial-up access at twice the speed of standard analog telephone service.

Java: Not coffee! Instead, Java is a high-level programming language developed by Sun Microsystems. It is used in programming pages for the World Wide Web.

Job bank: A database of job openings on a computer, like the classified advertisements in a newspaper, that can be searched by keywords, job titles, geographic location, company, and so on.

JPEG: Joint Photographics Expert Group—a common graphic image file format that supports millions of colors. Better suited for photographs than the GIF format.

kbps: Kilobits per second—a measure of a modem's data transfer rate (for example, 28.8 kpbs equals 28,800 bits per second).

258

List owner: One or more people who are in charge of a mailing list.

Log off: The process of disconnecting from a computer network.

Log on: The process required to dial in and identify yourself to a network's host computer. It usually requires dialing a certain number and typing in your user name and password. Log in has the same meaning.

Mailing list: A collection of people with similar interests who are connected via e-mail where they receive the messages automatically.

Modem: A piece of computer hardware that connects your computer to a phone line, allowing you to communicate with another computer. *Modem* stands for *modulate–dem*odulate, which is the converting of digital signals from your computer to the analog signals of your telephone line and then back into digital signals at the other end of the line.

Multimedia: A computer file that contains more than one medium: text, graphics, video, animation, and/or sound.

Netiquette: The etiquette of using the Internet.

Network: More than one computer connected together for the purpose of sharing data.

Newsgroup: An electronic discussion or information group distributed by the Usenet.

OCR: Optical Character Recognition—a special kind of computer software that can examine, via a scanner, the dots of ink on a printed page and determine by their shapes which letters they represent. This information is then converted into binary form that a computer can read in a text editor or word processor.

Offline: Disconnected from a computer network so you are unable to access information or transmit data. The opposite of online.

Online: Connected to a computer network and able to access information or transmit data. The opposite of offline.

Password: A combination of letters and/or numbers that you choose to access your commercial online service, bulletin board service, or Internet service provider. Don't use your first name, last name, initials, phone number, or anything else that can be easily guessed. A combination of words and numbers is the ideal password. Keep your password a secret. Anyone who knows your password and user name can access your accounts and any credit card information you have provided to those accounts.

Post: The act of leaving your information (like a résumé) on another computer. Can be uploading a file or typing your information into an electronic form at an Internet site and then clicking a button to send.

Protocol: SLIP (Serial Line Internet Protocol) and PPP (Point-to-Point Protocol) give you access to the World Wide Web and let you use graphical Internet tools. When information is sent over the Internet, it is divided into smaller pieces in transit and reassembled at a final destination. Protocols allow computers to exchange these packets with the Internet. These protocols work behind the scenes of your browser with little input from the user.

Queue: To wait in line.

Résumé database: A collection of résumés on a computer that can be searched using keywords. Your electronic résumé will end up in a database like this. A hiring manager can type in keywords to call up résumés that match job requisitions.

Router: A computer that determines which path Internet traffic will take to reach its destination.

Scanner: A computer peripheral (piece of hardware attached to a computer) that uses light-sensing equipment to scan paper and then translate the pattern of light and dark (or color) into a digital signal that can be manipulated by computer software.

Server: A computer on a network that provides a resource on the Internet. Client programs access servers to obtain data.

Shareware: Computer programs that you can try before purchasing. Although some shareware programs are free, most request that you pay the author a fee if you decide to keep and use the program.

Site: Also called Web site. The entire contents of a location on the Internet, including all of its multiple pages.

Surfing: Accessing the Internet and indiscriminately window shopping, wandering from site to site with no real plan.

SysOp: System Operator—the person responsible for managing a forum on a commercial online service or bulletin board system.

TCP/IP: Transmission Control Protocol/Internet Protocol—a set of protocols that standardizes the transmission of data over the Internet. TCP/IP stack programs (like the Trumpet Winsock) talk to the Internet behind the scenes while you run Internet tools such as Internet Explorer, Netscape, and Eudora.

Telnet: An Internet protocol that allows you to log on to a remote computer.

Terminal emulation: Communicating with a remote computer in which your PC acts as a terminal connected to it.

Text file: A generic file that can be read by any word processor or e-mail program.

Upload: The process of transmitting information from your computer to someone else's computer. The opposite of download.

URL: Universal Resource Locator—the address of an Internet site, for example *http://www.careerpath.com.* An URL is a road map to help you get to a particular Internet site.

Usenet: Users network—thousands of computers that are organized under a set of groupings known as newsgroups.

Virus: A computer program that is intended to cause damage to your computer files if it is allowed to enter. Viruses are not spread by simple e-mail messages but may reside in any files you download. Commercial antivirus programs are a must for any computer with an Internet connection.

Web: World Wide Web (WWW)—a graphically oriented overlay on the Internet that may contain text, graphics, video, sound, and other data. The original Internet was text only. The World Wide Web was developed as a part of the Internet to allow the use of graphics and sound.

Index

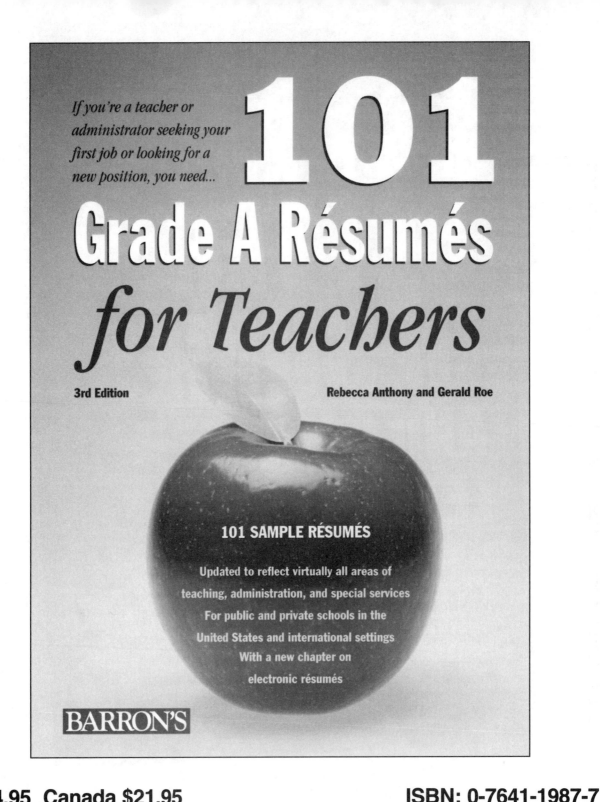

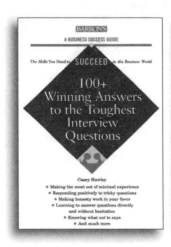
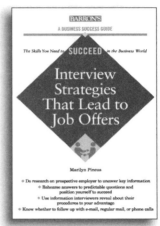

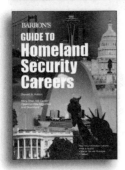